The Romanian
Bruce Benderson

snowbooks

LONDON

SNOWBOOKS

2 4 6 8 10 9 7 5 3

Copyright © Bruce Benderson 2006

First published in French translation in 2004 as
Autobiographie érotique (Rivages)

Proudly published in Great Britain by
Snowbooks Ltd.
120 Pentonville Road
London N1 9JN
www.snowbooks.com

A CIP catalogue record for this book
is available from the British Library

ISBN 1 905005 18 0
ISBN-13 9 781905 005185

Printed in Denmark by Nørhaven

FOR REMY

Have you sunk into so deep a stupor that you're happy only in your unhappiness? If that's the case, let us fly to countries that are counterfeits of Death.

—CHARLES BAUDELAIRE

The sex instinct created a world of its own which was outside the Party's control and which therefore had to be destroyed if possible.

—GEORGE ORWELL

I

The stranger's hands are cracked and callused, coated with something vaguely sticky. From the puffed-out shape of his pants at the knees and the worn fading around his lean buttocks, I guess he's been sleeping in a lot of different places lately. Over a wide black-wool turtleneck collar, his sharp features and high forehead offset a haughty, blasé bearing. Quickly I jerk my hand away from his.

This is my first night in Budapest. Five hours ago, when I set out from my hotel across the Szabadság Bridge, hardly anybody had braved the cold. The few introverted faces I passed seemed disembodied against the tar-colored sky. I'd come here to do a story about brothels for an online magazine. Something personal and literary, the editor had chuckled in his impishly paternal way. Planning to grope my way through the job by sheer instinct and horniness, with little knowledge of the city's history or present, I left the hotel without even checking a map. My rationale was that my own libido was enough to carry me into the unconscious of the place.

I zigzagged recklessly—playing with the dizziness of my jet lag—using the river as an obvious thread of orientation. Deep into the night, around two a.m., I ended up on the Pest waterfront, where chilly gusts sharded the light on inky water. That's where I saw him, through wind-teared eyes, in front of the Inter-Continental Hotel: a black form cut from darkness, topped by a fluorescently pale face; a nose like an enormous shield, over a pouty underlip; and eyes hollowed by hunger and fatigue. I broke the frozen silence by making up something—a club I pretended to be looking for—and he pretentiously claimed to know them all.

We crept along the streetcar tracks, enveloped by the echo of lapping waves and cars humming on the bridge above, leaving our wet, black footprints in the asphalt. That's when he grazed my hand with those rough, coated fingers of his and I jerked it away, afraid of the feel of dry cartilage on his knuckles.

But I've stayed here anyway at the foot of the bridge, as a match flares in his face, bringing out small, distrustful black eyes and their stagy melancholy. His eyes aren't searching mine for pity. They look dead.

He is, it turns out, a Romanian, one of the dozens who prowl this Danube promenade, called the Corso. Struggling to get by without papers, he's been surviving day to day through an underground network of other Romanians, on petty heists, hustling and borrowing from friends.

In a macho gesture, he hands me a cigarette and lights it in a cupped palm. Beneath his plucky gestures is a cynicism so unbending that it sends a shudder down my spine. His name is ancient: Romulus. No people, he explains, including the Italians, feel closer to the Romans, who once occupied the land now called Romania. In fact, the Romanian language is largely pure vulgar Latin and its closest modern equivalent.

With one laconic hand, he sketches a flamboyant biography meant to entice me. It's a smug story about disappointment borne with masculine fatality. This last year, he explains, was the worst punishment of all for being born in a country where the average monthly salary is the equivalent of about eighty dollars. "Not my fault," he mumbles, "that I was born there," like a confession an inmate unwisely whispers into an ear, his snake eyes glinting behind curls of smoke....

The noisy waterfront club to which he leads me is a bisexual mishmash. On the little gilded stage with its colored lights is a self-conscious drag show that most people are ignoring. The crowd has that smugness and prudishness that have begun to substitute themselves for hip wherever I travel these days. For the winners of global capitalism there's no more aristocratic sophistication to ape, just the bovine suburbanism of triumphant North America.

By contrast, my new companion has a waterfront scowl, not really hiding a kind of cunning. He may have injected a forced hint of hip-hop into his thuggish walk, probably picked up from music videos, but his half-shut eyelids speak of ancient transactions long before new markets. He is, I realize, as I feel anxiety coating my throat, the reason I took this assignment, and why, despite my American passport that could get me into any so-called sexual utopia, I've bypassed Amsterdam's chilly, predictable, well-run brothels. I'm tired of new Western liberalism. I want Budapest to take me to a vanished world of *Venus in Furs*.

Romulus is twenty-four, a child of the last years of Communism, having grown up during Ceauşescu's most oppressive and desperate attempts at industrializing the country. He was, he claims, well on his way to becoming a soccer pro, until his ailing mother put a stop to that by begging him not to travel. After two years of hopeless inertia, he left their two-room sardine can of an apartment in the city of Sibiu, where he'd been squeezed in with her, her husband and two of his half brothers. Then he set out on foot and by bus and train without a visa to a handful of Western European countries. He sneaked over borders, hid in container ships, rode rails. For a while, he even picked up cash as an illicit border guide, dodging bullets between Macedonia and Greece, smuggling Romanian refugees.

Finally, in Italy, he enjoyed one salad year as a successful hustler and car thief, but got thrown out on his ass for a failed heist. Budapest is the last of several attempts to escape bad luck. Pity that it's already dwindling into a sinister love story, a girl's life gone haywire, more about which he'll disclose later.

He shares a room with six others, who charge about three dollars a night for a bed that has to be vacated by eight a.m. for another guy with a night job, after which he spends each aimless day in a shopping mall, playing video games, fencing stolen goods, whatever comes up. Or he hangs out in a basement Romanian bar where the clientele specializes in forged passports, and late at night wanders the Corso, where which the wealth of tricks has dwindled to a trickle by the middle of winter.

His anecdotes of constantly narrowed horizons dovetail with descriptions I'll later read on the Internet about cloak-and-dagger human rights violations in his country during Communism, and after, until the late '90s. What will especially attract my attention are stories of the hunting out of homosexuals in towns and small cities by means of police maneuvers worthy of villains in silent films.

I wrench my eyes away from his death's head—the alcohol has lathed it with a blurry, drowned beauty—to glance once again at the dull, liberal faces of young bourgeois Hungarians milling around us, with their sensibly chic haircuts and inhibited expressions that seem so determined to master the vapid, hedonistic, athletic attitudes of the new economy. They and not he, of course, will be the inheritors of the European Expansion. Wouldn't it be delightful, I decide, to walk across a bridge over black water, in the middle of the night in a strange city and country, with this soon-to-be exile from liberalism? It must be a feeling, I fleetingly think, worth risking one's life for: snubbing up-and-coming Hungarians by putting myself in the hands of a gloomy, nearly homeless desperado. As Europe marches gloriously into the North American model, why not savor his keener feeling of exclusion?

Though I know very well that we're on our way to a sexual encounter—if not a robbery—his suave politeness feels like the kind reserved for an elder, a teacher—not a trick. Yet nothing in it promises that he won't suddenly bring out a knife on the bridge devoid of traffic at four in the morning or even push me into the Danube's razorish black crests. Each step across the bridge brings that lucky feeling of having gotten one more step across it, but always with the one I fear.

The Balkan-romantic, red-velvet-and-mahogany furnishings of the lobby add to this fantasy. The hotel, chosen by chance, is the 1918 Gellért, named after a saint who was slaughtered on the hill above. It's a medieval-looking monstrosity crouched right at the foot, close to the bridge, on the Buda side of the city. As if aware of the awful risk of our pairing, the doorman, who wears red-and-gold braid, lowers his eyes demurely, turning our walk to the elevator into a grave procession.

Our room is a tiny cell, offering little space between the mahogany wardrobe and the narrow bed. Tossing the black turtleneck onto a chair, he begins a mournful striptease. Slight, satin-skinned and covered with fresh bruises and old scars, he's nearly half the weight of my stocky, infinitely less wily body, cultivated by the ingenuous values of middle-class America.

He pounces for a seldom-had shower, while I stare at the worn-out pants and black turtleneck thrown across the chair...wondering whether I should go through his pockets, look for weapons or clues that he's been lying about his story. Instead, I lock the door of the room from the inside and slide the key far under the mattress. Only by overturning the mattress with me on it will he be able to rob me and leave. He'd have to murder me first.

The shower goes on endlessly, and then he's leaping into bed, his body snaky and slippery, his strong thighs quickly locking with mine.

"There's something Russian about you."

"Jewish," I add, as if he'd ended the word with a hyphen.

"Not a problem," he counters with blanking eyes, as my mind scans memories of old history books for the Romanian role in the Holocaust. Gently caressing my chest, he puts moist lips against my ear. "Put on the porno channel?"

Bare white concrete walls, lawn chairs, bodies, a fountain pool and potted palms, lit mercilessly by halogen lamps, explode from the screen in a utopia of flesh, aluminum and water.

German porno.

Upon a Mediterranean-blue chaise longue, a blonde lies masturbating. Ample breasts with large brown nipples pointing away from each other. Now a hairless, broad-shouldered demigod has stooped to eat her cunt in close-up. His tanned biceps bulge around her svelte thighs, against a fountain playing in the background. There's an unreal crispness to the digitized images flooding hallucinated libido into our room, now colored by the harsh, shifting, bright reflections.

I remember his name: Romulus.

He doesn't shed his social identity with his clothes as some people do. Nudity only sharpens his persona. Sex before the hard-edged German porn images becomes a feline experience—agile and evasive, always indicating beyond. His skin feels glossy, poreless. His rough hands spin out my excitement without sacrificing the gentlemanly cover of his cherished masculinity. They play across my nipples as he masturbates me, while I ponder the fact that such elegant sexual complexity as he's able to offer is in some way a handmaiden of the grotesque political prohibitions against homosexuals in his country. With proud narcissism he offers his body to be fondled, and when I ask him to put my cock in his mouth, he obliges. Sex as he sees it is a game of finesse and street honor, better understood by the disinherited. Through a drape of foreskin, droplets spray across my chest.

The German is bent back in an impossibly gymnastic posture, her legs straddling the gushing fountain, while the man's enormous cock slides in and out of her like a piston, his buttocks tensed like two planets.

It's almost dawn, but the privilege of lying next to such a petite, perfectly sculpted body keeps me entangled. I switch the channel to an American film, whose disturbing plot absorbs us as gray light seeps through the window. It's the story of wilderness scouts of the Old West, lost without food in a blizzard. Limbs freeze and gangrene, and food sticks to chilblained lips. Primal hunger transforms one of them into a deranged cannibal who must be kept chained, but not until he's eaten several people. The intricate, grisly tale of murder surging from hunger and Western pragmatism seems to suit Romulus well, who nods and clucks his tongue at each twist of plot, as if such occurrences were an ordinary part of life.

Several shifts of maids have knocked and gone before we disentangle. Doubtless, staying with me is a better option than going back to the shopping mall for the rest of the day.

Then we hurry. He has to meet four other Romanians at Nyugati Station. They're all going to Slovakia for the day to renew their visas. They have to leave Hungary once a month in order to live here.

Filled with nervous excitement at the chance of sampling his daytime life, I take him for a quick lunch at a bad Italian restaurant. Foolishly I offer to rent a car and drive all of them to the border and back, or take them to Romania for the day. My imagination zooms through the Hungarian countryside toward the forbiddingly exotic Romanian border, pressed between young vagrants who trust my generosity and courage. But my offer wins only a look of astonished suspicion, though after skipping a beat, he shrugs. "Okay."

On the way to meet his friends, he offers me a rapid tour of the station and points out a gangly man sidling through the crowd. "A Romanian," he says, with a grim smile, "a great pickpocket." We meet up with his friends, and the pickpocket is standing among them. Like Romulus, they're all spookily suave with their low-cost belled jeans, well-groomed hair and grimy hands. They size me up behind a restrained politeness. The gangly pickpocket looks relaxed, confident, but keeps refusing eye contact. A conspiratorial conversation in Romanian pitter-patters among them under their breaths, and Romulus informs me, "They say you are driving me to Romania too dangerous. Discrepancy between us will say to authorities that maybe we carry drug." He offers a hand stiff with pretentious camaraderie that the others scrutinize ironically. He'll meet me the next morning at eleven, at the Gellért, he promises. Off they go.

When—predictably, I suppose—he doesn't show up, the hysterical ecstasy of that first encounter takes a nosedive. It's as if I'd been plunked back into the West with all its deceptive marketing formulas. I go back to my room, sullenly change into a robe and head for the gloomy, cathedral-like bowels of the Gellért. They contain an enormous complex of baths filled with reproductions of classical statues and faux Byzantine columns, wanly lit by high, small windows in a vaulted, turquoise-tiled ceiling. There are a few curative pools featuring gnarled old men attached to monstrous pulley machines, intended with water therapy to correct skeletal misalignments.

In my mood of rejection, the lumbering locker attendant's frown seems accusatory. A burly masseur offers me an inexpensive half-hour mauling, but his hands are like an interrogation.

Feeling unpleasantly anesthetized, I go about my assignment for the online magazine. The only male brothel in Budapest is a tiny establishment with barely enough room for a horseshoe-shaped bar and seven stools. Three of them are taken up by the evening's trade. A platinum-haired adolescent, pasty and tubercularly elegant, and a darker, duller-looking hulk fix me in their sights. The underfed blond has a brutal effeminacy, a deprived Dietrich face, bony features set off by plush lips.

The bartender is a fat Ukrainian woman with a malicious smile and fast, greedy fingers, who increases the price with every drink I buy. Her hospitality is predatory, full of the threat of violence to enforce rules. The Dietrich boy, who speaks passable English, is fumbling in my lap with moist, wormy fingers. Nothing illuminates the underground chamber to which he leads me but the red coils of a heater and American porn glaring idiotically from a TV monitor. As I come, I'm instructed to shoot on the floor.

The next day I spend the afternoon wandering through the chilly catacombs of the castle district on the Buda hillside,

9

where female Soviet-style museum guards with steel-clamped expressions stand vigilant in their black costumes and white gloves. Outside, along the river, I pass svelte and busty women who exude Cold War chic like stewardess extras in *From Russia with Love.* A rosy-cheeked teenaged girl with longish, watery hair and dark circles under her eyes stares at me suspiciously. Everybody seems fiercely introverted.

Depressed, I walk over the bridge toward the stretch of waterfront where the black figure separated from black the night before. If I see him, I won't stop to speak.

Almost on cue, he's there, chatting idly with a group of underaged hustlers. He swaggers toward me with fake bullishness, as if ready to pick a fight. He'd waited, he exclaims cockily, in front of the Gellért for almost an hour. "But we were supposed to meet in the lobby," I protest.

Did I really expect him to make it past that doorman in his monkey suit of gold braid? Our dissonance of expectations produces an erotic, masochistic charge. What am I but a foolish tourist, blithely unaware of the class problems of a sex worker who, though without a future, is far savvier when it comes to social boundaries? He knows they won't let him into that hotel alone. Why didn't the ugly American think of it? This is when it occurs to me that it really is some unconscious feeling of discrepancy that arouses all of us. More than anything, I want to keep experiencing that epiphany.

Soon I'm swept into his sphere of control, while he stays grave and endlessly poised. Night comes, then grows blacker and more remote as we careen from bar to bar. With glum, masochistic eyes, he gives a vague, amoral report of the possibility of his Hungarian girlfriend's pregnancy, the opportunistic options for him in terms of bringing him closer to the European Union should they marry, and the confused, deadened affect produced in him by the idea of creating another life. His monologue is set off by numbed half-gestures of a cigarette-holding hand, as smoke curls across his luminously sallow skin.

When he met her a year ago, the possibly pregnant Hungarian girlfriend was, according to him, a good high school girl who lived with her parents. My vampiric empathy produces an image of her with the heart-shaped face, rosy cheeks and watered-honey hair of the teenaged Hungarian I passed that afternoon by the catacombs. Her moist, fragile hands poke from the sleeves of her oversized parka anxiously clasping his in hopeless excitement. When she's naked, I somehow believe, her body is pale pink and bruises easily. Her cunt hairs must be soft brown, with an overly sensitive slit that he has to coax open. And her gasping mouth saturates a strand of the hair falling across her face as he enters her, while she clutches his hard, slippery back, denting his skin with the cheap ring on her finger.

My stunned, mute gaze confuses him at first. It's too complicated for a john's. All he can say is, "I know you trying to read my thoughts. But truth is, me myself don't know what I am thinking."

He tells me that when the month in a rented room with the girl ended, there wasn't any more money. She was afraid to go back to her parents and became homeless with him. She would wait in the cold on the Corso while he combed shopping malls and bars for ways to make money or went off to one of the hotels to turn a trick. Then she, too, began working the Corso. After a few scary episodes, she found her way into a cathouse run by and for Asians.

"Every time I see a Chinese person I want to killing him," he spits.

*

We don't get back to the hotel until four a.m., and the sour desk clerk has had it. "Are you a guest?" he shoots out, before we can even make it to the elevator. I explain that my friend is only going up to watch television with me for a while, but the man insists on seeing his passport. When Romulus holds it out, he snatches it and locks it in a drawer.

We head for the elevator. I'm shaking with outrage, or is it fascination? Romulus has that stiff, sardonic expression of someone whose opinion of the human species has once again been proven. Inside the room, I barricade the door with a tilted chair and start pacing manically. What, if any, are the sanctions against prostitution in this country? I'd never thought to check. What's lurking on his record? Am I harboring a passport forger, or a murderer? How reasonable are the Hungarian police, so recently working for a Communist regime? What's their attitude toward homosexuality?

Holding a cigarette, he watches with sad bemusement, the way some people watch animals pacing in their cage at the zoo. Rapid footsteps in the hall are getting closer, but they just continue past.

My fingers shakily dial the desk clerk. "My friend is staying the night. Give us a double room and bring his passport back right away."

"Someone will be there to remove you," snaps the clerk, in what I hope is a case of bad English.

A formal, frowning bellboy arrives to swiftly gather our belongings, sweeping them, and us, to another, much larger room. I paste a dignified expression on my face and march Romulus down to the lobby to reclaim his passport. By this point we've fallen into a kind of corny intimacy based on my "heroic" behavior—in which formulas of gratitude, even little vows and cute recriminations, become the script. "I go with men, I think," says he, undressing on the velvet-upholstered stool, "because of something to do with the father. You would be the father I would wish to have."

To his vast credit, he plays this awkward part gracefully, even allowing new sexual liberties by putting them in the context of manly friendship. Of course, a blow job given in friendship isn't the most arousing, but it stays in the memory longer.

Then comes the quick exit: hurried packing, the exchange of money plus extra money, his rush to meet his girlfriend making her early-morning egress from the whorehouse.

The desk clerk has a surprise in store for me. Our new room has been billed as costing four times as much as the other—more than $350.

An hour into the transfer at Paris, a not altogether unfamiliar feeling begins its leaden crush. I could describe it, I suppose, by the term "sinking heart." It's part of a formula of erotic intensity, which, like most, never takes into account its own aftermath. Just before releasing subjects from the trance that causes their foolish behavior, stage hypnotists tell them, You will remember nothing. But maybe misgivings nag at the subject afterward.

My black despair has little to do with anything so banal as our physical separation but is, instead, that sense of shame and helplessness that comes from opening up to a certain type of hopeless person. Just days later, he'll call me in New York (collect) to tell me that his girlfriend has been stabbed at the cathouse by an irate client. He'll ask me to wire money, and I will.

II

I'm lying in my bed in Manhattan's East Village, surrounded by books on Central Europe and Romania, thinking about last week's trip to Budapest, so repulsive and enthralling. In this year 1999, the context of my life is changing. The trip has marked a new start. Strangely, I'm full of all kinds of new imaginings and philosophies. The silly idea has even crossed my mind that sex in the dark must have been invented by northerners like these chilly Hungarians, whose weak-lashed eyes would have found the sunlight too clinical.

I put down the book on the Magyar tribes, and my head falls back as if hypnotized. Lust for flesh under the smell of pelts must not have been very different from hunger for meat, I imagine, and I myself am in a swoon, famished for Romulus.

I roll the melodramatic name across my tongue. He's called twice already, each time in need of money. Charity needs images. When he asked for a hundred dollars to bribe the doctor of his stabbed, probably watery-haired girlfriend to get better treatment, I had to picture the white walls of the hospital, him perched yawningly, casually, by the bed.

His second call was to announce that he was leaving Budapest and the penniless mess into which he'd sunk. When he got to the train station, I wired a little more money, after which he disappeared. He never showed up for Christmas at his mother's home in Sibiu, Romania, as he'd promised. I called there four times that day, to the perplexed reactions of mother and brothers and cousins.

A week later, he did show up in Sibiu and immediately called collect. With weary, casual poise he detailed his attempt to get to Italy by way of Vienna—and my money. It was, he claimed, a spur-of-the-moment decision. He bought the ticket and hid in the train toilet when they got to the Austrian border but was caught anyway, and spent a depressing Christmas in jail that he didn't want to talk about. Still, I tried to picture him lean and inebriated from depression, squatting in a corner of the cell, waiting for the long unraveling of red tape that would ship him home on some hard train seat.

Home—Romania—is a shadow-desire for me; a few blurry TV images of a monster dictator and his wife assassinated—two crumpled bodies in black-and-white. It was the only violent anti-Communist revolution in Eastern Europe. And then there was that time, in 1991, I think, when I went to Hamburg to work on a film script. At the train station and in the St. Pauli district there were clusters of teenaged refugees working as hustlers who I found out were Romanian. I remember their brooding young faces, with similarly wolfish haircuts and that identical expression—what would you call it? Seductively depressed. A stylized, toreador-Elvis look, full of bruised machismo and oversensitivity, bewildered surrender.

Other images of his country, perhaps no less obscure, emerge from a book I choose from those scattered on the bed. They're morbid and fantastic like German fairy tales, full of romanticism and guilt. In a palace in Bucharest, across the room from a throne, a balcony veiled by gauze curtains; food on gold platters and champagne in a crystal flute are being carried to it by a servant in black livery. From time to time, a king in a white silk cloak imprinted with a crimson cross looks up at the curtains to raise his glass in a toast. He is Carol II (1893–1953), prince of the German house of Hohenzollern-Sigmaringen, the last king of non-Fascist Romania. The woman hidden in the balcony to whom the king raises his toast is his mistress—Elena, née Lupescu, from the Romanian word *lup* for "wolf." She's at least half Jewish, and her life is in danger. The country is turning Fascist and is against her. They've accused her of being a "voluptuous parasite," the king's Semitic manipulator, whose wiliness is degenerating the nation....

What kind of country can produce such risky melodrama? I actually know very little about it. According to these books on my bed, Romania has always been a land of necessary suspicion, hemmed in by larger powers greedily eyeing its riches. A manipulative Austro-Hungarian Empire lurking in the west, swallowing and regurgitating its western territories; to the northeast, the heavy fist of Russia clamoring for influence; to the south, an implacable, exploitative Ottoman Empire and an envious Bulgaria.

Its people date back to the year 101, when tribes known as Dacians are conquered by the Roman Empire, whose soldiers intermarry with their women. By the end of the thirteenth century, it has become two fertile principalities, Wallachia and Moldavia, which hug the Danube River. Centuries of occupation from nearby Turkey follow, aided by Greek governors called Phanariots, who bleed the country dry. The Romanian landed gentry, the Boyars, are in thrall to these foreign leaders; and to compensate for it, they in turn suck the wealth of the land to its marrow, leaving the peasants impoverished and bitter. To make matters worse, Russian and Austro-Hungarian neighbors are hungering for mineral-rich Romanian territory, playing for it against the Turks in a brutal game of Monopoly. But during all this—for some unexplainable reason—the people keep their ancient identity: they believe they are the only true surviving *Latins*, adrift in a hostile Slavic wilderness.

It's only in the aftermath of the Crimean War (1854–1856) that Romania finally emerges as a nation. In 1866, a foreigner comes to claim the kingship, hoping to put an end to power squabbles. The outsider is the German Carol I, a prince of the Hohenzollern-Sigmaringen dynasty, who governs Romania with the Teutonic discipline and iron hand of his royal forebears. In 1893, Carol I's weak nephew and future successor, Ferdinand, marries the stunning Marie, Princess of Edinburgh, the eldest daughter of the Duke and Duchess of Edinburgh and a granddaughter of Queen Victoria.

It is charismatic Marie, the queen beginning in 1914, who brings Romania to the attention of the West. During the negotiation of the Treaty of Versailles, she works seductively behind the scenes to acquire Transylvania for Romania and enlarge the country along the lines of its present dimensions. But soon she will be forcibly put on the shelf by her profligate son, Carol II; and under his rule, Romania slips irresistibly toward Fascism and Nazi control. When World War II ends, the country becomes a member of the Communist bloc.

A shudder, swallowed by a pit of longing. Is it any wonder that my new obsession comes from an amputated country with a fractured identity, a country that is like an abused child from a broken home? How much of this traumatic history is hidden in his dark, suspicious eyes? All I know is: I have to find out.

Such thoughts rattle through my mind as I call my editor to report on the assignment. His voice skips only a beat when I announce that the piece I'm going to write for him will be called "The Romanian."

"What happened to the brothel-in-Budapest assignment we paid for?"

"Trust me, this will slay you," I shoot back with the conviction of an addict. Then I launch into a breathless, rambling monologue. Heterosexual though he may be, my editor is a connoisseur of any form of sexual energy, and I can hear him savor each nugget. But when I try to explain who Romulus is, I'm at a loss for words.

"He's a..." I don't say "vampire." Romulus comes from the land of Dracula, and it would be too much of a cliché to resort to those kinds of metaphors.

"He's..."

I falter. Because he's no one, I suddenly realize, a person with no identity moving illegally and aimlessly from country to country. A vacuum sucking my lost life forward.

Then who am I?

I am, it occurs to me as I put down the phone and page obsessively through the books on Romania, a cultural leftover. An old-fashioned, pre-Stonewall homosexual. As recently as six years ago, I still spent white nights in the company of Midtown Manhattan hustlers, ex-cons and junkies, sponging up their speech and vampirizing their emotions to write about. This was, of course, before Manhattan became an entertainment complex for singles of a single class and gay life began turning into just another assimilation story. Now that gay life has grown blander and duller, it seems more and more identical to the world of family values I thought I was escaping. The field of my libido has shrunk; and since writing is desire, my texts have grown shorter. I long for new voices and accents, new worlds to mirror my loneliness and isolation.

To get back to the new world of Budapest and its offer of pure social disconnection, I've taken a job as a technical writer in a financial printing company going digital. It's the dullest job of my life. Five days a week I spend seven hours in a stifling, windowless room packed to bursting with Indians, Pakistanis and Russians, whose skills have bought them entrance to the United States on temporary visas. The room is white and silent, except for the tic-tac-tic of keyboards, endlessly producing 0's and 1's and 0's and 1's, for hours, days, weeks, months, without any programmer's looking up or stopping or speaking, for fear of being sent away from the West and back to poverty.

I gaze at my own dazed reflection in the poisonous cathode-ray screen, adding a tac to their tic every once in a while, checking expedia.com every twenty minutes or so to type the words "new york...budapest" or dropping my head to read the book in my lap about King Carol II's Jewish mistress, *Lupescu: The Story of a Royal Love Affair.*

In exchange for an impossible fantasy about a hustler, I've convinced myself that this temporary situation doesn't matter. My mind is full of strategies for fleeing the city into the next touch of his hard-rubber body. In this stuffy white room, excitement courses through me like sap. I imagine great bursts of inspiration. Books about Eastern Europe and love and risk and class dissonance. Sexual desire, I'm convinced, is merely the interplay of social inequities—or should I say dreams about the libidinal possibilities of the Other. But now that gentrification has increasingly separated us from a clash with those who are different, libidinal energies are becoming blocked and denatured. If we want to, we can go our whole lives without seeing someone from another background. The Other has been banished from our reach. Am I foolish enough to think that I've found a way out?

Earlier I claimed that arousal is just an unconscious sense of discrepancy, a feeling of imbalance. Then desire, or love, must be the servant of that same impression of injustice—a perverse urge to settle the balance.

These thoughts recur in fragmented form in a low-ceilinged suburban bedroom in Syracuse, New York, in the house in which I grew up. I've come back here to visit my ancient mother—another exile from Eastern-bloc turmoil. A Jew, she came to the States from Russia at the age of two, almost a century ago, with her family, so that her father could avoid being drafted into the czar's army.

Now, as I gaze out the bedroom window at the carpet of snow, drugs lick my nervous cells into bolder imaginings. Is this the eighth or ninth tablet of codeine I've taken—ostensibly for a toothache? I really should watch it, stop raiding friends' medicine cabinets to supplement my stash, popping them at the slightest sense of isolation.

It must be past two a.m. Like a mask of latex sealing off the head of a fetishist, the drug encases my brain, and my whole body disintegrates into a low-resolution image. Visions are pulsing, full of that energy that was killed off in New York with the last peep show. Periodically, the glowing silver shovel of Romulus's face leaps out, as in an old-fashioned photographic instant when the flash powder goes off. Then the image melts away, and the dark bedroom in Syracuse pops back into hard focus.

I open my eyes, feel the drops of fantasy evaporating from neurons, the bright emulsion fading, and I remember my stubborn, endlessly resilient but finally failing mom lying in the next boxy room. Our doors have been left ajar all night because she's awoken so many times by her bad heart. With a twinge of guilt, I rise unsteadily and tiptoe into her bedroom to check on her again, a glimpse of the bundled body I've known all my life, so still now and surrounded by foreboding; and then I come closer, bend with held breath until my face is nearly touching hers, to be sure she's still breathing....

Before we went to bed, we talked about my time in Budapest, which is—it comes to mind—only a few hundred miles from Shedrin, in White Russia, where she was born. I had to shout because her hearing is going. But despite her advanced age of ninety-six, her strong will and sharp intelligence are completely intact. I can picture her so clearly right now, frail but enlivened by the favorite topic of me—leaning forward on the very edge of her seat at the kitchen table so as not to miss a word, scrutinizing me with attentive, worried eyes, asking probing questions and desperately hoping for all the false answers; hoping I'll materialize by some magic into the prudent, cautious traveler I wasn't.

Fascination came early to me because of her. In a way, the stage was set early for the hypnotic hold of this new obsession. I've been told that I was a receptive baby, used to being gathered abruptly into the arms of this delighted, full-breasted woman whose china-blue eyes sparkled with joy as her charismatic, booming voice imprinted me with its linguistic mastery. From several family pictures, I can reconstruct her habit of holding me under my arms and hoisting me to my toes as if I were standing, then bouncing me up and down on her soft lap as the pleasure began to ripple.

If my senses mesmerize me, it must be because of her: those arrivals in rouge, perfume and a '50s veiled hat: moments of epic excitement. But I also remember her departures, which occurred more and more frequently as she became a community activist. Then absence stretched to infinity.

White-limbed and smooth-skinned as my mom seemed, she was already a woman in her mid-forties. I was a child of her old age, an unusual occurrence for that era. Almost from the beginning I could feel the morbid threat of her increasing years and impending death, and I suppose this intensified the romance.

I still remember the spell of her bedroom, which seemed like a palace of sensuality. From the large mahogany dresser emerged shiny costume jewelry, filmy stockings and bright snaking scarves, which she'd let me touch. After cinching her waist in a white clasp girdle, she'd smooth a nutmeg stocking up an ivory leg and clip it to the hanging garters. My fascination and anxiety—based on the fact that she was getting ready to leave—built as I watched her apply the dense powder and bright rouge that would turn her face into an abstract treasure under a veil. Over her shiny blouse she'd button the pearl-gray jacket that clung to her hips. Then she'd pin on the enigmatic hat and slip into the haughty navy blue heels. The spell caused by all this had the same quality as that excitement the moment I saw Romulus's hollow-cheeked face, cut from the black. For me, I suppose, he was some imago emerging from the dark past, like the fleeting figure of my mother turning off the light at night, then horribly vanishing into blackness.

How else to describe the transformation of a boxlike suburban room in Syracuse into one of high ceilings with peeling plaster walls and nicked, ornate molding, the shoddy splendor of an old room in Budapest with warped floorboards that creak if one dare change position? It's the room I imagine he rents in Budapest, where he probably sleeps with his head just a few feet from the triple-socked feet of the pickpocket from the train station.

Images of him come now just as they are said to do before

dying, when each nanosecond delivers a lengthy plot. The memory of clasping that hard, smooth waist and bending to tongue the nipples of that pallid chest. Or his mean rosebud mouth tightening with suspicion around a cigarette. Then another dissolve, murky and shimmering like water, into his silhouette getting smaller as he walked away from the hotel.

This afternoon, I could hear my old mother's voice crack when she made an effort to take my answers about my trip to Budapest casually. Like some puritanical bloodhound, she sniffed out my elation, which stimulated her fantasy life, composed primarily of worries about me. "You didn't meet anybody when you were there?" she interrogated. "In such a desperate place, I'd imagine." And, "Why do you go on taking such difficult assignments?"

Because she'd failed miserably in her attempts to fashion me into her aspirations, the sum of which created a cartoon dream, I was a constant source of anxiety—the type of writing I did, the fact that I'd swerved into bohemia early and never returned, after being such a model, adoring child....Even so, she's one stalwart soldier—I mean, general. Unerringly she tracks the path of her obsession step by step through its most exotic transgressions, always demanding to know everything. I can sense her on the road with me perpetually, pleading with me to give up "the Life." To this day I haven't been able to escape the persistence of her radarlike surveillance, wheedling for a return to common sense, mourning my transformation into something alien, unmanageable and male. Like an organism with no cell wall and thus no intact inner life, I've been forced again and again to vomit out my fantasies and desires for her approval that was never forthcoming, even as the loss of privacy deteriorated my ego. Over the years we developed a confession ritual. No matter how hard I tried to protect her and myself from the details of my private life, she always got them out of me.

"Well, yeah, I did meet one person."

Mom's eyes turned to steel and a chill crept into her voice. "Was it a man?"

My bowdlerized description of meeting Romulus—a preposterous subject to have mentioned at all—didn't seem to fool her a bit. She zeroed in with questions about how I'd been able to make a "friend" in a strange country in so short a time, and why he'd left home. And what had I said he "did for a living"? Somehow, she sensed the whole picture, despite my guarded answers and evasions, because deep down I wanted her to.

Yet never in a million years could she enter my world, which explodes in another burst of opiates...then ripples away again into the blackness....I can glimpse him once more, pale and slumped against the wall of that freezing Austrian holding cell, after being arrested on the train. And here I lie in this clean powder-blue room, with a full stomach.

Like comets, my charged neurons fly through space, swirl about the Austrian–Hungarian border and penetrate that prison, perhaps by smothering it with ugly American dollars. In the middle of the night there's the clank of the cell door opening. The silver spade of a face buried in a grimy sleeve jerks up in surprise, then floods with wonder and relief at the sight of me. He's being let out because of me.

Or perhaps I pull the limp, exhausted body up into my arms to feel the pleasure of it slumping against me like a life-sized rag doll, as the sharp, wet features and oily, straight hair press against my neck. For isn't such time-and-space travel what codeine and passion are for?

*

I wonder whether Romulus ever thought of me while he was in jail. At any rate, he couldn't possibly picture me here, on this absurd four-poster in suburbia. I know for certain he has fantasies about America. Only the feel of its pavement under his feet would be enough, he told me on that first night in Budapest. Maybe, as he sat in his cell, he imagined me in a New York gleaned from old movies, with spider-black skyscrapers and tarnished-silver sky, gangsters and amber liquor...while he crouched there, angry and depleted like a rat in a cage. And earlier...on that clanging train from the Communist period—not headed east to Romania, as he'd promised before I sent the money, but west to Vienna—was he thinking of me then?

The train pulls in at the border....He's probably crouching in a crawl space over the toilet ceiling. His half-bent knees, so long in that position, are starting to shoot pains. A wooden baton is banging on the slightly open partition in the ceiling. When it won't budge, the guard calls a colleague to lean on so that he can climb onto the toilet seat and bang harder. Romulus's head is jammed against an iron beam.

When a foot finally dangles from the crawl space, I bet they grab for it and yank down roughly. Romulus lands on the small of his back on the toilet seat and slides to the floor.

The whiz of the tires of the Syracuse city plow on wet snow loosens the luminous grip of these ideas. The ray of a headlight brings me back to the American suburbs, illuminating the insipid blue of the bedroom curtains. Restless, I think about getting up to check on Mom again, but merely recover the image of her chest rising and falling, her small form bundled in blankets.

Then the curtains are swallowed back up by the darkness, the half-dreams begin their rippling again, coaxed into larger and larger waves by the trails of codeine. Against my will, I'm thinking of that hypothetical watery-haired girlfriend of his, a little bloated from her late nights and beers, in a cheaply furnished room of the brothel located in a concrete high-rise. She is struggling against the drunken hand of a Chinese client whose pants are open at the fly. His arm is fumbling with her shoulder in an attempt to pin it against the hollow-sounding plasterboard, which makes an idiotically thudding echo, and all because he wants to fuck her without a condom. When she finally bites the hand that's trying to muffle her screams, he lets go of her; but as she's straightening her ripped black décolleté dress, a glitter of steel driven by an irrational flash of anger plunges between her ribs, after which protectors come running, the client is ejected and the girl taken to the hospital.

I don't know it yet, but soon I'll arrive in her psychic space. Black is leaking in from the hallway like tar. In the four-poster, my hand slides across my hip. A white hiss travels up my legs; it's as if my confused body were dissolving into these sharp flashes of pleasure, pulverized into black-and-white dots by my pumping heart.

Afterward, I stumble to the bathroom to wipe the come off with a paper towel. When I return, I stare out the shoulder-high window. The storm has let up, revealing the huge evergreen across the road. Then once again the air—and my mind—become a prison of swarming white, obscuring everything, scorching my brain cells with hunger—like those famished northern hunters—for the flesh of Romulus.

The following evening, after my return to New York, I flee to an old friend, the writer Ursule Molinaro, who, at her advanced age—after the turmoil of war and Europe and rebellious love affairs and a bilingual career as a fiction writer—is a fellow connoisseur and victim of risk. She's been bedridden for more than two weeks, but she disdains help from the medical establishment. After being imprisoned during World War II in France, she swore off all association with institutions, preferring instead to develop an open attitude to the meaning of death.

Molinaro's tired yet crisp, marquesa-like voice expresses contentment about the energy I'm bringing near her. We've known each other for years, and during that time refined our anti-Protestant, pro-Latin aesthetic ideology; our penchant for surfaces and ceremonies, bodies, discretions and perversions; our choice of drama over security. She's also a lover of languages, five of which she speaks without any accent.

Propping herself up in bed with several pillows, she professes herself delighted by my new entanglement, its connection to Latin culture and the Latin language, its displacement in the Balkan world, and Romulus's ominous allure. When I show her a picture of his balletically long neck and spectral cheekbones, it sends her fantasizing as a way of supporting me. How eager she is to approve what the Other can offer! Together we immerse ourselves in this new obsession, this palpable symbol of our alienation, feeling all the more content that he spells danger, risk, which is sometimes the messenger of death.

"You must get him on the stage, in theater!" she announces archly, gleefully, with the photo pinched between her pallid bony fingers. Her eyes, clouded by illness, gleam with approval, delight for my adventure into another linguistic reality, a sexual labyrinth.

"It's an ancient face," she decrees.

"Yes, it could almost come from the Roman period," I agree.

"Long, long before," she insists.

And so we sit in her tiny bedroom on East Second Street, celebrating my new adventure, which, unknown to us, is fated to overlap with her death.

III

My eyes are twin snails inching down a statue, past the hostile wings of the hunched shoulders, past the nipple red and erect and slightly askew from my nibbling, to the hyperlean stomach muscles, which tell the story of his multiple starvations. All caused by the accident of being born Romanian and leaving for countries where no Romanians are wanted—which means most.

I've flown back. I came as soon as he called me and mentioned that his relationship with the girl in the brothel was over. We're in Budapest, and we've had our first bout of sex. Things are settling in; they were at loose ends before. Before the plane left the runway, fear about flying to a Romanian vagrant whose features I could now hardly picture gripped me, until an image of him—lithe and sinister—sizzled in my brain like a branding. I buckled myself to the seat, and his spell took complete control of me again, put me back in that blank, teetering moment like the one before orgasm, just as the plane's takeoff flattened my body against the seat. For the rest of the trip I held on to the picture of his gaunt, big-nosed face, the ferocious irony in his deadened eyes.

My fantasy, however, was deflated when I saw that pale, chain-smoking kid, a little less than half my age, waiting for me with a crinkled smile, at Ferihegy Airport. Somehow he seemed too diminutive, inexperienced, to have sent me running for a plane, my wallet stuffed with cash-machine money. Our taxi ride to the Margitsziget Hotel in near silence seemed unreal and synthetic. Confused, I fell down next to him on the queen-sized bed and plunged into a deep, jet-lagged sleep.

When I woke up, he was in his underwear, settled patiently next to me, the way a cat waits for the next event over which it has no control. On TV was a soccer match, which he followed through heavy lids, shrouded by the clouds of smoke he exhaled. Instinctively, I burrowed my face in the crotch of his briefs while he kept smoking, getting more and more aroused, never looking down until I slid off the briefs and gulped him to the root, as he clasped my head and shoulders, and I finally pulled away as he ejaculated, but not fast enough to avoid the dribble that clung to my eyelash.

I rushed in a panic to wash it off, and he snarled an acidic observation about my lack of trust in his seronegativity. Then he chuckled fatalistically. He lit another cigarette and switched the channel.

When I came back, I put my face very close to his and let the trance that had been my reason for coming swallow me. Soon I was entirely inside what I'd longed for. What was it, exactly? Not just the thud of his coiled muscles against my body, nor even the roller coaster of genital contact; something else. Nothing short, in fact, of a generous portion of his inner life, which I imagined I could read, or hallucinate, in the hyper-close-up of his dark, Oriental face. From any distance it worked a harsh schematic on the eyes—it's a face that can look cruel, if cruel can be lazy—but very close up, just before my eyes began to blur, I thought it began to release a bizarre humanity—if, indeed, humanity can be thought of as a mismatch of parts, the poignancy of things not fitting together. His face was a cluster of cruelty, laziness, sweetness and vulnerability—built from the spotty patchwork of a life.

By this time the room was full of smoke, which cut it off from the sunny world outside. When I'd booked our hotel, I hadn't realized it was on an island in the Danube, a nature preserve protected from the hubbub of the city. I could immediately feel that for him it was a kind of cage. He saw no privilege in this isolation, in having nature served up to him, and glued himself to the television as if it were a lifeline. But I could feel that his body was tensed with expectation. His face was glowing, excited. I knew he was ready for a new chapter in his life.

I'd never noticed the roundish, quarter-sized scar near his jugular vein—though I'd been curious about another scar encircling the end of his large nose as if someone had tried to lop it off. Draping a soccer-defined thigh over mine, he languidly confirmed the violent cause of both scars, panto-mimed with a jocular arm the stroke of the blade that opened both places on the skin in one curved swipe. Between exhales of smoke, he described the brawl in front of a bar that left him lying in a parking lot as blood gushed from his jugular vein and sliced nose through splayed fingers.

There is a second scar on his neck, which I hadn't noticed. It was from the stroke of a scalpel, he explained, the sur-gical aftermath of a drunken car accident and an attempt by doctors to repair a broken neck by cutting in from the front. It happened in Romania. He was drunk, but the other driver, who came to the hospital weeping and begging him not to press charges, was at fault. Romulus couldn't lift the head attached to his broken neck and remembers only the trembling top of the kneeling man's hat. He identified so strongly with his desperation that he let him off.

Then he rebelled against the doctors, threatening to walk

out of the hospital, demanding a beer. He removed the brace to make it easier to get at a pack of cigarettes, swore there was nothing wrong with him, tried to leave—right up to the moment when the anesthesiologist held a dripping needle in the air, told him he was the most difficult patient the hospital had ever had, and gave the injection that plunged him into unconsciousness, and, against the odds, let him wake up repaired rather than paralyzed.

The scars on his legs are from attempts to cross into Greece through a Macedonian wood where he'd been lurking for a day and a night; he was shot at six times by border guards as he ran through brambles until he made it past the frontier into Greece, a lacework of blood pouring from his ripped shins.

Berries hastily nibbled in more woods until, two weeks later, he sneaks into the hull of a container ship at Patras on its way to Italy. There's nothing to eat or drink during a roundabout, sweltering voyage but a crate of melons. Weak and disoriented, he creeps into the blinding sun of Bari and steals food on his journey by foot and by hitchhiking to Rome, where, supposedly, fate smiles on him for six golden months.

The highlight of the Roman period comes with a rusty-fendered Fiat spitting diesel and making the late-afternoon rounds of viale delle Belle Arti, opposite the Galleria Nazionale di Arte Moderna. The driver shoots glances at him. Why? He's only one of several unremarkable hustlers leaning roguishly against the sun-dappled tree trunks. Astonishingly, the driver is a paragon of Italian beauty—or is it Sicilian? There's a touch of the African in her prominent lips rouged in luscious purple or the pale-sienna dome of her forehead above half-circle eyebrows, trimmed and penciled to the thinnest of lines. The car putters to a halt, and the young woman leans out the driver's window. He can't believe she's pointing at him with an arm sleeved in crisp linen, the cuff clasped by a pearl button. He floats to the car window, from which waft clouds of a jasmine-and-rose perfume. *Joy!* he exultantly thinks, having once made a mental note of the expensive scent when a trick took him shopping on via Veneto.

He sleepwalks into the front seat, the perfume overwhelming him, and stares in disbelief at her crisp pleated linen skirt creeping above the knee of her cinnabar leg. She shifts into first, her soft hand with its polished beige nails grazing the side of his thigh. She speaks in a thick, hoarse whisper, never quite looking him in the eye, and suggests they stop for a drink. Then there is that sumptuous dinner all paid by her, and afterward that club he considers the best in Rome, with the house music so booming that it makes the air between your pant leg and shin vibrate, although there are hustlers in the crowd who recognize him, but he ignores them all. Never has he felt this mesmerized by a woman's power as she leads him into the ladies' room and locks the door. After covering his mouth, neck and chest with her purple mouth, she bends and raises her skirt and puts her back to him, then guides him inside her effortlessly, her head thrown back to enjoy his hungry, gasping kisses and controlling bites.

But ever so quickly after: coolness takes over, a strange restlessness. It turns him into a cheap hustler again, something she picked up for an evening's pleasure. In her puttering Fiat, neither of them says a word when she drives him back to viale delle Belle Arti. All the next day, leaning against the same tree, discussing prices with potential tricks, he spends hours imagining their second encounter, how he'll show her that he's something more than she thought, maybe even reject her until she begs. The fact of this bounty fallen out of nowhere fills him with vertigo, panic. He must discover before she returns exactly how he'll win, since the chance won't come again. He's willing to spend some of the money on her that he's saved from hustling, and wonders, Could she really love him, will he end up leaving this life for her?

Late that afternoon around the same time, just as he'd hoped, the car reappears. He bounces toward it with an eager, cocky smile, his heart bursting through his chest. She's grinning, too; but with a hint of resignation creasing the corners of her mouth? Almost proudly—is it even with a touch of sadism?—she tells him there's something she must ask, but first she must know, did he enjoy fucking her in the ass last night as much as he seemed to? *In the ass?* He thought that they were...You were very, very drunk, my dear, but wasn't it delicious? It embarrasses him to talk about it like this, leaning into a car window, with all the other hustlers staring at his butt. Then you'll be patient? *Patient about what?* he wants to know. Until I get my pussy. I'm almost ready for my sex change.

A new kind of vertigo, like acid leaking into brain cells, makes him lose his balance. He can feel the other hustlers are staring...staring...maybe they knew the punch line all along. If it weren't for those heels, those stockings, he says under his breath, I'd teach you a lesson man to man. But honey, she says, we were so good together. His hand moves back to strike her, and as the Fiat putters off, forced, brittle laughter cackles from it.

Even so, this was a year of great accomplishments, rare pleasures. His Italian, a language with many similarities to Romanian, got so good that people couldn't tell he wasn't native. A trick even got him a one-time job posing for a perfume ad. They wanted a highly romantic Latin look—his black hair gleaming with gel, his thin eyebrows arched in sinister seduction; he can still remember the feeling of his Adam's apple rubbing against that crisp white collar. And then the red car, the convertible in which he's shown sitting, actually almost belonged to him. Another trick, an executive with the Hilton chain, leased it for him, along with a suite of rooms to live in.

In another picture, which the Hilton guy took, and which he thinks is at his mother's, there he is, on the beach, so tanned he almost changed races; and he was lifting weights at the hotel, gaining weight from eating so much pasta. But the worst thing about that Hilton guy was the sex. He wanted him to do all kinds of disgusting stuff; after a few weeks he just couldn't deal with it anymore.

That was a salad year, all the same, he claims, exhaling self-satisfied smoke rings. The money he made! He sent most of it home, over four thousand, which paid his parents' rent for four years when he got back. And not all of it came from hustling. He was an ace wire-crosser, a car thief. A Romanian network takes the car right off your hands. It's not such a big deal in Italy like it is here in Hungary. A lot of times they let you go, just make you give the car back.

Then, finally, he met Angelita, a real Italian and a real woman. And not far from a tin shantytown in a dusty Roman suburb, there they are dancing on the terrace of a club. The strings of colored lights leave glints on her satiny forehead, her wet lips and shiny brown hair, under a heavy, starless black sky impregnated by metallic music. The air feels humid, oppressive, especially since he's drunk too much; and the alcohol's moving through him like shifting quicksand. Each dance step he takes seems so perfect, in that minimal way he's learned to move, as if it's a gesture rather than a dance; but there's also that leaden feeling.

Out on the street, the polished fender of a Ferrari. He realizes he's yanking Angelita toward it. No, no, she's giggling under her breath, as he makes her go over to it, caress the shiny hood and ornament with the palm of her hand. Who in this lousy neighborhood could have such a car? Then he remembers the gold bracelet on the wrist of the silver-haired, bag-eyed businessman in the severely tailored suit and polished shoes, and the two scrawny African girls in bright blue dresses, needle marks on their arms, the hookers who were dancing with him. He thinks of the man's stiff expression of entitlement...which to his surprise makes him think of the tiniest newborn, the cutest imaginable, in a flowery crib, it's the businessman's child, and here's the father carousing in this sleazy neighborhood until dawn, fooling with skanky prostitutes.

He's suddenly so furious at this...this father...that in seconds he's accomplished the trick of prying down the Ferrari's window by twisting his knife between the rubber and the glass; and as Angelita keeps giggling nervously, he unlatches the door and pushes her into the car. And while her voice, now shaky, obviously drunken, is breathing, No, no, no...he shows her how he can break a lever to silence the shrieking alarm and cross the wires of the engine, which starts with a roar....

"But I crash it a couple blocks later, I was so drunk, and get arrested," he says with a grim chuckle. "And it seems asshole who owns car is what-do-you-call-it, government official. So police taking me to border of Slovenia and saying to me, you can never coming back to this country, buddy, you stealing a car, get out of here. And then the Slovenians having to ship me back to Romania."

*

The trees outside melted into the dark sky hours ago. Our first evening together is half over. We're still in bed in front of the television. His leg is still hooked over mine. Though the late-February weather is mild, all at once the room is chilly. Outside, the leaf buds look weirdly hardened, molded from some dark metal, their branches like black bundles of cable.

Shiveringly, we climb into a cab to ride to dinner. His peppery rankness fills the air inside. It's a perfume part rebellion and part musk of depression. Some of it still stings my tongue from the sex we had, plunging me deeper into his dislocated thoughts. Years of failed exiles have turned him into a language machine. I can feel his mind jigsawing through multiple lexicons—Romanian, Italian, English, Hungarian, Greek, German. Language for him is the cubism of survival. He'll speak a word and, under his breath, quiz himself for versions of it in the other languages he knows—in case he'll need them. Later a friend, the Romanian writer Carmen Firan, will describe this to me as a "Gypsy tongue."

In the restaurant, Romulus's ears are pricked like a spy's and his eyes blank. He's evaluating that couple across the room. A Pole speaking accented German sprinkled with bad English to a woman speaking good German and English who must be Czech, he decides. His foxlike face screws up in shrewd satisfaction.

Always next to his hip is the cell phone the ex-girlfriend bought him when she was in business at the brothel, so she'd be able to keep track of his whereabouts. I fix my eyes on it, ask about it. Now it can only receive calls, he says, not make them, the card's been used up. But just as my mind moves elsewhere, the phone jangles.

He holds it to his ear, speaks in Romanian. Who, who is it, I desperately want to know. His hooded eyes only grow more opaque, his pallor more pronounced. There is, he admits, after hanging up, another *girl* here in Budapest. He says the word "girl" the way you would say "job," dispassionately, with an air of bored utilitarianism. I told her, he goes on, that my American *uncle* was coming to visit. (He rewards the word "uncle" with more status than "girl," a tie of blood.) "And I told her that while my uncle was here for ten days, I could not be with her at all."

"And what did she say?"

"'Why?'" he says. "She say, 'Why?'"

"You can see her once or twice," I say, my eyes becoming more hooded than his. "Your *job* with me isn't all twenty-four hours a day." And of course, the word "job" cuts through him, my revenge for the word "uncle."

"Is not necessary," he says, getting stonier.

Two days later his very pungent cock dangles over my face as I sit on the floor between his legs and nip at the foreskin. It smells strongly of pussy. He'd disappeared for six hours with some of the money I'd given him to get a haircut, hooking up with his pleading girlfriend, I later found out. Supposedly, he took her to the movies, but then, he added casually, with a kind of masochistic pride in his vulgarity, fucked her in the toilets. While I lay in bed waiting and waiting and growing progressively more anguished, angrier, killing time by reading about King Carol's enormous sexual prowess in the disappointing and clichéd *Balkan Ghosts,* until everything seen through the haze of the many codeine tablets I took somehow faded into this *girl* I'd imagined: the watery hair, the easily bruisable skin...And now I didn't identify with her at all, or feel I was becoming her in that abject sense I'd felt before—and she became the *enemy.*

Insolently coaxing the girl into the bathroom as she murmured over and over, "But why can't I meet your *uncle?*" Sliding the latch of the toilet door shut. Covering her neck with kisses forceful enough to leave bruises. Taking her hair in one hand like a horse's tail and pulling her face against him, then lowering it slowly down his chest toward his open fly...

When my mind was so choked with resentment that I couldn't read the words on the page, I took a bus to the Corso, that boardwalk along the Danube where we'd met, and sat glaring at the windswept waves. Then I began to walk, as if through gelatin and surreal loss. There was the occasional wizened hustler sitting in one of the small parks, face scoured by months of cold wind, hands cracking with vitamin deficiencies....Until finally, I found myself sitting in a cab again, taking the useless trip back to the empty hotel room. It's really an annoying trip. I had no idea the hotel was so isolated, would cost so much to get to.

At the hotel a strange presence lurked about a hundred feet from the entrance, like an animal crouched in the bushes. And then slowly, abashedly, it appeared, like something that had no right to be there, creeping toward me with head bowed, and a timid, self-punishing smile that gave me a secret twinge of pleasure....He was a bona fide guest at this four-star hotel, but I'd forgotten, again, to consider his amazing sense of disentitlement, the effort he must have been expending to walk in and out of the lobby past the concierge. So when he'd returned and found me gone, instead of asking for another key, he'd loitered in front of the hotel and even hid in the bushes so as not to be shooed away. The animal he incarnated, skulking from the bushes when he saw me getting out of the taxi, wasn't a dog, despite the hangdog look, but a fox...a sly fox only temporarily cowed by my stony glance, my barking admonition, "If you don't want the *job,* then okay!"

"I disappeared on purpose," retorted the shy fox craftily, "just to see what you do. I was testing you."

That was ten minutes ago. Now I'm sliding my mouth up his thigh, licking at the scent of her arousal in the toilet of the movie theater with the thought of *her* fear and despair at losing him. "Always bring me your cock when it smells of pussy," I advise, as I slowly gulp it to the root.

IV

Romanian history has crept back into my story like an enticement; or is it a warning? King Carol II, of the enormous sexual stamina. And his Jewish mistress Lupescu, of the pursed Cupid's-bow lips and sashaying loins. In a landscape like my current life, it's natural to expect, or at least long for, the spectacular.

From the books I've been reading here in the Margitsziget while Romulus watches round after round of TV soccer, I can piece together life in Romania during Carol's early manhood, around 1915, when the new nation bristled with excitement, looking eagerly toward Western Europe for acceptance. I can picture the future king, Prince Carol, as a cocky, moody, blue-eyed twenty-one-year-old, with an extravagant mop of wavy blond hair and a weak Hohenzollern chin, pulled in even further by Hohenzollern propriety. I've also learned that Romania's capital, Bucharest, where young Carol accumulated his sexual conquests (including one, called The Crow, slender and witchlike with cocaine-dilated pupils), was already known as Little Paris at the time. It was a bustling nexus between East and West, built up by Romania's rich reserves of oil and wheat and its access to the Danube. The fashionable main streets overflowed with natty young gentlemen smoking oval-shaped Turkish cigarettes and often available seraglio-eyed women, their shiny black hair framing Eastern-kohled eyes, their undulating hips sheathed in Turkish silks or filmy French organdy.

These images of Romania's past animate the isolation of that hotel on Margitsziget Island, but it's still becoming a bad place for Romulus and me. There's an air of family groups and bird-watchers, and there's no sex at all on TV. Motivated by the stories of Carol's amorous exploits, I spice up our sex sessions by inventing turn-of-the-last-century scenarios, whispering into Romulus's ear minutely detailed descriptions of moist labia beneath frilly corset edges and rippling breasts.

One day I come back to our room after a short sightseeing trip to the Dohány Street Synagogue and find Romulus lying stiffly on the bed, a shade lighter than his usual pallor, with no television playing. Boredom had driven him outside, where he was astonished to see someone entering the hotel as he was leaving.

Who?

Well, just a person...

Eventually, I'm able to pry out the story of a choreographer, an obsessed john whom Romulus dropped as a customer a little while ago, after which an assistant was set on Romulus's tail, as in some spy movie. He was afraid to leave his room for a week, kept getting hang-ups on his cellular. And now... there the man was, entering the hotel.

The next day we switch to the Gellért, our original trysting place. A spectacular room awaits us there, since this is the offseason. It has a balcony overlooking the noisy square and the green-metal Szabadság Bridge spanning the Danube. The anti-Romanian clerk who seized Romulus's passport is the same to check us in, but he doesn't bat a contemptuous eyelash. In fact, now that we occupy one of the luxury rooms, his previous suspicion has transformed into a robotic

Old World servility. Henceforth he'll delicately refer to the vagrant I arrived with on the last trip in the middle of the night and whose passport he snatched as my "nephew from Italy," a role that Italian-speaking Romulus laps up.

Our room really does feel like a Central European paradise, with its fake-Biedermeier furniture, fringed lampshades, heavy brocade curtains and two individual snowy-white comforters for the same bed. The large bathroom has a heated towel rack and a spacious tub, which Romulus takes advantage of immediately, after which I perversely forbid him to pull the plug, so that I can bathe in the same still-warm water.

Time stops in this world of constantly replayed porn videos coming from the cherry TV cabinet and sumptuous dinners delivered on rolling carts covered with stiff tablecloths, as Romulus smokes cigarette after cigarette, blinkingly staring at the posh atmosphere with sullen lips. We take fanciful pseudo-historical photos with my digital camera, fashioning togas from the brocade bedspread to impersonate Romania's aboriginal Dacians, or Turkish turbans to represent its en-slavers; or we lean, sometimes naked, from the balcony at night to peer at the unreal congestion of streetcars, cars and pedestrians below.

None of the videos has changed. The big-breasted German woman in her white concrete tropical paradise still gets fucked over and over by her thick-dicked, hairless German partner. To supplement this we construct elaborate scenarios of what we could do together if we brought a hooker back to the room from an area of town Romulus calls the "prostitu-teria." It's an idea I keep encouraging to keep up his interest in sex. The plan is for Romulus to take her from the back while I fuck her pussy. My concern, which he pooh-poohs, is the whore's reaction when I suck his cock in front of her.

Our fantasies are sometimes fueled by the suitcase half full of books on Romania and the Balkans I've brought with me, perverse political fairy tales of Turkish kidnappings and homosexual harems in Panaït Istrati's 1924 novel *Kyra Kyralina,* or stories of royal intrigue in Paul D. Quinlan's exhaustive 1995 account of the life of Carol II, *The Playboy King.*

Carol II, whose mother was Queen Marie, is the figure who interests me most. Born in 1893, coming of age shortly before World War I, he was the first sovereign to be born on Romanian soil. And during the war, as the country saw itself hopelessly challenged by Germany, he was leading a dissolute, womanizing life. Later, his ten years of kingship, from 1930 to 1940, were years of capitulation to the Nazi threat; and his affair with the Jewess Lupescu during that period added a perverse complication to an already demoralized nation.

I'm becoming more and more astonished by Romania's dizzying political scandals, its schizophrenic identity encompassing Occident and Orient, its sexual legends and its aesthetic cultures full of mysticism, rural romance and pantheism. Romulus, it turns out, is surprisingly informed about the history of his country. Despite his street origins, he grew up in a Communist era that demanded at least a solid high school education for every citizen. Unlike me, he's always been aware of Romania's Turkish, Greek, Slavic, German and French influences and its relatively short history as an independent nation.

It seems to me that Romania's hundreds of years under Ottoman rule have left their traces in his sharp Oriental features and coal-black eyes; but when I suggest it, he's adamant about his pure Romanian origins. No matter, since in fact, the tale of the Romanian royal family that's gripped me to such an extent is really a Teutonic and British story.

Romania's only royal rulers came from the West and were all placed on the throne by Western powers.

I page through the history books beneath the high, chandeliered ceiling of our room at the Gellért, my leg entwined with a yawning Romulus's, who's incredulous that I have the patience to spend so much time reading. When I come to the reign of Carol II, I realize that this playboy's dissolute promiscuity was probably forged from early experiences that resemble mine. It's becoming more and more apparent that this rebellious Casanovite was oedipally inspired by his lively, charismatic mother, Marie, granddaughter of Queen Victoria.

Queen Marie, who is even memorialized in a humorous ditty by Dorothy Parker, reveals herself in her famous diaries, correspondence and autobiography as a headstrong, articulate woman with a high libido and a compulsion for political achievement. It is she, not her passive husband, King Ferdinand, who wins the acclaim of the peasants by venturing among them in traditional dress or puts herself and her son in mortal danger by suggesting they nurse cholera-stricken soldiers on the field during the Second Balkan War in 1913, the year before she becomes queen. It's also she who journeys without her husband to Paris after World War I, presumably to visit her dressmakers and put her daughters in school, and seduces the ministers at Versailles into enlarging Romania rather than partitioning it.

Inspired by some mesmerizing Internet photos of this blond, blue-eyed, regular-featured queen, we create havoc for the maids by using the duvets, curtain and brocade pillowcases to make fantasy costumes worthy of a Warholian send-up of Sternberg's *The Scarlet Empress*. One of the photos we discover on the computer in the lobby of the Gellért shows British Marie, called Missy by her family and friends, in a

Pre-Raphaelite pose over a marble-potted plant, in a light-saturated conservatory, wearing a filmy, nymphlike peignoir with a train. In other photos, she lounges on the ledge of a Romanian countryside balcony in a Turkish warrior's head-dress and tight, metallic costume, or sports a peasant's apron and kerchief, or leans seductively toward the viewer from her throne under a heavy crown and cowled dress that make her look like Nazimova in *Salome*. The enormous bedroom she designed for herself at the palace, part ecclesiastic study and part Turkish bath, so disturbed her mother-in-law, the poet queen Carmen Sylva, that the latter couldn't sleep all night the first time she laid eyes on it.

Marie is, quite clearly, an innovative powerhouse and a fascinating maternal figure, rightly called the first "modern queen." Beginning as a frightened seventeen-year-old English bride in a strange Eastern country, she blossoms into a figure synonymous with Romanian identity, nationalism and pride shortly before World War I. Abandoning her British past, she drinks in the culture of Romania in great draughts and graciously accomplishes more for it than does any other leader.

In the shadow of Marie is her thwarted son Carol II, originally adored as the firstborn, then later subjected to her Victorian prudery and lust for power. He rebels, of course; but like most whose autonomy has been stolen early in life by a strong-willed, magnetic person, his attempts at independence are perverse and sordid.

Oedipal vectors shoot from the pages of *The Playboy King* and *Lupescu: The Story of a Royal Love Affair,* revealing Marie as a doting, overinvolved mother at a loss when confronted with her grown son's sulking bids for independence; and Carol, her son, as an obsessively womanizing "priapist," destroyed by tortured love and hate for a mother who hopes to rule Romania through him.

I'm so immersed in the gossip about the allegedly enormous size of Carol's member that I don't even notice the sullen look my own charge has pasted on his face. Ever since he discouraged his girlfriend from annoying his "uncle" with constant calls, our relationship has settled into a narrow routine. We've even reached the point of talking about ways to be together permanently. Before me I can see an entire half-life forming around the dynamic of his boredom and whoredom and my money and desire. He's declared his intention to abandon Budapest and hustling and, as if it were an afterthought, the *girl*. When I leave, he'll take the money I give him and go back to Sibiu, where he'll wait for our next opportunity to be together. The rules of the game are to allow heterosexual dabbling as long as the primary relationship remains us.

I agree to all of this enthusiastically, hiding a certain misgiving. No one has to explain to me that the forces we depleted bourgeois intellectuals sometimes borrow for our transgressive narratives never free themselves from their unstable sources. That entity of teeming street energy, that exotic sociological specimen or puzzle of your own past you think you've captured, even reformed, is continually being lured back into those landscapes of risk he came from. And so, after a week in the lap of luxury, after several sumptuous meals and several bottles of wine from our suddenly accommodating hotel restaurant, as well as countless sex acts in front of the piped-in porno until his nipples grow increasingly carmine from my deep-pressure kisses, Romulus gets bored. He begins yearning for a shady Romanian bar in the Pest section of the city.

One rare day we bother to leave our fantasy chamber on a long trip along the river and up the funicular to the castle district. His lips shrivel with contempt when he sees the refurbished luxury apartments, picturesque church and sterile-looking café in that exclusive neighborhood. Even so, he obliges me by stopping for a drink. When a bevy of black-clad bourgeois Hungarian girls, holding shopping bags from an expensive boutique, glance at us through the window of the café, he makes a remark about wanting to fuck one of them. Perhaps it's with bitter pleasure that I explain to him that such a woman has to be courted more gradually, become convinced that you're mirroring her self-worth before you can have her pussy. When I do, he snarls that such tactics make the conquest not worth the trouble at all. And that is the night he begins wanting to go to the Romanian bar.

It is, as he describes it, a picaresque cellar in the Pest section of the city, where pickpockets, passport forgers, counterfeiters and smugglers meet to the tune of house mixes of horas, illicit traffic in boosted electronic equipment, frequent fist-fights and occasional knifings. I tell him that I want to go to the place, too, but he answers that he's afraid to take me. He fears blowing his cover and compromising his machismo, and we may run into violence. So I hatch a defiant plan. I'll enter the bar alone twenty minutes before he does and take my chances. It's my choice, isn't it? Then he can enter and, only if it feels right, casually greet me, probably not even sit that near.

At the Romanian bar, those few liverish-colored patrons, who look like Andre the Giant hulks in black silk shirts and black suits, seem too simmered in depression to offer more than an apathetic glance. I've seen those expressions before in more appealing form in Hamburg, at the train station and in the bars of the St. Pauli district, where I first encountered teenaged Romanian hustlers. Now I'm learning that most of the more unfortunate Romanian males of the diaspora are masters of this melancholic pose. Here in this hole-in-the-wall in Budapest, all the men have a version of it.

The music is deafening. It sounds part Hungarian, part Roma, part Turk, full of accordions and synthesizers and reedy things. There are rousing folk elements that sound shrill in their electronic form, frantic and hysterically Byzantine. The hyperdetailed, obsessively repetitive melodies spill into space, swirling into a kind of epilepsy. Thus I sit trying not to look at the large, black-suited men frozen in tango-inspired seizures of depression, as the music discombobulates my nervous system. But each twitch I make is greeted with a stony lack of reaction on their part.

Romulus arrives as promised, greets me in an exaggeratedly offhand manner. He takes a seat close enough for us to talk and whispers a few explanations. Across from us, the handsome, moonfaced, sloe-eyed but acne-pitted adolescent with the pompadour; the stocky man in black; and the skinny dark-haired girl, whose prominently veined hands stick like spiders from a black parka, are work partners. On late-night subways, the two younger people will begin to kiss, his hand will slip inside the girl's parka, moving toward her breast; and as people gape at this distraction, the older man will go about his job of pickpocketing. Then there is the tall, drawn man, also with a wolfish haircut, and sad, ringed intellectual's eyes. He's a master passport forger. An American passport, Romulus informs me, can be sold quite quickly for several thousand dollars, after being doctored by the forger genius with a new photo. Mine, however, is next to valueless because of my birth date. The people who buy these hot passports have a future.

Just a few doors from the Romanian bar is the Old Man Club, which has one of the most eclectic young crowds in Budapest. Romulus credits himself with opening it to

Romanians. It's a new club in a post-Communist New World, crowded and bursting with energy and noise. Americans and Africans, Poles, Germans and Romanians gulp whiskey and beer along with the Hungarians, dance alone or in groups. Romulus is sure that the waitress is overcharging us. Each time she brings a drink, he quizzes her about the prices of comparable brands. House music and '80s New Wave pump through the smoke-filled air.

Slightly heady with my risk-free visit to the Romanian bar, I careen through this new place, losing sight of Romulus. The two young men he shows up with a few minutes later have the hangdog look of people adrift; there's something greenhorn about them; maybe it's their clumsy, stale clothing or their eyes projecting a desensitized stubbornness that expects little. One is swarthy and slender, mute and shiny-lashed. The other is fair and meaty and Slavic-looking, with the oval, dull face of a butcher. Between them is Romulus, who now seems different. His grim, determined look borders on cockiness, or sadism. He shoos all of us to the same table, and I buy everyone a drink. Then he begins to speak as if he were holding forth at a board meeting:

"These are Marius," he says, pointing at the butcher boy, "and Francisc," pointing at the dark, slim one. "One of them will sleep with you."

I keep a steady tone, with a touch of haughtiness. "Excuse me, but I think it's up to me who I sleep with."

"Yes, as you wish. It's only that I must see the girl tomorrow night. When you go in the Romanian bar, and I am waiting to go in, you see, I see her. I did not plan this. Because she needs me so, I say yes."

"Go ahead."

"But you see," he explains, "if I think of you alone, I will not be able to enjoy."

I glance at Marius and Francisc, trying to determine how much English they understand. It's obvious that the details of this transaction are beyond them, but they get the gist of it.

"That's your problem," I spit, "just don't ever tell me who to sleep with. Would you," I say to the two boys, a note of impudence and superiority in my voice, "be my guests for dinner tomorrow night? Romulus, I assume your date will be after dinner. So the four of us will eat at the hotel. The Gellért at seven." Marius, the dulled butcher, nods eagerly and winks. The darker one agrees resignedly, letting his eyes go blank, looking at the hands in his lap. Probably my strategy is blatant: the invitation is meant to make Romulus seem cheap for offering fresh meat and also to make him worry that I may be taking the offer seriously.

"Bruce," says Romulus, with cold irony. "Is not necessary. You just have to give to them a little money after sex. A very little."

"I don't remember anyone mentioning money, Romulus, or sex, except you."

Slightly humiliated by the remark, he savors its motive: his decision to see the girl has obviously wounded me. "As you wish," he says conceitedly.

I'm switching from the porn channel to the French-language channel with one hand, while the other wipes my come off with a towel. Romulus is staring at the television with weary though glinting eyes, the hint of a rictus smile creasing his lips.

"You know, Romulus, I kind of regret inviting those Romanian guys to dinner. I think I'd rather be on my own tomorrow night, go to a bar. You never know who I'll meet. I want to be free."

"Oh, then you don't want Marius?"

"No, if I had to pick, which I'm not saying I would, I'd pick the dark guy, Francisc."

"The Gypsy?" His nose crinkles with distaste.

"Is that what he is? It's more respectful to call them Roma."

"We get rid of Marius."

"Wait a minute, I didn't say I wanted either of them."

He blows a smoke ring toward the ceiling. "Then we get rid of both."

"And how will we do that? They're coming to the hotel."

"Easy as a pie. We just don't go downstairs at seven."

I realize then that, of course, just like Romulus, neither Romanian boy would dare enter the hotel on his own and approach the desk and ask them to call our room.

"We can't just leave them there waiting."

"Fine. I go downstairs and tell them go away."

"No. I mean, they don't have any money or anything. Aren't they counting on it? Won't they be hungry?"

"All right, I go down and give four dollars and say go away."

"Four dollars, for both?"

"Is that too much?"

"I just can't do that to them."

"As you wish." He crushes out the cigarette, amused. Takes the remote out of my hand and searches for a sports channel.

By four in the morning he's asleep and I, despite the codeine I've been taking, am wide awake. Night cradles us like black cotton wool. The air is lazy with cigarette smoke nudged by gusts of river wind rattling the French windows at the balcony. This is not the vibrating black of that room in Syracuse, but something stiller and more perfect. Certainly things are tinged with doom, even if night makes a false promise of permanence. His leg on mine feels light as a wing, but when he moves away just an inch, it's like watching his body through the wrong end of a telescope. Slowly the vulgarity of our twin states of desperation dissolves, and temporary security washes over me. We're nothing but statues in some utopian tableau. Once again we've escaped the premises of our respective cultures, for the time being. I plunge into unconsciousness: that sweet prelude to betrayal.

V

Budapest's newly tolerant atmosphere makes Romulus cringe. We've decided to hit the baths in the basement of the Gellért, famous in Budapest and populous, but like several other ancient baths in this old city, frequented by homosexuals. They're looking at him and can't help it, despite the fact that he's relatively clothed. Though most—me included—wear only the muslin loincloth provided by the management and made translucent by hot water, Romulus is wearing his blue bikini, which I've just bought for him.

Flat and straight as a blade, buttocks steely, he rises from the scalding waters, colored pallid green by the skylights in the high vaulted ceiling. Desire glimmers, or should I say glowers, in the eyes of some lumpy older men. I do believe that when one sex desires its own, there's always a touch of envy.

All the frills of the out gay life cherished by today's contemporary Western gays leave Romulus in a kind of frozen repulsion. As much as he enjoys the wit, warmth and attentions of some gay males, he has no desire for, or conception of, a community in which groups of men who happen to sleep with other men eat together in restaurants, cruise each other in baths or dance in clubs devoid of women. Fine with me. I find life with him outside gay group culture curiously refreshing—as if I and my desire for him had been placed back inside the whole world.

Four hours later, the river and the cable-car stop below our hotel window are awash with golden light. Night and the "dates" I arranged at the Old Man Club are coming. With sardonic coolness, Romulus has made some well-timed, seemingly offhand comments to make me afraid of the supposed treacherousness of the Romani boy. Pancake-faced as the other one, Marius, is, I've decided to keep only him on the "payroll." While Romulus is on his date with the girl, I'll use Marius as my guide, hopefully penetrating some underworld sites to which Romulus is afraid to take me. But I don't tell Romulus exactly what my intentions are. A mild spitefulness is welling up in me as his "night off" gets nearer.

On the balcony, the gusts of wind are surprisingly balmy. It's only the end of February and the river is still partly frozen, but there's the feeling of an early spring. I lean over the railing, trying to pick out the two boys from the clusters of people at the tram stop and in front of the hotel. Twilight is so very luminous that white shirts under jackets glimmering against the black water look like blossoms in liquid tar. I can see Marius and Francisc hurrying across the bridge with exalted, confused faces. Then they hover uncertainly in front of our mammoth pseudo-gothic hotel like mechanical toys suddenly winding down. Their faces scan up the building without noticing me. In a moment, I see Romulus burst through the door of the hotel and stride toward them with that no-nonsense bow-legged walk, stiff with authority and efficiency. In the clandestine gesture of a drug dealer, he yanks the five or so dollars out of his pocket and presses them into the hands of Francisc, the Gypsy boy. Marius's face lights up, while the other's stays blank and he pockets the money. Looking as withdrawn as he did the night before, he heads back across the bridge.

Bold knocking on the door. Marius bolts into the room with an eager, avid look, followed by a contemptuous Romulus. Marius has probably never been in a hotel room like this before. Now he's hit the jackpot! He strides about with the troglodyte stare of a proprietor. He grabs a bottle of scotch as if it's part of the booty and hoists it above his head like a prize. I take a photo.

We make our way toward the wood-paneled hotel restaurant in a triumphant procession, past the desk clerk who once locked up Romulus's passport, whose mouth gapes in disbelief at the fact of my now trailing not one but two hustlers. Certainly Marius has never sat down to such a menu, either. His eyes bug in disbelief. If I intend to spend this much on dinner, how much will I give him to suck his dick? Romulus merely tilts back his chair and enjoys the farce. He's seen money wasted on fancy cuisine and fantasized its paying for a leather jacket or a new pair of shoes many times before.

There are wines and meats, salads and cheeses. Romulus keeps consulting his watch anxiously. Marius's glow over his supposed good luck hasn't diminished. It's time to get down to specifics.

"I'm wondering," I tell him, "if you'd agree."

"Yes, yes," he answers eagerly.

"But you don't know what I'm asking." It's obvious that he's expecting a sexual proposition, the chance of gleefully fucking my head like some stuffed dummy's while cash oozes from my pockets like sawdust. That's how he sees me: a pudgy gold mine, something squishy and exploitable. Who knows what the night will bring, if he's really eager enough to win my attention that way....But for now, "I'm looking for a bodyguard," I blurt.

Romulus sneers in amusement at the absurdity of it. "I

want to go to some places that Romulus won't take me," I add pointedly. His sneer freezes on his face, unyielding, stoic.

"Me strong. Good bodyguard," growls Marius.

"Really? Let's see." I put one elbow on the table in an arm-wrestling challenge. Marius grasps my hand. After an initial pause motivated by politeness, he flattens me. The silverware and dishes rattle. The waiter, in red jacket and black tie, watches in panicked disbelief. Marius guffaws with pride.

"You'll do, I suppose," I remark, my eyebrows arching campily. "And for your services, Marius, you will now be paid thirty American dollars in advance. Is that okay?"

His eyes are bright with elation. "Yes, yes." I take the bills out and push them across the table. "Now remember," I say, "I expect full protection."

I turn toward Romulus, and in an acidic tone, "Well, then, I won't be needing you anymore. You may leave."

Romulus ignores my comic impertinence and answers with an Old World sense of decorum. "Yes, yes, I am late. No dessert for me, thank you. She waiting for me. You excuse me, yes?"

"With pleasure."

He looks at me in bored disbelief, shakes his head bemusedly. "See you tomorrow...."

The pain of being separated from my obsession is searing, but it's a pain I embrace with grim pleasure. Wanting him is the only feeling of being alive, and at moments, having him isn't wanting him. It's unlikely, of course, that Marius can imagine any complicated level of attachment. We're in a taxi on our way to the Romanian bar, but even such a simple operation takes on awkwardness the way he handles it. He's sprawled in the front seat like a bumpkin who's won a buggy ride at a county fair. He's telling the driver, who glances at him with annoyance and then ignores him, to step on it.

The Romanian bar doesn't feel dangerous or forbidden to me anymore. Is it the absence of Romulus's squeamishness about my safety? The shrieking, serpentine music coils through me in an Asiatic intestinal pattern, flattening and twisting my thoughts into Francis Bacon–style distortions. Marius is slurping up the drinks as if it were his last night alive. I'm high on a weird sense of widowhood, the feeling of being cut loose and perfectly free to destroy myself. I look avidly at any gnarly wrist, jutting Adam's apple or tree-limb neck that promises a hard time, an onslaught of energy and resistance and force. Still, I feel there's something about my physical bulk and emotional gravity that protects me. Incredibly, this brings me into good rapport with the clientele. Among the severely deprived, my bizarre sacrificial state is interpreted as genuine confidence, even a type of paternalism.

Before long, a smooth-skinned, wiry man with reptilian lids is basking under my attention. He's got a bony, angry body, dry, dirty hands and bulging, meditative eyes. Marius comes back only on those frequent occasions when he wants another drink, for which I flamboyantly hand over more money.

English is limited between me and the Romanian with bulging eyes, but liberal Latin codes of male bonding allow for starkly sensual innuendoes. As long as body poses follow that impudent etiquette of the confident male, the face, I've found, can express many playful messages that we Anglos might interpret as flirtation but that these Latins call solidarity. At one point, I take his hand in mine, supposedly to compare its roughness with my smoothness. It's an old trick I learned with rough trade—a coded confession of femininity safeguarded by that thrilling message of class superiority: my hand is smooth not just because I'm a fag but also because it hasn't done any manual labor; it's the hand of a writer, which I explain by pantomiming the act of typing for him, watching his eyes light up at the novelty of it. Yet for me, sitting broad and sturdy with my knees wide apart, my grasped hand feels as thrilled as a young maiden's; and on the surface, no one will be the wiser.

From what I can tell from his quirky utterances and pantomimes, he's from the city of Cluj, the twenty-three-year-old son of displaced peasants whose village thirty miles to the northwest was razed by Ceauşescu so that they could be moved into Communist high-rise housing and work in a new factory. It was a common-enough occurrence in the last decade of the leader's rule, an attempt to sever Romania from its rural past and fast-forward the country's industrialization. But now, with the hundreds of layoffs in the soon-to-be-privatized factory, the deterioration of the housing project, his forty-three-year-old father's poorly treated heart condition, there seems to be no reason for anything but dazed wandering, a canine life motivated by following scents, vague leads about work, from one capitalist subsistence subculture to the next.

It's hard to judge people like me, I assume he's thinking. The way I'm dressed looks confusingly awkward, but he's seen Americans like that. How can somebody with all that money for drinks be wearing such unfashionable, dirty shoes, so broad and dusty? Even so, my face with its clean skin and wide, candid eyes reminds him of something positive. He's got nothing better to do than sit here and bask in those eyes, pouring out more approval than most eyes he's looked into for a very long time. Yet what, really, do they want?

Abruptly I've stood and announced that we're going to the Old Man Club. As we get up to leave, Marius runs after us. He's very drunk now, playing a bad Sancho Panza to my Don Quixote, trying to pump up his bodyguard role by walking like a soldier, albeit a drunken one.

The other Romanian isn't very comfortable in the Old Man Club, opened to Romanians by Romulus a short time ago. The tables are packed, the customers talkative and intense. On the dance floor, there's everything from Portuguese to African-Americans. Burning with excruciating freedom, or loss, I begin dancing, disintegrating. The pain of separation from Romulus is ecstatic and full of new possibilities, including doom. It doesn't matter that I outrank most of those on the dance floor in age. I weave through the spaces talking to anyone who interests me, oozing energy and generosity, buying drinks wherever I can. The other Romanian is watching from a distance with a patient poker face. He's seeing this peculiar dancing American in his clumsy shoes and boxy shirt throw money around, and something's starting to dawn on him; he probably can't quite put it together yet, but there's something—exploitable?—about this Westerner of ambiguous age, his balding baby face and chubby, nearly feminized paternalism, his sloppy openness and precise eyes and words.

The Romanian is used to associating an open friendly façade and precise eyes with artful fraud; and come to think of it, he's run into quite a few Gypsies who've used variations of that combination—with their loose casualness and sharp eyes—but this is different. Unless it's a genius version of the same kind of fraud, somebody who brings down all your defenses by appearing to be oddball and infantile, generous, careless, but whose substantial brain is calculating every moment to find your weakest.

On the other hand, what could the American want from somebody like him?...and then the thought occurs to him, just for a moment in passing, that it could be sex he wants; but the thought of it is like the thought of the weather, or more like the thought you have when watching another species eating or mating or preening, and you think, how curious, and then, as a momentary afterthought, what does it have to do with me, that living thing and its strange habits, could I eat it, or make use of its fur or feathers or bones?

In this case, though, the possibility of this clumsy, warm, stupidly generous American's wanting sex lingers in his mind a bit longer, probably he considers it, wonders how much money it might bring. Except that the American seems to be focused everywhere now, talking in that same intrusive yet merry way with anyone who comes across his path, but never forgetting to fill your glass again and then dancing away; but isn't he swaying a little now? Isn't he drunk? Your eyes can't help focusing on the bulge in his side pocket that's the wallet he's been taking out, over and over; you can't help wondering how much is left in it; you try not to stare at it; and now all you can think of is the sex he might want and the money he might pay for it, or other ways to get that money....

I do remember his glances at my wallet, but by then I was too caught up in the trance of the night, too excited by the absurdly small possibility that all at once a new Romulus would be created who was just like the original but more fascinated by me—until I reached into my pocket for the wallet and discovered that there was practically no money left. I'd spent most of it. Marius had disappeared, I could see the other Romanian far across the room, staring at me in an unsettling, unblinking way with those shiny, bulging eyes. Something told me to slip out, head for a cash machine and then hop a cab back to the hotel. But after the cash machine, I thought I heard someone calling. As I was turning away from the machine and stuffing the money into my pocket, I noticed the Romanian getting closer and waving frantically at me to wait, and I panicked and jumped into a passing taxi.

An abject elation over the risk I'd taken and the danger escaped held me in a kind of endorphinic paralysis. But when we got to the colossus of the Gellért, the fact that I was about to enter it alone penetrated the barrier of endorphins as if the entire building were crashing through them. I couldn't breathe, just stood staring at the dark gray surface, on which the long tresses of female Art Nouveau figures entwined over a side entrance to the baths. Then I walked drunkenly toward the Danube, remembering a comment in the István Szabó film *Sunshine* about all the Jews who'd been slaughtered on its banks. I climbed down the stairs near the foot of the bridge to watch two men in rubber boots and slickers, who'd cut a hole in the ice to fish; and I stared at the black meanderings of the water, until I thought I saw a flicker of light that suggested a glimmer of young legs twining.

I hadn't given Romulus enough money for a hotel, so there was a possibility they'd found a street-level window open in the basement of one of those buildings across the river and slipped inside, where there was probably at least a damp mattress and a broken chair. The mattress would have looked horrible even in the dark with its huge stains, so he probably took off his jacket and her coat and made a mat out of them; and then he took off his sweater and covered her with it. His small, strong hands began to wander over her body; they cupped her breasts as if they were made to fit them, while she kept complaining about his week of absence, that *uncle* who refused to meet her. And in fact, she felt so deprived about being excluded by that uncle that she greedily sucked the lips of the hawkish face, like a bird hungry for food.

On the mattress, the zipper of his jacket cut into her buttocks. All his hardness pushing against her, like metal the temperature of a body, crushed out the week of loneliness. He kissed her and nipped at her tongue. She sucked the nicotine off his. The sting of cold air on body parts felt as if the cold were mocking her, or fucking her, so she climbed on top of him because it made her feel safer. She straddled his narrow hips with her thighs, and her breasts swung above him as he lay underneath, lean and pale. She touched her clitoris with her fingertips and then took hold of that sharp weapon and pierced herself with it fast enough to hurt. And after its first stinging insult, she knew whose it was. Hers.

VI

We're a mile from the Romanian border in a rented car because Romulus has to leave Hungary to renew his visa. The road is narrow, and there are potholes.

Gnarled, nearly branchless oak trees. Amputated, scarred. Why do they look the way they do? I'll learn later that they're cut back again and again for firewood, or to stimulate growth. But over decades these oaks have become monstrosities, their trunks covered with humps from which sprout tiny misplaced buds. Romania is a country of wood, where woodenness is inspiring enough to create an artist like Brancusi; for now, though, the woodenness of these deformed oaks plunges me into a grim fairy tale.

We're entering the country the way Queen Marie entered it, from Budapest. The asphalt looks darker than I'm used to—liquid and black like oil. So do the tree trunks, smudges in the failing light. The grass of the fields looks greasy, coarse and swollen, a species I've never seen. There are big blotches of black in front of my eyes, and the feeling of being in a black-and-white movie.

Inside this movie, he's changed. Friendly and familial, he studies the map, patiently encouraging me when I grind the gears of our standard shift or, astonishingly, gently clasping the back of my neck or shoulder while I drive, as if we're a real couple. He's grateful that I've decided to take him to

Romania to renew his visa. He keeps repeating it.

The buses crowded with the poor, their gigantic cloth-wrapped bundles and rolled rugs clot the entrance to the border crossing. We inch forward. The Romanian immigration officer in his gray uniform, in his glass cabin above the car, bends forward to study us. His glance is deadened yet full of queer complexities. It's obvious that his boredom has achieved an imperturbable contempt, but I can tell that he's proud of his imagined Byzantine cleverness, whether or not this really exists.

It's not that he has any respect for law or order. He merely wants to protect his position, project an identity. If we're drug dealers or holders of false passports, it might behoove him to unveil us; yet the possibility of his having to account for it even if we are seems unlikely, so he's filled with an unbudging laziness, civil-servant style. He's made up a game for himself with at least a minimum of amusement, supposedly in the name of doing his duty. It involves harassing those who look used to being interrogated.

He hands my American passport back to me immediately. Then he takes his time with Romulus's. The alleged problem is that Romulus's passport looks too trampled, rain-streaked. He'd put it in his shoe during one of his flights across Macedonia. The officer thumbs through it again and again, pretending to gauge the thickness of the paper between thumb and forefinger, making a show of focusing on the ink where the rain has made it run, folding the bent corners back and forth and looking meaningfully into Romulus's eyes. He clearly has little expertise in identifying counterfeit documents, but he's casually hoping his act of suspicion will make Romulus edgy and break him if he's concealing anything. He even locks the passport in a drawer while he does a lazy search on his computer. His movements are impudently slow. Then he looks up from the computer screen and asks Romulus to explain what he's been doing in Hungary for such a long time.

Working at a travel agency, Romulus answers. And where is he living? With his girlfriend. And why is he crossing the border with this...person? The officer gestures at me as if at an object. Romulus tells him that I'm a writer and that he's come along to translate for me.

The officer takes the passport out of the locked drawer and begins the ritual of thumbing through it again, peering periodically at Romulus with a crafty look. He does a poor imitation of someone studying the official stamps on each page. And why have you come back and forth so many times?

Isn't it obvious? I want to shout. He needs to renew his visa once a month to stay in Hungary.

I keep coming back to visit my family, says Romulus. My mother's sick.

Finally, the officer hands him back the passport, staring rudely in another direction at the same time. We drive through. I'm in Romania.

According to Alice-Leone Moats, one of several 1950s journalists with a gossipy appetite for the scandal of King Carol II and his Jewish mistress Lupescu, the Hohenzollern side of Carol's family were squeamish about sending their German blood to Romania. They feared its Oriental and Byzantine elements and were shocked by its Latin sensualities. The country had been free from Turkish rule and Greek exploitation for not even fifty years when Carol's father Ferdinand came to the throne, and they literally thought it was contaminating their royal family.

"I feel safe here," Romulus says, as the road becomes

narrower and pitch black. Other cars shoot past at eighty miles per hour. Their style of passing is to do it whenever, especially on curves. It's up to me and the car coming from the other direction to slow down, or even drive off to the shoulder of the road until they're safely by. After the last car passes, all around me is dark, empty. The small, callused hand caresses the back of my neck. Elation and fear peak through me in jagged cardiogram bumps. My hands tingle.

King Carol's mother, Marie, called Missy, came to this country with her heart in her mouth at the tender age of seventeen, from a sheltered, rural English childhood. Her first experiences of the family into which she'd married felt unreal, when, in 1893, shortly before her marriage, she was taken to meet her mother-in-law-to-be, the poet queen Elisabeth, also called Carmen Sylva. On a bed to which she had taken in a fit of hysterical paralysis, Carmen Sylva lay all in white, beneath an enormous skylight, which had been cut into the ceiling to allow her to paint. Missy was clasped into her arms, and a feeling came over her:

"...A curtain was being lifted, giving me a glimpse into a world unknown to me, where all things had other names, other meanings...."

I feel the same way. It seems impossible to trace my path back to my first sight of Romulus, some three months ago. How have I gotten this far? As our car speeds deeper into the country, on a route paralleling that of the Orient Express that brought Missy to Romania in 1893, the shadows of branches make fleeting, eerie patterns on Romulus's face. All familiar contexts are peeling away. The air is coated with bizarre possibility. New York, my mother and the other benchmarks of my life are being drained of color. All I can feel is this funnel of desire through which I'm speeding.

A little past the border, in the city of Arad, a gang of street children pound on our car. All we have is Hungarian money, but I open the window to hand some of the coins to the youngest, who throws them back as hard as he can at my face, bruising my temple. Shakily, I pull the car over to rub it. Romulus is pale with embarrassment, but not with fear. As more children run to the car, he shouts coldly at them in Romanian and they retreat, but only a bit. They hang at the edge of the road and offer a passion play of misery, chanting and whining in an imitation of pitiful piety. "Ignore them," Romulus says in a clipped voice.

To our left is the municipal building, outlined in white Christmas lights. A taxi is parked in front. "Ask him for the best hotel."

Romulus climbs out of the car, resorting again to his efficient swagger. There is much discussion and pointing. Returning, he tells me, "The most expensive is the Intercontinental, about a hundred meters down this street."

We pull up at a dilapidated high-rise. Across its top, in letters that are askew, is the word "Intercontinental." We've been driving for four hours. I'm not at all used to standard shift, and I'm exhausted. "Go in and get a room. I'll get our stuff." When I come in, dragging all the bags, Romulus informs me, "It's about thirty dollars."

"Okay."

Something clicks in the head of the tall, thin desk clerk, dressed in a funereal black suit. "He says now," Romulus tells me, "that the fee for foreigners is different. Now the price is seventy-eight dollars." Rage simmers through me, but I take out my credit card. We change some money for Romanian lei.

Our room is large enough, with two small beds, thin mattresses and some wood paneling. Mildew fringes the red-flocked wallpaper. "It's a nice hotel," says Romulus.

The enormous restaurant is red as well, with those narrow, high-backed upholstered chairs I'll eventually see all over Romania. Stiff, spotlessly white tablecloths are set with heavy plates and silverware, thick linen napkins. Above our heads hangs a baronial wood-and-iron chandelier, a sort of Roger Vadim version of something rural and aristocratic. Our food is incredibly delicious, and Romulus shows a new confidence in handling the waitresses, never exhibited in any of the Hungarian restaurants we went to. We taste *ciorbă de burtă,* a velvety tripe soup with cream and butter; *mămăligă,* a spongy polenta plastered with fragrant sheep cheese; and a mixed grill that tastes fresh enough to be the booty of that afternoon's hunting party. My reactions are exaggeratedly ecstatic, with all the naiveté of the gung-ho greenhorn, and Romulus puts up with them with princely gloating. I choose to take this infantilizing of me as a triumphant sign of intimacy, start feeling happy about my "wifely" role.

As Romulus's bubbly American wife, I suggest we see downtown Arad before we go to bed, so we head along the main street past shuttered shops until we come to a courtyard with a place that looks like a tavern. All that are left on the street are children and a pack of insistent money changers and fences, offering cut rates for dollars, marks and forints or trying to sell battered tape players, an old flashlight, a torn plastic agenda. Romulus seems more and more tense about my bright-eyed, overly appreciative rubbernecking. When street kids ask us for money, tugging my sleeve and even pushing their faces against my belly, I take my camera out, intending to give them some money in exchange for a photo, but Romulus grabs it from my hand. "Do not take a picture of them," he warns. "People could think you being a child molester." I defy him and do it anyway. They pose, gloatingly holding up the bill I gave them the way Marius held up the scotch bottle. But it's obvious that crossing the border has brought about a change in Romulus's attitude about appearing with me in public. He's struggling, I realize, to find a legitimate image for our pairing. Delighted wifey just won't do. In fact, nothing will. Our intimacy as imagined by me starts to dissolve, and in its place is his uneasiness, which makes our dyad grotesque, awkward, illegitimate. The dissonance creates an alienated zoom view of myself. Suddenly I can see us standing in the street, this blatantly underclass hustler with sharp, cheap clothes, and this pudgy bourgeois American, twice his age yet so much less hardened, and I know the open book we must present. My only alternative is proud defiance, a false show of independence in this unknown, possibly hostile environment. "I'm going in here," I tell him, pointing at the tavern. "Are you coming?" He nods, and as he follows me I can see that he's reverted into a nervous bodyguard with an unmanageable charge, whom he sticks with out of a sense of honor, but who he wishes had never come here with him in the first place.

It's a nightclub with a traditional orchestra and a very good singer wailing a doina, while the audience sits at long picnic tables sopping up huge quantities of beer. Romulus is absolutely appalled by the way I march clumsily past the dozens of seated locals to an empty space and make a show of casually signaling the waiter. Everyone is staring at me, tense, startled, and although I now understand that every detail—my shoes, my bouncy walk, my comically assured look—is under scrutiny, I'm simmering with anger at his lack of solidarity. So I ostentatiously order us whiskey in booming English and make a show of avoiding his glance, of enjoying the music and the crowd with big, bold eyes and a smug smile. All the while, I'm becoming aware of the special compartmentalization of his life as a hustler in Hungary, which has to clash with his identity as a normal Romanian man on the home turf—a realization that opens a trapdoor in my stomach and sends me into a nauseating slide of cognitive dissonance. Valiantly trying to collect himself, my prince makes conversation. Do I like the music, he wants to know. I grunt a noncommittal answer. Finally, he looks at me wearily and says, "Do you know what are saying those people next to us?"

" 'Look at the ridiculous fat American'?" I venture.

"No, they are talking an argument. The woman says, 'And why not I go to Greece and work as prostitute if I have chance for more money you'll see ever in your life?' And he, her boyfriend, is saying he kill her on the spot if she is saying she will do. Until finally he says, 'I don't care what you do.' That's what they say."

The urgency of the story puts a dent in my bravado. But all I answer is, "Thanks for the translation."

Out on the street, Romulus suggests that we return to the hotel, but I'm fueled by four whiskeys and have no intention of admitting my naiveté yet. "Look at that place over there," I say, pointing at what seems to be a respectable-looking bar. As soon as we sit down at a table, a girl who looks fourteen signals me to her table, while two middle-aged hulks scrutinize me. "What does she want?" I ask Romulus. "She wants to talk to you," he answers with a weary, vengeful passivity. When I sit down next to her, her hand shoots out, grabbing my member through the cloth of my pants. I can't pry it loose. Meanwhile, one of the bulky men in black suits towers nearby, watching with stern approval, irony. "Tell her to let go," I say to Romulus through clenched teeth. He does, she releases me, we leave. "She was hoping getting you outside and then the guys in black to jump you," says my friend, with grim, nearly pleasurable resignation. "I know because something this I used to do," he adds slyly. I glance at him with disgust, and now, for the first time, he glows with pleasure, the pleasure of my disapproval.

By the time we get back to the mildewed room, I've really had it. I want my satisfaction. I move the night table into a corner and shove the beds together. "Is it all right in this country?" I ask acidly.

"Of course. Just push them apart in the morning."

Lying on the bed, I watch the overlarge black turtleneck and the pants bagged at the knees and worn at the seat sliding off to reveal the body of reptilian economy, nearly hairless and terrifyingly compact. He leaps noiselessly into our tiny beds, and then the silky skin is gliding against mine; his legs, wiry and threatening as springs, are interlacing mine; his hard, dry, dirty hands sliding over my back. For me it's as if all the aggression and fear of the last couple of hours, all the longing, are about to be settled by one experience. I plunge my face into his neck, his armpit, savoring that tart, frustrated power transmitted by his odor. Is it loss, melancholy, steely resentment? I pull off his shirt and he dangles an arm backward in surrender. With tongue and teeth I begin slowly working on his nipples.

"You love me, don't you," he sneers.

And I do. Or is it that I'm in love with his culture, hoping for a chance to go native?

How ironic that Carol II, the blueblood German-English son of a queen who sought to rehabilitate Romania in the eyes of the West, ended up acting out all the clichés of Latinity and Orientalism. For more than thirty years, from 1916 until the 1950s, journalists reported every exploit of the Eastern monarch who spoke a Latin tongue, clucking over his "orgiastic" interest in his harem of women. Thus did weak-chinned Carol, the product of a stuffy Hohenzollern upbringing, become a locus of libido, a titillating hybrid of the Oriental, the Slav and the Latin.

Now that Romulus is asleep, I open one of the books I've brought along to a photo of a kind of zaftig Garbo, with a wistful Flora-Dora smile. Her Pollyanna simper of a voice reaches me from a 1908 childhood in the Carpathian resort of Sinaia, where she and her mother were allegedly invited to high tea with Carmen Sylva.

On the same terrace of the royal mansion stood a brooding fourteen-year-old Prince Carol, so mesmerized by the girl's sunburst of strawberry hair that he offered her a box of Belgian chocolates. At his request, she ate one, but when she refused another, he tried to place it in her mouth.

Some seventeen years later, the now grown-up strawberry blonde is crossing a military parade ground near Bucharest. Sunlight ignites the ringlets around her face into another burst of fire, reflected in the eyes of a mesmerized grown-up Carol, now a libertine of a prince. Who could the stunning woman be?

Lupescu, they tell him. But she's a Jewess.

VII

Bronchitis means opiates again. In New York, I ask the doctor for something stronger, hydrocodone syrup instead of codeine tablets. He gives me antibiotics, too.

I'm back on the job at the financial printing house, in the white room with the keyboard-tapping immigrants. Nobody noticed that I was gone. No one seems to be noticing what I'm doing. No one pays any attention to my eyelids falling shut, my head bobbing and jerking up again.

I talk to the doctor about it, without telling him how much hydrocodone I'm taking. He thinks it's a symptom of sleep apnea.

The plan is that Romulus and I will meet again for two or three weeks in Bucharest, in about a month and a half. Meanwhile I'm to research options for being together longer—his coming to New York or some other place that lets in Romanians.

Romania may be a figment, a fantasy, to me, but for Romulus, New York has the aura of an amusement park. To him the advantages of life in America seem so disproportionate, so unreal, that it's almost like another planet. He can't imagine the humdrum steps of making a life here, only the thrill of the pavement beneath his feet.

Maybe his attitude isn't all that unrealistic. Calls to a couple of immigration lawyers make it just too clear that

Romanians applying for tourist visas, like people from other poor nations, are assumed to be intending to emigrate—are guilty unless proven otherwise. Romulus would probably need a large bank account, property, a business and family as proof of ties to Romania to get even a one-week tourist visa.

Sunday night, the tingling of hydrocodone, sparkly globules coursing through my muscles and nerve cells, instills me with infinite patience. My body feels like a phony hologram of murmuring dots. I begin an Internet search. There are, it appears, a few countries that don't require visas from Romanians. Turkey and, unexpectedly, Costa Rica, are on the list. The latter conjures New Age fantasies of Romulus confined in a house on the beach, cheap prices. Indolent as he seems, he could be the perfect candidate for beach pet. How much competition could the impoverished local girls be, in the long run? This infantile Tarzan fantasy, idiotically fueled by images of him in swimwear, hardens into a scenario wrapped in red tape when I begin researching the voyage from Bucharest to San José, Costa Rica. Martinair, with stopovers in Amsterdam and Miami, looks like the cheapest, but even its fares start at $2,500.

The following morning, a searing migraine slices through my brain vacated by opiates. I call in sick to work, then spend hours on phone trees, gathering information from the Immigration and Naturalization Service. It turns out there's such a thing as a transit visa, needed by some travelers from high-risk countries who want to pass through a U.S. airport on the way to somewhere else. I wonder whether he'd be able to get one.

That afternoon, after lubricating another two teaspoons of hydrocodone with a glass of scotch, I call him. Over the connection fading in and out, his purring voice sounds amoral, charged with ill-intentioned excitement at the idea of setting foot in Miami, even in a cordoned airport lounge. For months afterward, I'll see the airports I freely use for changeovers in a different way, my eyes obsessively searching the doors and windows I pass as possible escape routes. I'll imagine his foolhardy dashes into parking lots where I'm waiting with a rented car.

I bring my crusade to my vague job at the financial printing company. One wearing afternoon, I become fixated on a doubtful Internet site that claims to be in the business of selling information leading to passports. According to this site, a certain Caribbean country will issue passports to those willing to stay for more than forty-eight hours. This citizenship changes an individual's immigration status radically, allowing, for example (and this in all caps), TRAVEL TO CANADA WITHOUT A VISA. For a mere $30,000, the identity of this amazingly welcoming country will be revealed, and all arrangements for passport application taken care of.

Since no one is watching, I lapse into a deep fantasy about importing Romulus to the passport-granting country, where we're surrounded for forty-eight hours by soldiers of fortune and corporate criminals on the run, as tongues are stung by rum or slaked with bottled water without ice cubes, in scorching heat where dust encrusts ceiling fans—all followed by a trip to a chilly Toronto in autumn.

Next comes a three-day weekend in Syracuse with my acutely alert but failing mom. Somehow her fantasies about me seem more desperate and romantic than mine about Romulus. And of course, they're as narcissistic as those of Queen Marie for her son. It's no accident that both he and I became libidinists. As a shield, I bring my opiates with me.

She's been ill, another bout of pneumonia. My older

brother came up a few days ago to watch over her in the hospital. Now that she's home, he's left and I've come to take my turn.

Just as I sometimes do, my brother has left angry. Nearing sixty, with huge responsibility in a government executive job, he can still become the target of Mom's reformative criticisms. This time the argument was about his weight. But unlike me, my brother finds the autonomy to leave the house when he's up there, abandoning her for an afternoon, in the midst of grumpy judgments, to visit old friends.

Even a recent hospital stay hasn't kept Mom from having her pure-white hair arranged into a stiff artichoke at her weekly hairdresser appointment, or instructing her home companion—a warm, affectionate gay guy who lives next door—to help her into her girdle (so rare these days that she had to replace it by mail order), hose, pressed gray slacks and spotless royal-blue blouse, which enlivens the color of her glittering, inquisitive china-blue eyes. Without his help, she's covered her pallor with the usual liberal doses of powder and rouge and brightened her mouth with red lipstick. Now she stands stiffly, as straight as she can despite her arthritic hump, with one hand grasping the back of a chair, and minutely surveys my clothes, skin and hair, searching my eyes a little anxiously for inattention or irony as her gnarled hand adjusts the collar of my shirt. Her eyes well with disappointment as she checks out my pants, which have lost their crease and wrinkled in the train ride up.

The phone rings and Mom hobbles to it, then bellows, "Who is it?" several times until the caller is shouting loud enough for me to hear every word. It's someone from the Housing Authority, on which, at ninety-six, she still holds a seat, calling to ask if she'll be attending the meeting. "Of course!" she booms into the receiver, with the voice of a young cheerleader, a voice temporarily infused with an astounding force. It's a fresh, energetic soprano she can still muster, to the extent that friends who call often ask me who the young girl was who answered the phone.

Even at this stage of her life, she treasures her resolve and community involvement and is fixated on her social status. These values stem from immigrant girlhood in a tiny town in upstate New York at the beginning of the twentieth century, when her poor family, who spoke only Yiddish, was also the only Jewish family in town. Her parents didn't learn English until my mother entered kindergarten, picked it up herself and came home to teach it to them. During years of exclusion and loneliness and anti-Semitic gibes, my mother struggled to prove her worth to this provincial, bigoted Anglo-Saxon community. She became the highest achiever in school and then entered Syracuse University for a degree in library science. Her vow, which she fulfilled, was to make a name for herself; and as she was appointed to more and more county offices or offered directorships of more and more women's groups and charities, I spent more and more time wilting at the big picture-window in anticipation of the crunch of her tires on the graveled drive.

After digging out details about my last trip to Budapest, Mom settles down to read, borrowing one of the books from my suitcase—*Lupescu: The Story of a Royal Love Affair.* Always a voracious reader, she takes easily to this tale of intrigue in early-twentieth-century Romania. She's quick to condemn the Jewish mistress Lupescu as a tramp and a home-wrecker, and she sides immediately with Queen Marie, that establishment figure who suffered at the hands of her disobeying, philandering son. I divert Mom's swift progress toward yet another discussion of my own misbehavior and a mother's suffering by claiming that she's partial to Marie because

Marie was a relative of the Romanovs (her mother was a Russian grand duchess). It's a joke we've been sharing for years: the idea that Russian-born Mom might really be Anastasia. True, Anastasia was born in 1901 and Mom claims to have been born at the end of 1903, but she's the first to admit that the year may be off, since at the time there were no birth records. Then there's the similarity between my mother's married name—Ida Benderson—and that of the woman—Anna Anderson—who claimed to be Anastasia. And finally, there's that picture of Anastasia as a child, who had the same light-colored eyes and dirty-blond hair as Mom's, arranged in the same sausage curls Mom wore as a child. It's one of our timeworn routines based partly on my childhood fascination for the hilarious absurdity of Mom's immigrant name change, from the Russian Itke Mariashka Olshansky to the anglicized-Norwegian Ida Mae Olsen, both of which, I teasingly maintain, are actually aliases of Anastasia.

As usual, Mom plays along, averting her eyes, pasting a mysterious, regal look on her face and vowing, "I'll never tell. I can't reveal this." She's always been a good sport. A year ago, I convinced her to pretend to be a still-surviving silent film star, whom my friends at an Oscar party heard on speakerphone being interviewed about D. W. Griffith and the pink Surrealist-inspired Schiaparelli gown she once wore to an Oscar ceremony. If I brought up this episode, she could recall every syllable of it. My mother has a photographic memory.

Our moment of hilarity is enough to exhaust her, so she trudges to bed, using the wall of the hallway to correct her teetering, and continues to read, but just for a moment, until she's fallen into a labored snooze. I tiptoe into the other bedroom to check my e-mail but become fixated on a favorite photo of Romulus I took and uploaded to the Internet, in which he's wearing the brief blue bikini I bought for him and doing push-ups on the floor of our room at the Gellért, his spare, muscled body straight as a blade, parallel to the carpet, his cheekbones casting sculpting shadows into the hollow of his cheeks.

My trance is broken as I feel Mom's stiff arthritic fingers on my shoulder. Tortured by the fact that my consciousness may have wandered into some sphere beyond her conventional grasp, she has awoken and come to hunt me out, like an officer doing a surprise barracks inspection. Squinting with troubled eyes at the image on the screen, she asks in a dead, cynical, almost accusatory tone if that could be the reason for all my traveling.

Her acceptance of homosexuality has come a long way in the years since she learned about mine, in contrast to my now deceased father, who could never overcome his disgust at the thought of two male bodies in clumsy postures of coupling. Mom's love, on the other hand, caused her to work hard to dredge up memories of old-maid librarians living together in the 1920s, and she was able to come to the sentimental conclusion that love can exist between any two people. Even so, no amount of biographies of Rock Hudson or Liberace, nor any Christopher Isherwood novel or gossip about Garbo, can enlighten her about my kinds of obsessions. Confused by what appears to her as pure perversity, she pleadingly and repeatedly demands an explanation of why I choose such objects of affection, why my affairs can't be more like those of the charismatic middle-aged gay couple who live next door, with their decent professional income and well-appointed living room. Despite her knowledge of Rock Hudson's preference for blonds half his age or Liberace's suing chauffeur, she's at a loss as to my interest in younger bodies from coarser backgrounds.

Her words sting me, and my harangued mind flees to the equally painful story of opinion-fearing Queen Marie meeting her son on a train in 1918 at Creţeşti-Ungheni, as he's being shipped to imprisonment, after deserting an army post to run away and marry a commoner named Zizi Lambrino. "Is it possible that you should have lost to such a degree your sense of honor and duty," she rants. "Wouldn't it be better for you to die, a bullet in your head, and be buried in good Romanian ground...?"

There are women like her and my mother who spend most of their lives hoping that a miracle will inject the be-loved with their image of decency. That's the reason why my mother keeps my serious fiction, written under my real name and so unpalatable to her, out of view, proudly displaying the coffee-table books that I cynically wrote under a pseudonym for quick bucks. This deeply intelligent, somewhat intel-lectual woman pretends to be perplexed by the fact that I wouldn't put my birth name on those wholesome books and use a pen name for the others.

Every five months, in fact, in the middle of the night during a bout of insomnia, she takes a copy of my novel *User,* about old Times Square, down from the shelf, having conveniently forgotten what it's about. After reading until dawn about the junkies, hustlers and transvestite prostitutes memorialized in its pages, she telephones me in helpless alarm, wanting to know how I could possibly have garnered such information. Then, magically, the subject is forgotten until the next bout of insomnia and rereading several months later.

VIII

Mom's unyielding intentions bring up the question of magical thinking and make me question my own impulses. Can vivid wish-fulfillment fantasies of the beloved, motivated even by compassion, produce a miracle and ever change him? The question occurred to me that morning, at the breakfast table with Mom, in the midst of an opiate-withdrawal headache. Would all my longing for Romulus, my good intentions, my fantasies, have the same lack of effect on him that my mother's have had on me?

I worried about this as I lay against the seat that afternoon on the train to Manhattan, in a mood of paranoid yearning, two big tablespoons of hydrocodone flaring into imagined scenarios of Romulus's betrayal. Like a sponge polluted by unclean water, I soaked up pathetic notions that seemed to replay endlessly.

From my mother's I'd used a calling card to telephone him in Sibiu, and he'd mentioned that he was planning to strip for the girls at the club where his brother was a bouncer. It sounded like a harmless idea at first, but snagged my attention, the way a piece of yarn from a sweater catches on a casement nail and has to be worked off slowly in order not to unravel the whole thing. And that afternoon, before the five-and-a-half-hour train ride to New York, I kept trying to clear my throat and couldn't. I remember supposing that a couple spoonfuls of the hydrocodone would relieve it as well as that armored stiffness in my body that came from my mother's expectations.

Slowly, the opiates lulled me into hypnogogic snatches. Made-up stories came into my mind, based on my insecurity about Romulus. Then I'd wake with a start, before sinking back in and finding the same scenarios gone no further in time, waiting to torment me. Romulus was leaning over the balcony of a formerly Communist high-rise in the city of Sibiu to the soft explosions of a beaten rug. It was a few weeks before Easter, so the beaters in this Eastern country, like the ones I'd seen in Arad, were at it probably from morning until dusk. Standing next to him on the balcony was a new blonde. Her blue-veined skin seemed infused with the lead-ridden air, a condition I'd read sometimes occurs in Eastern Europe's overindustrialized cities; from the look of her skin-tight jeans and impossibly clumsy platform heels, she and Romulus were about to go to the club for the striptease he'd mentioned, which suddenly began to overlap...that meaningless noise of a beaten rug becoming a musical beat charged with aggressive sex, as brazenly parted legs lowered jeans to reveal pubic hair inches from leering female faces....

The images flared up in a white-hot kiln, then wilted into something taunting and sticky in the mildewed corner of a bedroom—my idea of the bedroom of his apartment in a concrete ex-Communist block. Romulus was gyrating on a bed the way he did during the best times his cock was in my mouth, and into the bedroom came that same mercury-skinned blonde, her rubbery breasts bouncing gently in a harsh shaft of light.

I flailed away from the image and tried to stand, but couldn't unstick myself. Now the dank bedroom featured a nest of undulating hips and slapping thighs, until the train finally pulled into that satanic, rubbery smell of rot that greets you each time you come back to New York, and jerked to a stop.

Little by little I would become amazed at the accuracy of my fantasies as I learned about Romulus's real life in Sibiu, the city to which his family had moved after a decade in the town of Râmnicul-Vîlcea. There really is a mildewed bedroom, similar to the one I imagined. And there really is a bouncer brother, named Bogdan, two years younger than Romulus, who's full of bombast and bullish good humor. He's a big, meaty fellow with a generous, confrontational grin. Then there's the next-younger brother, Vlad, who's blond and tubular as a Russian doll, has a dazed grin, a low IQ and a narcissistic habit of pulling a pocket mirror out of his pants every few steps to examine his hair. Finally, there's sloe-eyed brother Renei, the insular genius of the family, just seventeen, who's discreet and cagey but sweet and depressed. And as for the dilapidated Communist high-rise with the rug beaters, that's pretty much what I found when I actually did visit Sibiu.

Romulus is the darkest and smallest of the children, the oldest, his father an unknown quantity who disappeared into the army after getting Romulus's mother pregnant. Her real fiancé, the father of Romulus's brothers, was himself in the army when the infidelity transpired. When he came home, he found his bride-to-be with a swollen belly. The only way he'd have her was childless, so Romulus was shunted to his maternal grandmother in Sibiu, while the young married couple escaped to the nearby town of Vîlcea.

So Romulus began life thinking that his grandmother was his mother and his mother his sister. All he knew of his real mother, whom he rarely saw, was based on a few of his grandmother's bitter comments about her daughter, "that bitch from Vîlcea." It wasn't until his little body and judgment had grown capable enough, at, let's say, seven, that his mother realized he had some potential as a babysitter for his three younger half brothers, while she went to her factory job and his stepfather to his construction job. Romulus was shipped from his grandmother's to their home and informed, to his shock, that he was going to live with his real mother.

It was like a fairy tale come to life, when the boy was suddenly banished by a doting grandmother to a strange town to work for a beleaguered woman whom he had heard called a villain for the last seven years. Here in Râmnicul-Vîlcea, he had his first practice as a fugitive, an émigré, slipping out of windows while the family slept (he couldn't walk past the kitchen, where his stepfather lay in bed next to the gas stove) and sneaking onto the train back to Sibiu. Then the child's ability to play became an ability to plot, for he had to play at playing, skipping from train car to train car until he found a couple who looked like they could be respectable parents, and loitering near them with the false expression of a normal boy having fun, until the conductor was out of the way. This sham of normalcy would soon develop into a major conning skill, but it didn't keep them from sending him back to his mother again and again, until he got used to it and learned to see life through that veil of blood that some call family and that ties one abject relative, or hostage of a situation, to another, encouraging him to view the rest of the world in a pitiless or predatory way.

All of which must have somehow struck me as we said good-bye at the Gellért, and I watched him walk farther and farther away, his back slightly stooped, carrying the five hundred dollars I'd given him, which was more than five times the average monthly salary for a Romanian. From my departing taxi I watched his rather bow-legged stride across the bridge toward a bus that would take him back to the place of his old confinement—his mother's house. Like many people of his ilk, he would spend most of his time merely waiting, his coiled muscles set at bay in front of a TV, smoking cigarette after cigarette, eyes ringed with boredom and insulted sensitivity. Waiting and always waiting, that's how it was. Waiting for the time with me to be over so he could see a girl, waiting for the girl to be over so that he could start waiting for me all over again and get some money. It certainly was one more aspect of him that excited me: his talent for submission. Perhaps I should have remembered that he was also known for bolting, onto trains and across borders.

Given his background, he may have been prone to plotting. Even out of idleness. Several times I put myself in his situation, trying to see myself through his eyes as someone who could never be kind enough no matter what I did, unless I were to relinquish all my power—in the form of money and freedom. I saw him crouched before the TV in the living room of his mother (who had now moved back to Sibiu), predatorily questioned by the whole family. What, really, did this educated American who was twice his age and had so much more money want from him? I saw them drilling like miners toward the mother lode of our sex acts, and his embarrassment and swift realization when they hit a vein, so that it was more than easy to draft him into their plan of exploitative outrage, their fraudulent project to right the corruption that had been visited on their son, by setting up some kind of sting.

Homosexuality is no longer illegal in Romania per se. In 1996, under pressure from the then forty-nation Council of

Europe, the country amended the language of its sodomy law, known as Article 200. Formerly, the law forbade homosexuality in all situations; but at the time of my most intense involvement with Romulus it still called for prosecution in cases of a "public scandal." Because the term "public scandal" is so vague, it can mean anything from having sex in a public toilet to forgetting to close the curtains as you kiss your partner good morning. And because the law explicitly condemns proselytizing for the legitimacy of homosexuality, it could undoubtedly be brought to bear on anyone thought to have corrupted another into a homosexual relationship.

In the mid-nineties, the prosecution of the homosexual lifestyle in Romania was grisly. Police in towns and small cities sometimes offered the most flagrant queen amnesty in exchange for helping them hunt out more closety homosexuals. Or else the information came from a family member. A well-known case is one from 1992 involving Ciprian Cucu, who was in his last year of high school, and Marian Mutascu, who was twenty-two.* The young men, who met through a coded newspaper ad published in Timişoara, lived in the town of Sînnicolau Mare, with Cucu's family. Their love affair was intense and secret. But Cucu's sister and her husband began to suspect, and when the sister discovered Cucu's revealing diary, she went for the only help she could think of—the police. During the interrogation, Cucu denied everything, but Mutascu confessed. The police confronted the "whore Cucu," as they termed him, with the diary, and he, too, broke down.

Trying to establish without a doubt who was the active and who the passive partner—which the prosecutor and the forensic doctor insisted were essential to the case—the interrogators forced Cucu and Mutascu to undergo painful examinations of their genital and rectal areas. Finally, after pressure from Amnesty International and the Romanian Helsinki Committee, the two were released and given suspended sentences. But by then, both had served jail time. Mutascu was suffering from a severe skin infection that had erupted on his legs. Cucu was banished from high school and not allowed to finish his last year. The reason was ostensibly too many absences, but he later learned it was because his lifestyle was considered an unhealthy influence. Mutascu committed suicide.

In a few of my many fantasies about Romulus, I'd considered the possibility of blackmail. I'd heard accounts of it in the gay world now and then. A few American gays had been subject to extortion by ex-members of the Communist secret police, in regions where draconian laws against homosexuality were still in effect. What would happen, I remember wondering, if Romulus's impoverished parents persuaded him to set up a bogus police sting with a local former member of the Securitate? The fake charge could be propositioning and sexual corruption of a citizen. Like Cucu and Mutascu, I might be beaten and held in a deserted barracks, while Romulus played innocent, explaining to me that the only way to get out of this was to have my traumatized mother wire huge sums of money.

However, this fantasy wasn't connected in my mind with any moral defect on Romulus's part. It had become all too clear to me that there's a kind of person who by some historical accident is born into a mess, which leads, paradoxically, to more and more messes of the person's own making, for him and for those around him. Finally, I was aware that just a glimpse into such dead-end trajectories can brand the heart of an outsider like me and lead to all sorts of entanglements. Society is structured to prevent the toxic effect of any meaningful contact with these people.

But once you've crossed over, there isn't any turning back from that reality.

Even so, each time these worries came up, they would drown again in the sea of my passion. I'd all but forget them, immersed instead in schemes to get to Romania, to create a future for Romulus by getting him some money or to make my mother or friends understand or even envy my passion. My blinding visions and sudden eclipses were like Coleridge's on opium as I skated from idealized fantasies of perverse bliss with Romulus to demoralized concoctions of betrayal. My dream worlds had no logical connection to one another, unless it was the connection between polar opposites, inexplicable joy and sudden fear. Shuttling from one state to the next, I'd squeamishly shade my eyes from the light of a Manhattan street, or close them against the sun coming into my bedroom window. On damp sheets, my body twitched with memories of our past encounters and visions of our future. Despite the dysfunctional state of things, and despite the current normalizing politics engulfing culture, I still saw my homosexuality as a narrative of adventure, a chance to cross not only sex barriers but class barriers, while breaking a few laws in the process. Otherwise, I told myself, I might as well be straight.

IX

Here on Piaţa Victoriei in Bucharest, Romulus has zero patience for the street urchins, those grimy kids who attach their sucking tentacles to us every time we step out of the hotel. With eyes shiny and hard as pebbles, glistening with a paint-thinner high, they never stop their operatic chant for a handout, appealing to us and the Savior in whines, or wailing soft sophistic arguments about charity. They grab the sleeves of our jackets and let themselves be dragged along until Romulus shoos them away with curses sounding like a witch's imprecations.

One of the more articulate, who looks about eleven and likes to play soccer with a balled-up newspaper after he's sniffed, constantly catches my attention. He acts courageous but strikes me as slightly oversensitive, with a pouty mouth and luxurious mop of shiny hair cresting his chocolate-brown eyes.

"Why can't we kind of adopt just one while we're here?" I ask Romulus. "Set aside twenty dollars a week."

He chortles at my naiveté. "Go ahead. Try. Give to him first installment."

I take out five dollars and the boy pounces on it, inhaling it deep into his stained athletic suit. If he does mumble a thank-you, it's quickly curtailed by the torrent of begging for more. Then he's ripped backward onto the grass in front of the Benetton store, as four other kids furiously attack him for a share of the take. Limbs cartwheel and small bodies roll through the grass as yelps of pain come from the jumble. Romulus shouts out for them to stop, like an athletic coach, but they ignore him, and he meets my eyes briefly with a look of being right. "You see what happens?" he says, clucking his tongue.

"But they're homeless."

"I do not believe it for any moment. I as kid did same."

As soon as I saw him striding across the busy street in front of the Bulevard Hotel, at that puzzling, unsettling instant when fantasy suddenly becomes flesh, I realized things had taken a step forward. We hadn't seen each other for six weeks. This time he looked older and more purposeful and was carrying his own luggage, a gym bag with a couple of shirts and two pairs of underwear. On my last visit, he'd come to the Gellért with nothing but a razor.

The Bulevard, our nineteenth-century hotel, is in a perplexing state of disrepair. The sour desk clerk looked past our heads with veiled contempt when we filled out the registration form. The lobby didn't feel like that of any hotel I'd ever been in. Among the marble columns and the peculiar array of vases attached to the walls, which I later found out held surveillance microphones during the Ceaușescu era, were stone-faced, bulky men in black suits like those I'd seen at the bar in Budapest. Cher–look-alike beauties in black designer miniskirts, their shiny hair cut Louise Brooks style and their long legs ending in gleaming sling-back shoes, lounged pantherlike on the scattered banquettes, scrutinizing us with tinges of hope but mostly undisguised boredom. Every once in a while, a cell phone would ring. One of the thuggish guys would extract it from his suit and answer it, and one of the girls would leave. It seemed like a pretty active hustling operation.

Our immense circular room has four bay windows. It's high-ceilinged and aristocratic, except for the fact that the counterfeit Louis XVI furniture keeps collapsing. But with our heavy drapes, mirrored vanity table and brocade couch, as well as the cavernous round space of the room, we soon forget about the rest of the world. Eventually I get the idea of filling a plastic jug with water to make the pull-chain toilet work; and since no one ever appears to make up the room, we learn to put our garbage outside.

A lot of phone numbers have changed in Bucharest shortly before our arrival, and an updated system is being installed. Not only do we never find out our real hotel telephone number, but the few contacts I have—such as the film critic Alex Leo Şerban, who's been recommended by my French friend the writer Benoît Duteurtre—turn out to be unreachable. The old phone numbers just ring and ring, and the new ones aren't listed in the directory.

Our lack of outside contacts has thrown us into that Cocteauean netherworld of *enfants terribles* that worked so well for a while at the Gellért. There's no greater accessory to romantic passion than an absence of context. Within our *Traviata*-style stage set we can enact hackneyed plots of sensual sloth, intense sex, encroaching boredom and jealousy. Our first sturm und drang occurs even before we've unpacked our bags, when I ask Romulus for a hundred dollars. A couple of weeks before, on the telephone, he said that the last hundred dollars I'd given him in Budapest had had red-felt-marker stains along the edges from the bank, and that no one in Sibiu would change them. He asked me to wire an extra hundred and promised to give me the stained bills back.

"What do you mean, you don't have them?"

"Not no more. Finally in bar they agree to change those bills with red."

"You were supposed to hold on to them."

"I did not know I need them."

"How in fuck am I supposed to trust you?"

"Then now I will leave."

"Hello? Are you a pure sociopath? You spent money that you promised you'd give back to me."

"Yes, yes, I needed, you see."

"Goddammit, I don't trust you."

"Good. I am leaving because one hundred lousy dollars is enough for you to lose my faith."

"All right. Forget it."

"I cannot."

"What?"

"No."

"Look, put down your bag. You're not going anywhere. Fact, I'm taking it out of the next sum I give you."

"Of course." He drops the bag to the floor.

He pulls on the striped velour shirt I've bought for him. It brings out the pirate and makes his black eyes look velvety. It's almost dark outside already, and wind is rattling the windows, so we throw on light jackets.

The vast hallway is unlit, like the set of *Last Year at Marienbad* after thirty years of cobwebs. In the lobby, one of the working girls follows us with X-ray eyes. Penetrating, bewildered, resentful. We hit the street, mowing through the begging children clustered at the entrance.

For me, this city has a baffling *Cabinet of Dr. Caligari* feeling. You imagine the buildings of Bucharest leaning at weird angles, but just as is suggested in Expressionist films, it's really your own grounding that's off center. You're faced again and again with that amputee, History. Then you yourself begin to feel dislocated.

Dissonant twosome as we are—Romulus young, lithe, short and sharp-faced, with shiny, stony eyes; me older, taller and much bulkier, eyes burning—Bucharest begins to feel like our landscape. It's part *Blade Runner* and part Boulevard Hauss-mann. Twilight doesn't seem to come to the city; it smudges it, I don't know why. We're walking past the sumptuous nineteenth-century Cercul Militar and its hopes of Parisian glory. An elderly woman stops us, her eyes bright with memories, a weird, wild compassion in her trembling voice. When she finds out we're visitors, that we haven't suffered what she has, it sets something off. She recalls Bucharest's old glory for us—and the memories shoot like sparks from her eyes to the tips of her wild, gnarled hair—she blesses us, begs us, as tourists, to reconstruct the Bucharest of the past for her by eating at Capşa, a once famous restaurant with velvet-and-ebony furniture.

As we leave her and walk up Calea Victoriei, the Haussmannian look of Bucharest brings back my literary memory of that fantastic promenade during the teens and twenties, the days of Lupescu and Carol, when seraglio-eyed women in masklike makeup and dyed fox stoles sauntered past moustachioed men in severely tailored serge suits, brilliantined hair and patent-leather shoes, puffing oval Turkish cigarettes with their pouting, gleaming lips that made off-color comments about the parade of "possibilities"; but this is swiftly interrupted by an onion-domed Russian church, sprouting like a mushroom between two dank housing projects. I make Romulus enter with me. Its small, musty interior holds gleaming icons and genuflecting women with covered heads, all clustered together to leave little walking space.

On the street, wild dogs and even wilder homeless children keep crossing our path. A Soviet-style housing project looks like it's caving into a shiny new adjoining bank. Everything looks pieced together by Krazy Glue, fighting for space and contradicting everything else, like Cubist structures on a baroque wedding cake. Most interesting to me are the pharmacies. You see, I associate my desire for Romulus, that sense of dislocation he causes, with the syrup and white tablets I've been taking: hydrocodone and codeine that exaggerate my fantasies of passion and make me forget my anxieties about my mother's health; as well as the white lorazepam tranquilizers—also available here—that I now swallow in order to sleep. From the glass-doored wooden cabinets of the pharmacy we've just entered, the bony-fingered clerk extracts what I tell Romulus to ask for.

Just as exciting is the discovery of a line of face creams called Gerovital, which I will begin to use regularly and will later maintain has magic properties. At barely four dollars a jar, it ends up filling my suitcases on every departure from Romania, as requests from friends for the magic substance multiply. The creams are based on a formula developed by the legendary scientist Ana Aslan, who until her death claimed to have discovered an anti-aging chemical. Today, all over the world, elderly people are still swallowing Gerovital pills. I buy several jars of the cream and then stock up on fifty-pill boxes of lorazepam and opiates, leaving the store with flushed excitement.

Calea Victoriei leads us to a vast square, a crossroads of historical trauma. There on my left is the palace where Carol II's Jewish mistress Lupescu hid behind gauze curtains while Carol, in his white cloak, raised a toast to her. Now it houses a national museum of art. It was the palace in which Carol felt most at home, whereas his father preferred the more remote Cotroceni, on the outskirts of the city. There were rumors of secret passages running underneath this palace, bringing Lupescu undetected to Carol at night and allowing him to meet secretly with deal-makers and his cabal of scheming advisors.

The Central University Library across the street, as well as the palace, were nearly gutted by fire during the Revolution of 1989, and thousands of priceless volumes in the library were reduced to ashes. Behind the library are the charred ruins of a once stately house that was destroyed during the revolution and left as a reminder. Not far away is the wide, stern façade of the old Communist Party headquarters, riddled with bullet holes, from whose roof Romania's last dictator, Nicolae Ceauşescu, escaped by helicopter. A white marble plaque indicates the spot, with the words *"Glorie martirilor noştri"* (Glory to our martyrs), in remembrance of the revolutionaries who lost their lives.

Unaware that Capşa, the restaurant the old lady mentioned, is across the street from where we met her, we take an eerie cab ride in search of it through back streets with decaying mansions, whose pitted wooden columns, stagnant gardens and shady gables keep leading us into dead ends. After several days, we'll realize that most of the taxi drivers don't know where anything is. We give up on our search and look for another restaurant, Mioriţa, named after the primal Romanian myth. Only later do I ponder that legend of a murdered shepherd and realize how deeply it seems to articulate some of our experience.

It's eight p.m. already. Dying of hunger, we hurry shiveringly on foot north of Calea Victoriei, still in search of a restaurant, past a large late-nineteenth-century palace fronted by two stone lions. We stop and stare at the scallop-shaped glass canopy leading to the entrance, just as the iron gate is being locked by a grizzled man in a moth-eaten sweater and wool cap. He is, he claims, the conservator of this museum, Cantacuzino Palace, where George Enescu, the composer and musician, used to live; and he wonders—looking us up and down—whether we'd like a private tour. We follow him up the stairs into a terrifying well of pitch blackness, after which he throws on a series of switches that illuminate heavenly, elegant rooms of polished wood and stucco, decorated with plaster cherubs, winged trumpeters and a rosy-fleshed nude sprawled across the ceiling. Casually, he pulls open cabinets containing the personal belongings of Mr. Enescu and removes priceless musical scores for us to examine, finger. He tells us—and this turns out to be confirmed in *Romanian Rhapsody*, by Dominique Fernandez—that Enescu lived here with his wife, the princess Maruca Cantacuzino, who was a former wife of the Boyar Cantacuzino and who kept the palace in near darkness, because of a disfigured face resulting from gasoline burns she'd inflicted on herself after an unrequited love affair. She appeared in the light only when her face was hidden by a plaster mask. Later I'll also find out that she was a confidante of Queen Marie.

He takes us to a smaller house in back of the main building, where, he claims, the composer, who was of peasant origins, felt more comfortable and spent most of his time. It's only after we've thanked him and given him a ten-dollar tip—an average Romanian's two-day earnings—that we realize he must be a museum employee, hoping to make some extra cash.

We make another attempt to find Miorița, and our cabdriver gets lost again. The ride ends in a mud path, where eerie light from an Art Nouveau window in the unlit street illuminates the uniform of a soldier, working in this city in conjunction with the police. I want to ask directions, but

Romulus grabs my arm and keeps me from crossing the street. It seems no one asks the police for help.

We cross to the other side farther down, through mud. Why do I feel that I'm becoming lost in a marsh? I'll eventually discover that Bucharest was built on forested wetlands and a tangle of roots. Once across the mud, we end up in front of a large red Victorian house that could have belonged to *Psycho*'s Mrs. Bates. There's a sign in front of it that says "Opium." We enter out of curiosity, and a woman in a revealing red cocktail dress asks whether we prefer the smoking room (we aren't sure what substance she's referring to), the "bath lounge" or Purgatorio, a room in the basement with chairs decorated alternately with red devil horns and white angel haloes. The establishment is owned by the Romanian actress Ioana Crăciunescu, whose much younger partner, the director Bogdan Voicu, is working with her to create theater entertainments for the special few.

There are, says the manager—who has appeared to give us a tour—weekly performances in the bath lounge, a bordello-red room featuring an immense golden bathtub. And in Purgatorio, a new trend of stand-up comedy in English has begun, because, he says, Romanian stand-up is just a bunch of potty jokes. Next door, in the yellow smoking room, spooky pantomimes are going on among the Oriental cushions. But there's no food here. Someone calls us a taxi, and we return to the hotel, defeated and hungry.

Too tired to keep looking for food, we switch on the television. In front of it and an endless soccer match, we learn a series of passional attitudes designed to fit his smaller, steelier body into my padded bulk. I'm stretched out on my back with him using my stomach as a cushion, or we lie entangled like two tarantulas, a perfect balance of lighter on heavier limbs that avoids bone pressure. Or I'll be lying belly-down with my head by his waist, so that my hands can wander over his body like tortoises inspecting every blade of grass on a beach.

Because he doesn't complain, I've decided we're in paradise. Visions of him change, but they're always highly sexual, with elements of the predatory. I feel like a falconer with his hawk, that beady-eyed, sharp-beaked and alert but dependent creature that pecks ever so carefully at its master. At other times, his sinuous muscles enlace me in the fantasy of a python, our corkscrew intertwinings thrilling me into believing myself some circus performer who's ready to chance being strangled for the right to be caressed. But then, every so often, he suddenly diminishes to a poor wren, for what is the real difference, except in the sense of motive versus action, between vulnerability and predation? Isn't each part of the same formula?

It's his emotional hunger, often presenting itself as stoical machismo, that keeps promising a trapdoor into his heart. And as we lie here, the unreal atmosphere of the room is as disorienting as the description of some powdery scent in a decadent novel, while snippets of his fairy-tale past float into the air.

"And then what happened?"

"Why you want to know? You will write a book about? The story of my life, such a book that will make."

"How you ended up in Budapest. You were telling me."

"I got to go to the toilet. Toss me those cigarettes."

"Can you hear me?"

"Say?"

"You were telling me."

"They threw me out at eighteen...."

"Who, who?"

"Say?"

"Can't you hear me?"

"My parents, when is no more money from state for me, even though they keep money they get for me when I still live with my grandmother. Toss those matches in here at me, please, will you?"

"Your parents threw you out?"

"Surely. They fabricate this fight in Vîlcea to make me exit when I was eighteen," he claims. "Say I steal from them. Which is how I end up on Corso in Budapest where you find me. But you know, my stepfather waste what little they have for drinking, and soon as I am to coming back, it is money all the time, they take it from us all, me, Bogdan."

"But tell me again about Macedonia. Come on, come back on the bed."

"All right, give me the remote, you know they have this erotic evening on TV every Friday, they showing one of the *Emmanuelle*s."

"I saw them in the seventies. What'd you say happened in Macedonia?"

"I am crossing Macedonia two or three times, with two other guys, mostly walking, you know? They throw us out of train at every stop because they don't like our passports, but we just keeping walking and get on at next station. But then they throw us out again."

"And that's how you made it to Greece?"

"Hm, hmm, three weeks there, my Greek becoming very functional, but I not write it, not write any of the languages I speak except Romanian."

"Did you ever get caught in Greece?"

"Yes, yes. First time they send me back in closed train with other illegal Romanians. But I climb through window at station. Two days later they catching me again. 'Let's see you jump from this window,' they say. They put me on a plane.

Bring me to plane handcuffed."

"A regular plane?"

"Of course. I get the meal, the drinks. But is November, still warm in Greece, and we land in Bucharest and freezing. I wearing only T-shirt. Have to hitchhike back to Sibiu."

"What about the time you got shot crossing from Macedonia into Greece?"

"Which time? I went over so many times, I start to make money that way, border guide, you know? I prefer bullets to staying home. Listen, this Mexican border. I read in a Romanian paper that plenty of people cross over to U.S."

"Come on, Romulus, there are easier ways."

"You do it your way, I mine."

What did history do to him? The question sounds absurd, for we're all to some extent victims of history; but I'm convinced that, as my friend Ursule Molinaro suspected, Romulus is ancient. His half-finished projects and sudden departures, his enslavements and sullen betrayals are micro-recapitulations of the fate of his land.

Like my beloved Times Square, Romania was a crossroads of cultures and clashes—Byzantine glories, wily Levantine schemes for survival, the nexus of three empires: the Ottoman, the Austro-Hungarian and the Soviet. Romanians are, they themselves believe, Latins lost among the barbarians, the Roman victims of Turks.

It's midnight and we're finally eating dinner, the only customers in the hotel restaurant. The mottled marble and enormous mirrors are exquisite, baroque and unreal, the room immense. The way the waiters and whores who walk through look at us says that we, too, are lost, isolated. Romulus's eyes, I can tell, see doom and are perpetually disgusted by it. But such a stance is overruled by courageous passivity, which the Romanian poet Lucian Blaga once called the "Mioritic space."

According to the great Romanian myth of Miorița, three shepherds from different regions came down with their flocks from the Carpathian Mountains. Two of them began to plot to murder the Moldovan shepherd, who was warned of the scheme by Miorița, a magical ewe. The shepherd didn't flee. With a vast and perplexing sense of spiritual acceptance, he planned his own funeral, which took on the character of a wedding with Nature, a return to Eden.

Critics have debated the ancient myth's meaning since it was first published by the Romantic poet Vasile Alecsandri. There are those who have associated it with pessimism and passivity, going so far as to call Romania a "suicidal" culture. But Mircea Eliade, the controversial Romanian historian and mythologist (who has been accused of being a Fascist early in his career), saw the myth of Miorița as being about an active transformation of fate, the will to change the meaning of destiny into something self-empowering.

In light of this, Romulus's surrender of his body to me takes on a morbid and transfigured aura. It may be an arrangement of circumstance, but to him it's part of a timeless cycle. I can see it in his eyes. His prostitution has a sacrificial, portentous significance. And so it is that the fixed expression of his eyes, the angry near-piety of his touch are signs of sacrifice that can't be possessed by me. But in any case, the buyer can never control the ritual of prostitution.

His face is getting paler during dinner as I flounder to stake a claim, shamelessly offering him long-term financial schemes as if they were car insurance. The obsessive-compulsive nature of my feelings for him makes me spit out vulgar maintenance plans whose function is to take away the guesswork of our relationship. I want marriage instead of doom. Each of my offers is an insult to his approach to transgression. He's getting increasingly furious at my attempts to buy him.

Eventually my attack temporarily obliterates his machismo. Back in our room, he strikes me as a little boy, an effeminate one, as he angrily tosses his few possessions into a bag. Now I must beg him to stay yet again. And so we're back in our trance once more. He puts down his bag.

It's two a.m., and we've decided to have a drink at a tony club we noticed in our wanderings. It's called Byblos and it features a fancy restaurant with live entertainment and nearly New York prices. How can I explain the despairing rage that fills Romulus at the sight of its Armani-clad clientele? This isn't simple resentment of the bourgeoisie on the part of an outsider, an underclass person, but something even more inherently political. His rage is, in part, Communist. It could even be interpreted as prudishness. But Romulus is himself in many ways a crass materialist who dreams of killer sound systems and flashy cars. Even so, the discipline and conservatism of real wealth, such as those exhibited by the privileged young people in this bar, crush his spirit. What repulses him most is the lack of Mioritic sacrifice in the comfortable lifestyle of the young people around him. He's looking at the faces of children of politicians or publishers, and he knows what strategies their parents have employed to achieve such security in this impoverished country. He wants to put out the eyes of their children, whose blandness negates all the wisdom of his suffering. Once again, his rage leaves me feeling helplessly inferior. There's nothing I can do but slavishly admire this odd man out of global capitalism.

Back at the hotel, he strips for bed and I gobble two of my fortuitous codeine tablets. I know what my duty is. Within an hour, I'm in that sparkling night gallery made of little explosions of codeine. It blots out most of the sociological details surrounding our situation, leaves only his hard, shadowy body inexplicably laid out for me, dappled by the streetlight piercing the gaps in the heavy curtains. This is a funereal, or should I say vampiric, scene. I fall to my knees in the darkness because I know that to worship his abjection is to drink at the fount of cultural doom and play at entangling my fate with his. He's a door out of the repetitive banalities of North American capitalism. His penis plunges into my throat like an eel into inky water.

X

My favorite picture of Romulus is the one he took of himself. Sitting naked on the absurd lilac brocade couch in our hotel room, he held the camera at arm's length and snapped a picture. Because of the effect of foreshortening, his forearms look as enormous as Popeye's. His chest, over the middle of which runs sparse, matted hair, shows the ribs at the sides. And above it is a face grown oval and generous. An enormous nose over smiling lips. It's a face he hasn't shown me yet, but I know it's there.

Try as I may, I can't reproduce the angle myself, so we decide to begin our shoot for a porn magazine that I contracted before I left New York. It's a scheme I've cooked up to make him money. I'd called a contact at *Honcho,* a gay magazine, and proposed a spread on Romulus with a text by me. Out of it, he'll make a whole $800.

It's more than obvious that this room is an ideal backdrop for a hilarious send-up of European eroticism; it's a camp porn set ready to be exploited. He's sitting on the upholstered bench before the mirrored vanity table, removing his pants, which are about to fall onto the pretentious paisley rug. Reflected in the mirror, the scene looks like a homosexual parody of one of the *Emmanuelle* movies we've been watching on television, or maybe it's a cut scene from *Belle de jour,* that surreal take on bourgeois infidelity.

Each time I click the shutter, the environment of the shoot is brought home to us. Just a few years ago, this room, like most hotel rooms in Romania during the Ceauşescu regime, was wired for eavesdropping. The bedside lamp, the overhead chandelier, the upholstered chair probably once contained microphones. And if these microphones still exist, as a nongovernmental security measure, or just to satisfy someone's curiosity, the earphoned spy at reception is privy to the groans, suckings and perverse requests of our little session. The possibility sends us into fits of giggles. We pump up the action, shouting orgasm noises at the lamp or smacking our lips at the chandelier.

To camp up the idea of the Eastern European call boy, I tell Romulus to strip down to his bikini underpants and count out a stack of bills on one bare thigh. *Pop!* goes the flash as I snap picture after picture, sliding the briefs halfway down his leg, bending to suck him, then pulling away with a wink to snap more pictures.

The bills have slid off his leg and are lying in a scattered pile at his feet, though one of them is still stuck to the inside of his thigh. *Flash!* I've got another good one. Now he's sitting on the bed, legs spread, washboard ripples prominent under the harsh light, curved cock snaking up his belly. He grasps each nipple between thumb and forefinger and winks as I push the camera button. The flash of white light electrifies his body. I dive onto his cock again, then take a close-up of his crotch. He throws himself into the upholstered chair and with a silly grin on his face pretends to doze, cock standing in a stiff curve amid the curls of pubic hair. He rolls onto the bed, pushes up against the headboard to a half-sitting position and puts his hands behind his head to reveal the large hollows of his armpits, whose hair he's shortened. I click again, suck again, click, click, click...Come sprays through the ragged foreskin and covers his belly and chest in droplets. I throw some bills onto him, which soak up the drops. *Flash! Pop!* Done.

The film is due in New York in five days. So we hurry to the post office. On the way, we stop at an Internet café, where I compose a cheesy text. But before I slip it into the envelope, Romulus grabs it and reads. My cardboard erotic metaphors send him into gales of laughter.

"'Red-hot Romanian'? Hah! So, my 'lazy, cocky gestures' drive you to 'frenzy'?" A burst of more laughter as he throws the page in my face. "Beware, Bruce, soon I become big, big American porn star. Soon you are growing old, and then... then I become the one who pays the bills!"

XI

In Syracuse, I grow closer to another body that has, sad to say, surpassed the probable. It's almost as if Mom's entire biology had been reduced to her enormous will. She's thinner than when I last saw her, a month ago, with nearly skeletal arms and legs, swollen ankles and a drooping belly. Miraculously she keeps running on empty, struggling in a chirping voice to the kitchen with her walker, looking determined, then bitter and disappointed, when she can't lift a half-gallon of orange juice by herself.

A few days after I got back from Bucharest, she fell and broke a hip; or rather, her porous hip may have crumbled, sending her to the floor. My brother flew up immediately for the surgery, and it went unbelievably well; but her recovery became a purgatory, truly an infelicitous term for the effects the morphine had on her.

She'd ended up by chance in a Catholic hospital. After each morphine injection, which sent her into delirium, she became convinced that the crucifix her bed faced had been put there by the nurses to mock her, in a kind of teasing crucifixion of a Jew. This was obviously a resurgence of her childhood agonies as the only Jew in her tiny village in up-state New York, when she bit her tongue in a red, humiliated face, as the Gentile English teacher harped on the despicable personality of Shylock in *The Merchant of Venice*. Luckily,

Mom's regression was temporary, a common reaction of the aged to opiates.

Strange that the very substances that stretch my thoughts into vaulting ecstasies should plunge her into doubt and grotesque imaginings. But then Mom has always looked askance at painkillers. She feels they interfere with the exercise of the will. I remember how astonished I was as a teenager when I found out she had refused Novocain when she visited the dentist for a tooth-pulling.

After just a few weeks in physical rehab with either my brother or me by her bed, Mom regained her ability to walk and all her critical faculties. She learned to laugh at the experience. Now her mind is little changed, but her body, with its replaced hip, arthritis-twisted hands and bowed spine, looks years away from how it looked when I last saw her. It doesn't prevent being near it from filling me with waves of painful sweetness. To me her ravaged flesh is...desirable. It's still the body that wore the bright scarves and the pearl-gray cinched-waist suits, bouncing me on her lap and letting me play with her costume jewelry.

We haven't had a very pleasant business. Mom's nearness to the end has only made me yearn more intensely for approval. And she's become even more relentlessly determined to know and correct every detail of my life. I've tried to ease her into the story of my attachment for Romulus, leaving out the underclass details and portraying him as a toiling but disadvantaged working-class boy who sincerely cares for me. Impishly, she keeps forgetting his name every time she mentions him, calling him instead Chaim Yankel, the comic Yiddish pejorative for "village idiot." This causes me to bristle and sends her into peals of naughty laughter. Her gibes wound me and make me redouble my efforts to get her to like him. How long will the child keep crawling back to the mother's breast? Until he's crawling back to her grave? Seeking solace on a carcass so close to the time when flies will come buzzing has a certain value. In some strange way you're approaching the ultimate meaning of generation as well as your own death.

My first futile attempt to escape her control is also the content of my first memory, just before I turned two. The sun is blazing and the sand near the green water is burning the soles of my feet. I'm walking in my tiny bathing trunks between my mother and father, each hand in one of theirs. Mom offers to pick me up off the hot sand, and I exultantly say, "No!" It's that delicious moment when the living being experiences its first sense of autonomy. The sand bakes the soles of my feet to an unbearable intensity, and flashes of white light turn my "No!" into something dangerous and metallic, an addictive adventure, one that will be squelched until adolescence, when it flares up again in contempt for her values and a compulsion for sexual adventure.

After our conversation, her many heart pills aren't functioning at peak. Her chest is tight with angina, her head reeling with fatigue. We're sitting on the bed and she's clinging to me in fear, her brittle white hair crushed against my chest. Is there anything sweeter, more oppressive than this painful intimacy? My own helplessness invades me, sickens me, as death invades her. But I deserve this. I'm swallowed up by it. I savor our moment of closeness, which, abruptly, is broken when she takes my chin rudely between thumb and forefinger. "I can still see traces of your former good looks as a child," she says.

In truth, Mom's imminent passing is merely giving birth to another mother. That fleshly, nearly obscene bond between me and Romulus has the fatuousness of the infant's dependence. That's why, sitting at the kitchen table with

Mom, I can think only of Romulus instead of her, only of my corruption, my infatuation with a prostitute.

The codeine I brought back from Romania relieves my longing for him and takes away some of the anxiety generated by Mom. I can rub her back for her as I feel my own muscles letting go, getting more elastic. The armored tension in my body eases, and Mom hums with relief. Later, if I swallow enough pills, Romulus will even materialize—sometimes becoming the way I want him to be, but other times animated by my fears. Too bad that she doesn't have a similar device to rely on. Instead she has only her memory. She stays relaxed for a moment after I've massaged her, then once more comes out with the same story of my birth. I've heard it this way a thousand times. "When they brought you into the delivery room, I asked, 'Whose beautiful baby is that?' You were so gorgeous." The implied question being, "What happened?"

A chance occurrence has made a long cohabitation with Romulus more likely. The Centre Pompidou in Paris has invited me to have a public discussion with the French writer Guillaume Dustan, all expenses paid. The offer comes by e-mail while I'm still in Syracuse. Mom is delighted but can't understand why they would be interested in someone like me. Ignoring the slight, I dash off an e-mail to Marianne Alphant at the Centre Pompidou, accepting the offer, then claiming that a certain Romulus T. is essential to my literary project. My presentation, I say, will make no sense without him. Immersion in my love affair has made me foolhardy. True to my derangement, I'm actually fantasizing giving a talk to the museumgoers with giant pornographic images of Romulus projected on the wall behind me, as if everyone else would automatically find him compelling enough to enter my world of significations. Without telling Mom any details, I claim that Romulus has been invited to the symposium with me. She looks at me oddly, then returns to *King Carol, Hitler and Lupescu,* which I've lent her. As she always does, she's taking a crash course on the subject of my latest obsession. But when she goes to the bathroom, I glance at the page and see that she's rereading some of the same material she read on my last visit. The reason is painfully apparent: Carol and Marie's oedipal trajectory is identical to our own. It begins with a utopian childhood and a joyously encompassing mother, only to swerve into perverse rebellion and sexual adventurism and the defeat of the more conservative, female figure. In Mom's eyes, the story is about a mother's tragedy, the irrevocable loss of a love defined by complete control over a submissive charge.

Two days after I write her, Alphant sends back a polite e-mail inviting Romulus to attend the symposium as well. But sensibly, she doesn't offer any help with a ticket or a visitor's visa. Next I write to Elein Fleiss, the publisher of *Purple* magazine, for which I'm doing a column, and ask her to invite Romulus to the magazine's presentation at the Centre Pompidou. It's a pushy, inappropriate request. Even so, she answers warmly, without asking too many questions. She sends me another carefully worded, noncommittal letter, at which the French, a rhetorical people, are so gifted.

According to my Parisian strategy, Romulus will come to meet me in Paris after I fly there for free. We'll live there together for several months with the help of friends. He'll stay on illegally past his visa, supported by me, while I do translations and writing to earn our living. While Mom and I are eating dinner, which she stubbornly prepares despite her reduced mobility, I offer her a more bourgeois version of the plan, complete with Romulus looking for a job in Paris. The fact that I'll be in Paris instead of Romania soothes her, but she can't resist pointedly admitting that she was hoping for something better, a nice middle-aged professional, perhaps. With a 401(k)? I shoot back. Then I can't resist reminding her of the only rebellious act of her conventional, law-abiding life: defying her mother and marrying my smolderingly handsome father, who came from a family beset with mental illness and poverty. The very same year they decided to marry, his sister was accused of embezzling. My mother's mother tried desperately to stop the marriage. Well, that was different, Mom says. Once again I lure her into discussing a facet of my father's childhood that fascinates me. I'd always been stymied when trying to decode his sweet, rather passive personality, so often dominated by hers. It seems that at the age of twelve he fled his turbulent home with a younger brother, and they survived for a while on their own like vagrants—like a near-homeless Romulus in Budapest—in an abandoned house. As always, dwelling on the incident makes Mom anxious. So I leave her and go to the mantel to stare at a picture of Dad's face at twenty-one. Sultry, with hypnotic eyes and full lips, he had a shy, shady appeal, like the best of the *beaux ténébreux*. With his slicked-back hair, he had a Valentino look, and the photo dates from the same period.

As a backup to the European plan there's an American one. Unbeknownst to Mom, I've convinced P, a flamboyant, resourceful Russian-émigré poet and male prostitute living in New York, to reveal all his information about asylum, which he's about to be granted on the basis of sexual orientation. It's a long shot, but it just might be a way of getting Romulus into the country. However, as his bow-legged swagger fills my mind, I admit to myself that never in a million years would Romulus publicly label himself a homosexual, regardless of the benefits.

His immigration has become a new obsession, fraught with longing, then fear. On the one hand, having him here in the

States seems like the simplest solution. On the other, I can foresee all the potential painful complications. I'm kneeling to pull Mom's shoes off her swollen feet as my thoughts careen toward Romulus and me having a vicious argument in my apartment after he's emigrated here. He storms out, and I have to run into him night after night at New York's one remaining hustler bar, which will be his only means of support. Later he's rail-thin and unwashed and cursing at me on the street, threatening to blackmail me, reminding me of my illegal role in helping him lie to obtain a visa. The fear gains momentum when I remember the gossip about a certain restaurateur in Manhattan's Greenwich Village who imported an impossibly attractive Pole, only to have him fly off eventually with his cash and credit card, until, some time later, the restaurateur, still deeply in love, actually went back to Poland and unraveled the legal mess of charges he himself had brought against the Pole, and then re-invited him to New York.

More blasts of desire erase these qualms as I help Mom pull her blouse off her arms and shoulders. Overwhelming as the problem of loving someone in the former Eastern bloc may be, I'm convinced that my desire can exterminate every obstacle. During a short trip to Montreal, I met a Panamanian dancer who'd just smuggled his sister to Texas in a gas truck. It cost him only $2,000. At the moment it seems like a viable option. Then there's that Moldovan actor who told me about the people his troupe had transported to the United States by letting them pose as members of the company. Finally, there's that sympathetic Lithuanian gay professor from a certain university who's willing to write a letter inviting Romulus to a Slavic symposium. By the time Mom's in her nightgown, I'm reaching to take her hearing aids out of her ears and cockily grinning with confidence.

What are you smiling about? she grumpily demands.

Potential cons are swarming through my mind at the very moment that—in all probability—Romulus is taking my love in vain. I'm assuming she's blonde, his preference, and that he's spending every penny I've given him on her. Sometimes I imagine her as that watery-haired teenager whose existence I found so annoying in Budapest, or that other blonde with the lead-infused skin I've concocted.

Here I am, peeling off my mother's old nitroglycerin patches, which have a gunpowdery odor, from the right side of her chest, and pasting new ones on the left, while in Sibiu, where it's five in the morning, Romulus is likely to have just spent some of the money I gave him on a last couple of liters of beer and those sunflower seeds he eats incessantly, like a parrot. He's going to share them with the buxom blonde waiting patiently outside the grocery kiosk. Isn't it probable that his girlfriend was never Hungarian but a Romanian immigrant living in Budapest, say, a refugee from that polluted glass-factory town known as Turda? And that she followed him back to Sibiu? For some reason an image of Turda's lead-ridden air stuck with me after I read about it in a travel guide. Smile fading from my face while Mom scrutinizes me, I nimbly construct a paranoid imaginary biography for this new character. On a daily basis—since the age of six—her drunken father has driven her out of the house to make money for the family. She probably sold some of those used anti-Semitic books like the ones I saw in Bucharest, from a table on the street in the icy snow; or she sat all day in the hot sun with an old bathroom scale, like that old man I saw on a Bucharest boulevard, hoping to convince passersby to weigh themselves for the price of a penny. Then she quickly figured out selling herself was a lot more profitable. That's how she met Romulus, while plying her trade in Budapest right about the time he met me.

For the first time her face shifts into clear focus in my imagination, plain and oval, an oatmeal complexion with steel-blue eyes and a slightly bulbous nose, the kind of potato-faced girl who looks like a chambermaid until she's lightened her hair and painted her lips a glistening pink to become a disco queen, a flashy trophy with long, lithesome legs, pert breasts and a high ass.

Four days ago, from Syracuse, I'd overnighted letters of invitation from the Lithuanian professor and Moldovan actor, with instructions for Romulus to go to the American embassy in Bucharest to apply for a visa. Now I call his cell phone and he answers distractedly, with a television baying annoyingly in the background. He's in Bucharest, he claims, as I instructed, staying at a cheap hotel near the embassy. But something about the incessant puffing of his cigarette, interrupting our conversation, hints of disconnection and disappointment. The embassy is demanding papers to prove his residence and his income, he tells me sadly. Is he really there? I squelch the doubt. Don't worry, I tell him, we'll find another way. What astonishes me is the tone of his soft, caring voice, his obvious comfort in hearing mine. It washes away all the paranoia, until Mom's abrasive voice barges in on the conversation, demanding to know immediately where I am and what I'm doing.

Instead of anger, a tenderness for her, overlaid on a sweet, sentimental need for him, washes over me and floats me into her bedroom. Her cool, waxy hand grasps my arm weakly, and she whispers into my ear that she approves of him if that is what will make me happy. But her voice can't lead me into the world into which she's rapidly sinking. Perhaps not so strangely, her failing is intensifying my Romulus fantasies. I seem to be substituting some harder, crueler comfort for what was once so soft and protective. All my life, from infancy to now, bodies have been my most cathectic points of signification. I never believed that the mind was any more important. Now I feel my own body calmed by fantasy, floating on Mom's touch, the conversation I've just had with Romulus and the white codeine pills I brought back from Romania.

Later, an unspecific distrust and fears about my exploits return, bringing back, for some reason, a memory of that last day in Bucharest. I'd awoken with him in my arms and that splitting headache that comes from a codeine hangover, feeling sudden regret about having neglected the city in favor of his body. As he lounged in front of the television with the curtains drawn against the afternoon light, I decided to separate from him for the first time, even though our nights had been saturated with more and more intimacy and physical pleasure. What cinched it as far as I was concerned was that I couldn't take the sound of another day's soccer marathon on TV.

Having become as accustomed to my constant touch as I was to his, he was startled at my decision to venture out alone; he sat up in bed and insisted on going with me as guardian. But separation seemed the healthy thing to do, so I left alone, ignoring his worried face and assuring him I could take care of myself.

Guidebook in hand, I headed for Bucharest's Village Museum, an outdoor exhibition of rural architecture that features thatched roofs, wooden houses, woven-twig fences and other authentic peasant productions. The feel of Romulus's embraces still hovered around me, like an article of clothing that has just been shed. The headache had dissipated, and I felt deeply relaxed. At the museum, as I neared a romantic clay cottage painted in vivid blue-wash, I heard devilish giggling coming from inside. This confused me, because the building was surrounded by a rope fence with clear indications forbidding trespassing. Out of it stumbled a gorgeous teenaged couple, an elfin girl in tight pink pedal pushers whose waistband she struggled to button, and an almond-eyed boy in tank top and too-large red athletic pants, the fly of which gaped open. Still giggling, they glanced at me in humorous complicity, then leaped over the roped fence and ran away. They were a far cry from Carol in his natty English suits or his mistress Lupescu in her black silk Chanel dresses, yet somehow they recalled the thrill of those illicit trysts I'd been reading about. A happy excitement shot through me like an injection, as I realized that the world was full of spontaneous sensuality always in reach if you had the courage to spit in the face of convention. Or at least that's what I thought. Months later I would read in a newspaper that guards were arrested for taking up to three dollars in bribes from such lovers and letting them use the cottages in the museum to shack up, but on that day the scene had the aura of a romantic comedy.

It was sunny and breezy as I strolled down Bulevardul Kiseleff, among stately lime trees, wisteria vines and dilapidated mansions, full of hope and excitement about my future with Romulus; then, out of curiosity, I turned into a tiny street with brown gabled houses and prim little gardens. Almost immediately, a sunken-eyed man appeared from nowhere. There was a sensual, almost desperate tension in his piercing expression that at first I took as sexual. He asked me where the InterContinental was, which is an inane question, since you can see this high-rise hotel from practically anywhere in central Bucharest. He wanted to change money, he claimed. Did I have any dollars he could buy?

Before I could refuse, two burly plainclothesmen in black

suits had surrounded us. They flashed badges and meaty arms and began accusing us of buying and selling money on the black market. When I tried to protest, they raised their fists toward my face. They roughed the man up and tore his shirt a bit, while explaining to me that they were sure he was the instigator but that I was implicated as well. When they demanded my passport, some instinct told me to keep a grip on it as I showed it to them. What resulted was a tugging match worthy of the Three Stooges—to which they finally succumbed. Then one grabbed my nearly empty wallet and began sniffing in the tiny recesses, supposedly for drugs. I thought of explaining that I was just an innocent American fag here to pleasure one of their countrymen, but fortunately, kept my lip buttoned.

After I returned to the hotel, Romulus's face was swept with relief about the fact that I hadn't disappeared. Then his attention was again glued to the soccer game; however, my story about what had happened became the first ever to distract him from it, perhaps only because the story was connected to soccer in his mind. It turns out that the whole plainclothes routine was a con well known in the streets of Bucharest. Two guys pose as cops and another as a perpetrator. The object of the game is to nab the tourist's passport and then, as he pleads, sell it back to him. "It's a trick we call a 'Maradona maneuver'"—Romulus chuckled—"after Diego Maradona, the ace Argentine soccer player." His eyes filled with comic irony. I could tell he admired the subtlety of the ruse.

XII

The continental sun is mocking my folly through a hole in the ozone layer, beating me down in my jet lag. It's the middle of May. This marks the sixth month of my relationship with Romulus. I'm waiting desperately for him in front of the InterContinental in Bucharest. I'm fresh from Paris but I haven't given my Beaubourg presentation yet—it's a month away. After our failure in getting an American visa, I've deemed it best to bring Romulus to France myself for the Beaubourg appearance. I have, luckily, come to my senses about the idea of projecting nude images of him on the wall behind me, but I still want him to be there. Then and hopefully, we'll stay together in Paris for a few months. So I've flown to Bucharest to try to take care of the French visa. The only trouble is, he isn't showing up.

Three hours later, when the sun is lower but just as scorching, when anger and humiliation are leaking through all my pores with the perspiration, he arrives with his gym bag, grimy from an interminable, local-stop bus ride from Sibiu. The bus took nine hours to get to Bucharest, delayed by a flat tire, a lazy driver who took hourly breaks and an unbudging Gypsy caravan on the road. But as usual, Romulus's manner is composed and uncomplaining, too dignified and soldierly to express any frustration. Because we have nowhere to stay, he persuades one of the many idle cabdrivers to take us on an exhausting trek through the city in search of a hotel room. After one night in a moldy hotel near the post office, we discover Hanul Manuc, a country-style Romanian inn built in the early nineteenth century by an Armenian merchant, Manuc Bey. It sits like an anachronistic hallucination across from the ruins of the royal court in a corner of the old quarter. Our cab bounces across the uneven road into a large, tree-lined space surrounded by intricate wooden balustrades. A couple of homeless dogs are prowling around the straw-filled covered wagon in the immense cobblestone courtyard. Romulus extends his hand to one of them, who lunges to bite it.

The place is magical, full of scalloped Moorish arches over wooden galleries, reminiscent of the rural Romanian world in Panaït Istrati's novels, two of which are in my suitcase. Our spacious suite has two rooms, a bedroom and a Romanian-style sitting room, with a Deco-ish dresser, high-backed wooden chairs and a wrought-iron candlestick with electric bulbs. We eat an enormous, tasty meal under the roofed gallery, with all the traditional dishes: *sarmale,* stuffed cabbage; *cascaval,* a kind of hardened cottage cheese; *ciorbă de burtă,* the tripe soup that Romulus chokes with sour cream; and *mititei,* an oblong meatball, which, despite its lamb and pork content, is served rare. Lackadaisical, overdressed waiters with very little to do hover over us, then lose attention and don't come when they're called—to Romulus's great displeasure.

That night the Romanian news hour is chattering on the television screen when Romulus gets up to take a shower. It seems that Ceaușescu's daughter is trying to repossess some of the jewels that belonged to the family. The climate is turning since the murder of the dictator. What seemed a pure act of patriotism is slowly becoming tinged, yet again, with corruption. Romanians are just beginning to realize that those who killed the dictator were also oppressors, who belonged to his inner circle. Now these same people are seizing political and economic control, after constructing new democratic identities for themselves.

Romulus's body is even leaner and more rippled than the last time we spent together, his ass like two polished rocks. But why that concave, crouched posture permanently stamped into him? His cock curls out from it like an angry garter snake, against the shields of his thighs. It's a sign of the rigidity and defensiveness that will get clearer as time goes on.

The next day is tinged with fatality, like a myth or ritual. It certainly provides a lot of evidence against that utopian cultural interfacing we sometimes talk about in America. What global village? The ironies of class have only grown more glaring in the über-capitalist age. As soon as I tell Romulus that he should dress up for his appearance at the French embassy, our tastes start clashing. I suppose it's the timeworn story of Pygmalion. At the moment, he has on tight maroon jeans, a two-toned polyester T-shirt and blunt-toed platform shoes. It's a look I associate with the underclass chic of Manhattan's Fourteenth Street shops. The likelihood of his overstaying his visa is written all over it, ready to be read at the French embassy.

The pleated wool-and-nylon slacks, the conservative gray viscose shirt with just a touch of pearly iridescence and the thin-soled dress shoes I'm trying to buy him, at a price that could be used to furnish an entire wardrobe, would really please my mother, but they fill him with stony alienation. It's the same angry sense of being excluded that he exhibited at the club Byblos. This time it's worse. He's a trapped pigeon in an airshaft, struggling against the realistic formulas of success. My insistence on these boring clothes threatens his lifelong fantasies about luxury and power. Can success really be a question of being this accommodating? He'd thought money was power, speed, color. With terminal bitterness he puts on the stodgy clothes. Maybe there are flashes of excitement when he gets to put his papers in the computer case I lend him to carry, but he knows the act will soon become tired. He dreads a life like this in France, full of quality fabrics and sensible shoes, energy spent seeming inoffensive. He's already waxing nostalgic for the easy girls, big-screen TV and quick money of his recent past and glaring like a whipped animal. Even worse is the emasculating effect. He'd rather look like rough trade—whose straight sexuality is obvious—than like the possible well-behaved member of a bourgeois gay couple. I can feel him cringe as we walk down the street toward the embassy and he fearfully scrutinizes my step, wondering if it gives us away.

Our audience is quick. Aside from the letters from Marianne Alphant at Beaubourg and Elein Fleiss of *Purple,* I have a more informal letter from another friend who is French, Victoire, inviting him to visit her in Tours. You'd think these documents were big guns, but the low-level clerk barely glances at them, looks neither of us in the eye and coolly requests a notarized letter of financial support from Victoire. I just can't ask her to go out on a limb like that. It's settled. If I want to be with Romulus, I'd better find a way to stay in Romania.

The inevitability of it makes me feel close to him, fills me with sentimentality. In a small way, I've become part of his curse of limitation. Like him, I'm trapped in Romania. We have to start looking for an apartment, so we head away from the embassy and trudge up a wide boulevard in the crushing heat.

As we do, the rhythm of his footsteps opens some door, plunging me closer to his reality. I can sense his relief at not having to bother to emigrate to France. He's sick of traveling and feels at home in his own country. Now that I've committed to it, our walk, in perfect time with each other, feels pastoral, like a dreamy tango with death and doinas, the music said to represent the emotional consciousness of Romania.

Some have described the doina, that melancholy, lilting song of extended rhythms, as a psychic landscape of spiral meetings with fate. It's an artful arabesque around the inevitability of death that is also the myth of Miorița, about the shepherd who transfigures death as a wedding with Nature. For me, entering Romania is like being in touch with that sensibility, like entering a trance. Our walk is an undulating consciousness, hovering and circulating around defeat. It's as if we were out of historical time and in that other *eternal time* conceived by Mircea Eliade. No matter that the cosmic spirit of Romulus may be dulled by prostitution, corrupted by fantasies of fast cars and cool sound systems. His macho fatalism, which I finally understand for the first time, instills everything with elegance. He notices everything at its most abject and shakes his head or clucks his tongue like an ancient for whom it's already happened, as if each detail represented the story of humankind.

I'm addicted to his curiously soothing discontent. Others would see a sulky hustler, walking with an overweight, wide-eyed tourist, but I see an endlessly rolling carpet beckoning us and all life toward extinction—which is why we make a smooth twosome, even without a place to live, as we stroll through Strada Lipscani in what is left of the old city, idling at a Romani stall to examine a bottle of cologne purporting to be Issey Miyake, though I notice the top is different, and

Romulus grabs the icy, translucent bottle, wants to buy it, but I make him put it down, promising a real bottle when I return from Paris.

To the swelling, hypnotic tune of our own personal doina, we amble through the ruined patchwork of the old city, always enchanted by its discrepancies. We stop at the ruins of the Curtea Veche, the Old Court, the remains of the fifteenth-century palace of Prince Vlad Țepeș, or Dracula; then, across the boulevard behind it, at an Internet café, which is plunged into darkness except for the glow of screens. White hands emerge from the shadows and pass me a card. Above them radiates the face of a small, excited woman, literally inebriated by the fact that I'm speaking English. "Call me," she coos, pointing to the number on the card. Romulus gives me a cynical glance, iced with resignation.

Later, on Calea Victoriei, as he floats away in search of cigarettes, a teenaged boy in a T-shirt threadbare-thin from too many washings advances through an invisible gelatin in smiling slow motion, placidly wanting to know, he says, where I could be from with such blue eyes. In our banal conversation he makes dents of intimate possibilities, somewhere between erotic and paternal, boasting gently about another older American who pays him as a photographic model; then he gallantly runs to a nearby bakery with the money I give him to buy us sweet rolls.

On Bulevardul Aviatorilor, near a movie theater, is an outdoor Internet station where a crowd of boys gestures to us. Delighted by the free access, they cajole me into showing them how to use it. Gesticulations and arms thrown around shoulders, while I keep feeling for my wallet. The whole experience seems faintly rural. This magic-forest feeling of Bucharest comes, I think, from the innate pastoralism of Romanians, which has been described by the scholar Traian

Herseni as pastoral loneliness. Add to this the fact that most Romanians were isolated during the reign of Ceauşescu, who prevented almost anyone from leaving the country, and you get a very singular sensibility.

This is only a walk in a modern city, but primeval fate seems to be curling its tendrils about us wherever we float; loss, extinction feel sweet to me, as they must have to the shepherd in the Mioriţa myth. I'm caught in this realization as Romulus and I stroll down Bulevardul Brătianu toward Piaţa Unirii, past the bullet holes from the Revolution in the walls of the underground street passage. Not far from our hotel we saw a sign advertising apartments to rent. It led us into a dingy courtyard bordered by buildings ornamented with fissured stucco. We went through a creaking door, up a cracked marble-and-wrought-iron staircase to a tiny real estate office, where a woman started as if she'd seen a ghost when we walked in. The fact of our wanting an apartment seemed to astonish her. As if in shock, she went through a faded roster of listings in a book with a broken spine, made a call and handed us a card.

The walk to the apartment, which is located near Piaţa Unirii, feels effortless, like standing on a moving sidewalk, gliding easily toward fate. Until I come smack against the wide, wall-like body of a Romani woman with back and buttocks of brick, who has stopped stock still in the middle of the street. As I slam against this wall, I feel spidery hands fluttering against my pants and realize that I'm in the middle of a Gypsy pickpocketing scam. The movie in gelatin is shattered by my piercing scream. Everyone stops to look, the three Roma involved in the scam hightail it up the avenue.

Romulus's face isn't sympathetic, but stony with disapproval, embarrassed. Of course, he knew what was happening. I'm such a target with my bulging pockets. But why did

I have to shriek like a woman? In fact, he's been meaning to tell me I walk funny, too much on the balls of my feet.

In a split second, I've slid out of the magic forest, been changed back into a possibly effeminate fag in a sector closed to me. I'll never get in again, either, beyond brief moments. When one of Romania's greatest pessimists, Emil Cioran, came to France, his first impression of Western intellectuals was that they thought only of money. He claimed that any of his people's shepherds was a more profound philosopher. Now I feel like one of those overembellished Westerners he scorned, a victim of Romanian feudal clannishness.

Our apartment-to-be is in a spectacular Teutonic-looking turn-of-the-century house in a middle-class neighborhood, on Mihnea Vodă, a dead-end street behind Piaţa Unirii. I'm drawn to the glass-and-wrought-iron door, the gabled roof, the garden of sweet peas. The staircase is creaky and dark, with a musty smell I associate with books about spells. On the first landing, a door creaks open, and the sweet, bewildered face of an old woman with soft, disheveled hair peeks out at us. She looks thrilled, relieved at seeing our faces, as if she'd been waiting for a hundred years. Eagerly she ushers us into her living room, which is dark and nearly empty, with a worn-out couch and a gleaming black-tile floor; and I realize that she really has been living in a kind of prison, guarded by the pitiless and unstoppable passage of time. On shelves lining the room are crinkled mementoes: roses, faded colorless, wrapped in yellowed cellophane; a wedding picture whose tones have sunk into muddy reds and browns; a plastic-framed photo of a blond pixielike child who must be in his fifties by now. She pauses in front of a dust-laden samovar and makes thrilled, nervous shrugging gestures at me while explaining in Romanian to Romulus that there's nothing to offer us for tea. She ate a last small cake for lunch an hour ago. She's humiliated by her inability to provide hospitality, she explains, accompanying her words with apologetic, cultured quiverings of her wrinkled hands and obsequious little bows, while her soft eyes transfix me ecstatically. The apartment above her has stood empty for more than a year, and here we've come to remedy it, she assumes. She apologizes for the fact that she speaks no English, but some instinct makes me try to address her in French. She's probably old enough to have lived the tail end of that time when Romania looked toward France as a sister nation—not so long ago as when Princess Bibesco socialized with Proust, but possibly when Paul Celan, a Romanian Jew, lived in Paris and translated Cocteau and Rimbaud. And after a few words in French, her eyes do light up and she begins to recite Baudelaire's "L'invitation au voyage" with a heavy Romanian accent:

> *Mon enfant, ma soeur,*
> *Songe à la douceur*
> *D'aller là-bas vivre ensemble!*
> *Aimer à loisir,*
> *Aimer et mourir*
> *Au pays qui te ressemble!*

But then she stops, confused. It's the only fragment she can remember. She explains to Romulus, who translates for me, that she's going to call her son, who'll arrange our renting the upstairs apartment. We spend the rest of the time in a nervous ritual of courtesy: the old woman, who has forgotten her French, bowing and shrugging apologetically, and me trying to keep a stiff, affectionate smile on my lips.

Her son, a middle-aged man in shorts, probably the child

in the faded photograph, looks as if he'd been released from a long sentence on death row—his eyes staringly fish-angry, like pieces of dull green glass in milk. He has a hunched, alcoholic manner and wet tentacles, frustration and defeat pouring out of him like sweat. He wants the twelve hundred dollars for three months' rent of the big apartment upstairs in cash, and he wants it in dollars, right away. When I protest, saying I'm not going to change lei back into dollars, he spends thirty minutes studying the newspaper for the exchange rates. Finally he writes the exact amount up to the fourth decimal on a scrap of paper. Then Romulus and I go with a large paper bag to one of the city's few cash machines. Since the highest Romanian currency offered by the machine equals about eight dollars, and it's impossible to get more than five of these bills at a time from the machine, I spend almost an hour removing money and stuffing the bag, while Romulus stands guard. It won't be the end of the drama. Our landlord will call us almost daily asking for electricity and telephone money in advance or maintaining that the exchange was figured out wrong.

Our new, spacious two-bedroom apartment is full of Romanian books—the literature that the landlord's daughter studied before moving to America. One of the bedrooms, which has a desk, will be my own separate study, and there's even a terrace. I'm a bit baffled by the fact that the kitchen is kitty-corner across the outside hall. Its ancient spice cabinet, which has herbs and remedies more than sixty years old, fascinates me. We settle onto the king-sized bed in our large bedroom, trying not to focus on the fact that the landlord's mother has a key to the back entrance and has claimed the right to mount when she pleases to use the washing machine in the bathroom, just outside our bedroom door. We can't, however, keep from noticing that our windows look onto the vine-covered windows of the adjoining building, so Romulus closes the shades and pulls the heavy curtains over them to muffle our noise. Both of us are aware that a revised version of Article 200, the law against "public scandal," is still in effect. Technically, we could be arrested just for being seen making homosexual gestures. This obsesses me for a while, I talk incessantly about it, until Romulus harshly silences me by saying, "Don't you know sex is dangerous?"

A few days later, we'll go back to Strada Lipscani in search of a VCR for playing porn. In a secondhand shop, we'll bargain with the grim owner, who seems to be threatening us, predicting all kinds of disasters, rather than negotiating a sale. Romulus assures me that if the VCR doesn't work when we get home, he'll quickly return it to the shop by throwing it through the plate-glass window. Finding porn on the street is easy; there are tables every few corners with pirated tapes, some Romanian but mostly German—none, of course, homosexual, but Romulus wouldn't want that. And I can't compromise myself in front of him by watching them.

Sex in our new home begins when the temperature has reached ninety degrees Fahrenheit. A terrible heat wave has started to hit Romania. There's no air-conditioning, and we fear opening the shades or curtains in the bedroom. Romulus watches one of the porn tapes, an artless German costume drama in a harem, as he slaps at mosquitoes, while I lie belly-down across the sweat-drenched sheets and put my head between his baking thighs.

We're just a few hundred feet from the Dîmbovița River, which has dried up in the heat, leaving ankle-high mud and rotting fish. I can smell it penetrating the curtains. After you get across the bridge over the river, the odor grabs you by the throat, you want to get away from it as soon as possible, but sometimes the stoplight hasn't changed. This seems to be the inevitable moment when the small boy at the intersection, pushing a wooden wheelchair carrying a legless grandfather, comes toward you begging for money, the grandfather's outstretched bony hand shaking a metal cup. If you give, the boy says, "God bless you," in English. Much later, in Budapest, a Romanian hustler will tell me that when some of his fellow hustlers need more money from a "benefactor," they tell him that their father works for the railroad and that his legs have just been cut off by a train. Yes, in the case of the boy at the intersection, the grandfather's legs really were missing, but then, the very idea of the imagination exploiting amputation...

XIII

During some of our white nights in Bucharest, I think of my friend Ursule Molinaro, whose blessing of my relationship with Romulus came as her health was failing. I remember how she claimed to have once visited a canyon in Maui, Hawaii, where a particularly horrible military slaughter had taken place. Although this strife was more than two hundred years past, its anguish and horror were as palpable to her as if it were happening at that moment. Through eyes swimming in vertigo, she saw a welter of dislocated limbs, smelled blood covering the canyon.

If you think about it, there isn't a place we can walk where someone wasn't probably murdered, where a bloody battle or some painful death hasn't taken place. Bucharest is just a decade away from the violent uprising that ended Communism, where members of the militia shot indiscriminately into the angry crowd gathered before Party headquarters. A little more than ten years ago, the streets on which we're walking were full of snipers, or students squeezing a blood-soaked shirtsleeve at the point where a bullet had entered. It's true that most of the bullet holes in the old Communist headquarters have been repaired, but near the university there are plaques commemorating revolutionary martyrs, a balustrade still dented by gunfire.

Yet loss in this city is not a question of tangible artifacts.

It's the very atmosphere of displacement, a hollowness of setting like a de Chirico dream. On the faces of some of the older people you can see the wizened traces of trauma, accentuated by current problems of poverty. Their eyes have a faraway look. Their body language is dominated by vivid memories, lives lost, which makes them seem only half here. Even the very young, who wouldn't be old enough to remember Communist repression or revolutionary violence, have a somnambulist manner, a pure stare as they walk through the streets. I think I see a numbed, almost blissful look on their faces that I associated before with the pastoral. It could be their isolation that gives them this expression of Edenic muteness. Few were allowed to leave the country during Ceauşescu's reign; and at this time, it's still next to impossible for them to visit Western Europe or America. They don't have the money, and it's very hard to get a tourist visa to any richer countries. What might be depression on their faces strikes me as the innocence of those who've never traveled, a life lacking the complications about which we more privileged complain. These may be the faces of people living in poverty, but they're as yet uncontaminated by the vacuousness of global capitalism.

The days in this city have begun to extend the heady displacement of my frequently codeine-filled nights. A few pills before bed prolong the REM period of my sleep, often producing the illusion that my eyes are open when they're closed. I see the room we're in just as it is, but peopled by characters and objects from my past and imagined future. Hopes and fears produce shadowy specters that waft through the air like dreams, toes barely grazing the floor. They're a symptom of the queer sense of rootlessness I feel here. This doesn't appear to be a city where Romulus and I can establish bearings. But maybe that's the point. Not only the unplanned clusters of buildings of several centuries contribute to the disorientation; it's also the people on the street, probably unemployed, who come across as floating in a kind of clear, viscous medium.

Within this world of fits and starts we gradually make our way to a gym in a run-down neighborhood south of Piața Unirii. Since Romulus has nothing to do, and since I'll be busy making money for us through translation, we thought that a gym might come in handy. After a labyrinthine walk through a half-deteriorated athletic center, we find the weight room, which is crowded with young men lifting impossibly heavy barbells. They ignore us totally, a nonchalance that borders on hostility and that only accentuates my feeling of living in a hallucination. When Romulus asks for an explanation of the hours and facilities, I can see him being drawn into their secretive mentality. Delicately but pointedly they pay no attention to my increasingly visible presence. I'm obviously such an enigma that they fear even to ask questions. Oddly enough, this pleases me. How many places have I been where people don't reveal their curiosity or other feelings about an American?

I can sense Romulus's brain being torn between our connection and the stringent codes of his fellow weightlifters. When they take us to the pool, the suspicious glares of the swimmers create an even greater tension. This time it feels as if they fear we're going to take their women. I find myself staring demurely at the tile floor rather than looking at a girl in a bathing suit. We pay the required twelve dollars each for a one-month membership, but by the time we're two blocks away, Romulus has decided not to exercise there.

As we walk through Piața Unirii, I say that the two shirts Romulus alternates weekly and doesn't wash nearly enough won't do, and offer to buy him another one. Inside the large, shabby galleries of the Unirea department store, merchandise is scanty. Salesgirls in black skirts and white blouses lounge against glass counters in such dreamy boredom they wouldn't notice a fly crawling across their faces. We take the escalator from floor to floor, encountering one nearly empty cave after another. I suggest we try Calea Victoriei instead. Its days of sumptuous, fashionable shops are over, but at least there are a few stores with Hungarian and Italian imports, even a Benetton. Romulus vehemently refuses. The high prices and the entitlement they presume fill him with a fury of insecurity. So for hours we thumb through the paltry acrylic merchandise at Unirea, while he seeks a shirt that will maintain his image as a street dandy. Nothing is right. Either he doesn't like the price, or the style isn't restrained enough for the particular pimp effect he wants.

Exhausted, I tell him I'll meet him at the cosmetics counter, where I cajole a sleepy yet guarded salesgirl into showing me the entire line of Gerovital. There are face creams and toners, face masks, eye creams, hand creams, body creams and foot creams. Some contain a magic substance said to slow or even reverse the aging process. It's called H3—later I find out it's buffered procaine. The Romanian gerontologist Ana Aslan, who developed the substance, is still a controversial figure, with some scientists claiming her work was a hoax and others—mostly in Romania—carrying on her studies. At any rate, I've already verified that the cream can produce surface miracles—it's the best moisturizer I've ever tried—so I buy three jars.

Lunch with Romulus at home fits into that strange time warp at which I've been hinting. It's only part of the chemically induced dream I extend from night to day. It's also like a trip into the past, as I haven't experienced anything like it since the late fifties, when I came home from school at noon for a hot meal. This anachronism only pushes me further into my shadow world of desire. It's nearly a hundred degrees, but that doesn't stop Romulus from frying lamb-and-pork *mititei* or spreading soft sheep cheese over *mămăligă*. Under the cabinet and its sixty-year-old spices, we sit at a fifties kitchen table like any working-class couple scarfing down a high-fat meal. After a glass of wine, an eerie domesticity settles over us. Fairy-tale as our world seems, it's getting narrower. Given the circumstances, Romulus as housewife is perfectly natural, as well as a discomfiting thought for us both.

Occasionally it strikes me that he must feel confined. But used to keeping his feelings to himself, he rarely expresses it. Nonetheless, at certain times of the day, grumpiness seems to take over. I try to tell myself that it's just a facet of his naturally reticent personality, despite the fact that every once in a while I sense an argument between us brewing, for no particular reason. I tiptoe around it, warmly coax him back into a good mood. What frightens me most is my own sense of not being able to tolerate an outburst. The idea of its happening seems unbearable.

Using hearsay and fantasy, I've been piecing together his nonprostitutional sex life, which fills me with fear and compulsion. I savor each story and add it to my repertoire. His body has become the number of women he seduced, their pubic hair, what their nipples were like, their buttocks, assholes and odors. Later this afternoon, they lightly envelop us in our hellishly hot bedroom as he lies naked on the bed in a near faint, puffing cigarette after cigarette and fiddling with the remote, while I explore his body with my hands and mouth.

His lassitude and muteness are so fascinating that I begin to snap pictures at close range. The flash exploding in the dark room produces surfaces that appear flawless and reveals his armpits, which are now cleanly shaven as a measure against the heat. Flat sheets of smoke hover above us as if issuing from his pores. His smoking seems to have lowered his body temperature, and so total is his repose in the heat that his skin actually feels cool. Still, the oil in his body has been extracted by the heat and coats his nose and chest with a sheer glaze. Eyes open even when the flash goes off, he stares obliquely at the camera past an outstretched arm, or lets his head hang from the edge of the bed as I cover his body with a hungry mouth.

Slowly but surely the female specters intermingle with our play. I sense their young limbs enlacing ours and scenting his cock with their juices, interposing their lips between his flesh and mine. Obviously he's thinking of them. As long as they're nameless while their silky hair dangles ghostlike above us, they send us both into a perfect world of sensation and belonging. But when a name or my idea of a face creeps into my mind, I'm frozen with jealousy. Still I know that, for the time being, Romulus belongs to me. His corpselike placidity doesn't speak of his leaving anytime soon.

The girls seem to linger while we dress for dinner at a restaurant across the square. As soon as our front door clicks shut, ghostly barks and howls reverberate down the street. These are some of the voices of the several hundred thousand homeless dogs of Bucharest. Possibly because my lips are smarting with the salts of his groin, I associate the howls with sex, the trailing presence of our phantom women. At any rate, the story of the dogs seems unreal, dovetails with my trancelike feeling of being here. They're the result of the displacement of thousands of families when Ceauşescu bulldozed a fifth of Bucharest to build an enormous new palace, not far from where Romulus and I are living. When the residents of these neighborhoods became homeless, some committed suicide; many abandoned their pets to the street. The multiplying animals divided neighborhoods into territories. Inhabitants tolerated and even encouraged these metaphors for their disenfranchisement and displacement during and after the Communist years. The animals also act as xenophobic watchdogs, keeping Roma and other strangers off the block, and they decrease rat infestations.

Eventually Brigitte Bardot, that fervent animal rightist, came to Romania to pressure the mayor, Traian Băsescu, into choosing sterilization over euthanasia and donated money to modernize the city's veterinary clinic. Băsescu had planned to murder the dogs as quickly as possible, an essential step in gentrification. Bardot's crusade had already made papers around the world when she adopted two strays, who urinated copiously on the carpets in her expensive Bucharest hotel suite. Băsescu finally gave in to most of her demands and started a campaign to sterilize and inoculate the dogs without killing those that were healthy. Months later, according to Bardot, he reneged on that promise.

Dogcatchers sent by the city government are regularly met with a volley of potatoes, flower pots and even rocks. As a people with a pastoral history, comfortable with animal metaphors like the myth of Miorița, that cosmic sheep who announced a shepherd's coming extinction, Romanians see the dogs as symbols of their amputation from culture, of the myriads lost to Communist repression who still seem to circulate like ghosts around imaginary homes long since torn down. To me the dogs' nighttime howling sometimes sounds like wolves', suggesting kitsch notions of "children of the night" made famous by Bela Lugosi. But the bewilderment felt by many residents of Bucharest is painfully concrete, after having seen a fifth of their city, including landmark buildings and centuries-old churches, sacrificed to one of the most absurd vanity projects in history.

For the last several evenings Romulus and I have been watching from our terrace the motley pack of mongrels that haunts our street. At sundown, residents gather at the circle beneath us to hand out treats. Their relationship to the dogs seems familial and affectionate, but sympathy for the creatures doesn't always stop these dogs from attacking, mostly at night. Pedestrians in the less central neighborhoods—especially if they're strangers—have the habit of walking in the middle of the street to stay away from parked cars, from under which lurking dogs might lunge. Many people regularly carry dried bread or biscuits in hopes of discouraging aggression.

Such precautions haven't prevented about fifty reported dog bites a day in the city; and because Romanian hospitals lack the modern version of the anti-rabies serum, victims have had to submit to the old-fashioned method of inoculation: a series of twelve painful injections in the abdomen. There seem not to have been any actual cases of rabies yet, but the disease has been found in foxes hiding in forests just outside the city. And recently there have been a few isolated cases of gruesome attacks. In Cornetu, a village near Bucharest, an entire pack mauled a sixty-two-year-old man and ripped the flesh off his legs until he bled to death.

Like most people in Bucharest, Romulus and I have made personal symbols of the canines. We're walking across a dark parking lot toward Piaţa Unirii when growls accompanied by perhaps imagined hot breath seem inches from my ankle. Romulus eyes me with an animal contempt that suggests the dog's hostility is being caused by my embarrassing walk. Ever since the Gypsy pickpocketing incident he's been harping on it. He's right that my gait is slightly peculiar; at the age of sixteen I was stricken with aseptic meningitis, and my legs never recovered one hundred percent. Before, I'd always walked a bit on the balls of my feet, and since then, mild cramps occasionally put the tiniest of jerks in my walk, which doesn't make macho posturing easy.

My friend Ursule Molinaro wrote a story that begins with a pack of wolves chasing a debilitated member to its death. She presented the scene as a contrast to the death-phobic sensibility of high-tech medical values. The snarl in Romulus's voice, which really covers a sense of embarrassment, plunges us into the reality of these homeless creatures. Metaphors of sick animals transform the floating female limbs and their perfumes into those of competitive bitches. I imagine that Romulus is preparing to eliminate me brutally because of my deformity. One of the dogs actually is barking at my heels now, as I force myself not to speed up. It rushes at us in fits, stops, then lunges forward again. From the corner of my eye I can make out black gums and yellowish incisors. To my walk that stiffens further, Romulus reacts with a sadistic smile showing his fangs. His cruelty makes me furious, but the anger comes out as effeminate hysteria. This makes him chuckle all the more derisively.

To shorten the walk, I try insisting we stop at another restaurant, at the edge of the parking lot. He wrinkles his nose and spits from the corner of his mouth: "Those Gypsies? In there you will take me? We will be poisoned."

The restaurant across the square has an outdoor eating area with two televisions. We sit so that my back is to the screens and he can watch a repeat soccer broadcast over my shoulder. I'm wondering if this abrupt reversal—Romulus as caustic husband contemptuous of feminine foibles—is some kind of revenge for his housewifely luncheon duties. I'm certainly not the first spouse to sit in a restaurant with the aftertaste of her husband's genitals on her tongue, while he stares past her at a sports replay. Insipid house music booming from the restaurant speakers crowns his pleasure and augments my annoyance. I put one of his cigarettes in my mouth and light it to cover the acrid taste on my gums. The waitress delivers a mediocre red wine. Romulus takes a sip of it, then brings his cigarette to his lips and inhales deeply. His eyes shift away from the screen. "Bruce, I must ask to you something."

"Yes."

"Why me? I want to know. Why *me*?"

"What are you talking about?"

"I want to know why you choose me from all boys at Corso."

"Why do you ask that?"

"Because, Bruce. You are so much...*better* than me." He savors the word. "So much higher up than me."

"Romulus, there are a lot of things about you I feel are better than—"

I stop, fearfully. His features are so distorted with contempt that he looks like he's about to spit. "Do you think," he says craftily, "that I did not notice when you hide key under bed? Such a stupid thing you do."

"I didn't know you, Romulus. I had no idea who you were."

"And do you know what I am thinking when you do that?"

"No."

"How stupid. That is what I am thinking. All I must do is knock you out, then take key."

"Why didn't you?"

He doesn't answer.

We're served various meats cooked in oil, and a salad that

is mostly white cabbage. Eventually I realize that something else over my shoulder has caught his attention. Through the filmy windows of the banquet hall inside can be seen a wedding party. Raucous laughter seems to propel several guests out the door. In the arms of one man is a kicking bride, alternately laughing and screaming. According to Romulus, the man carrying her isn't the groom. A traditional Romanian wedding diversion has begun: the best man and other male members of the wedding party are kidnapping the bride as a joke and challenging the groom to find her, claiming he must pay a ransom. We watch. Hurriedly, the man carrying the struggling bride disappears with her into a black car, which drives away. Romulus rubs his hands together, lights another cigarette and explains: "This joke much loved in Romania can bring to bride and groom great heartache." I stare with awe at the bitter pleasure that seems to have invaded his features. Intuitively I know that thoughts of the possibility of corruption have instilled him with sardonic confidence.

"You see, Bruce," he exults, "the character of the bride-robbers, though they even be best friends, cannot always be trusted." He winks leeringly and says, "Do you see where I am driving?"

"No. Which way?"

"More times than you are possible to imagining, the kidnapping turns into sour."

"I don't follow."

"I mean the bride gets raped." His face cracks into a delighted grimace, a startling gesture for a person who's usually so poker-faced.

"You're kidding."

"Kid you I not, Bruce."

"But the best man, the wedding party. Aren't they usually relatives, brothers, best friends?"

He nods enthusiastically, savoring the idea.

"I don't believe—" I begin. Before I can finish, a worried-looking man in a tuxedo emerges from the restaurant, holding a cell phone. Then two other male guests come out, gaze around and hurry down the street in the direction where the struggling bride was driven.

"Something goes wrong already, you see?"

"No, I don't see." Something may have gone wrong, but then, there are certainly no signs that anything as disastrous as a rape at a wedding party has taken place. I doubt, as well, that rape is a common occurrence at Romanian weddings. I sense a lurid desire on his part to invite me to see his culture as shameful, to reject it. I study him incredulously, but his smile is opaque, self-satisfied. Whether rape has occurred or not, he wants me to think so.

XIV

"He simply howls for her," wrote Queen Marie in her diary in 1918. Howls like the wild dogs in the Bucharest streets of today? A mother even more meddling than my own, Marie/ Missy was referring to her son's passion for a certain Zizi Lambrino, a commoner with "a shallow, cold, vulgar nature quite incapable of any better or nobler feelings." Missy was convinced that she knew what was best for her son.

Her words come to me in my study on Mihnea Vodă in June, where I've decided to sleep, minutes after finally being told by Romulus that he's had it with living here with me, and seconds after a call from my mother, asking, When, oh, when are you coming home? Now, in a fit of grumpiness, he's half dozing in a heat coma in our sealed-off bedroom across the way, waking to slap at a mosquito or glare at me if I come into the room, the TV booming an inane variety show and sheets of cigarette smoke layering the air.

Zizi Lambrino, the woman to whom blonde Queen Marie so objected, was her physical opposite. Née Ioana Maria Valentine, she was dark and plump, a Romanian bourgeoise of Greek Phanariot descent. In the summer of 1913, she met Prince Carol, who was not quite twenty; and in the months that followed, her bedroom became papered with pictures of the prince, the way girls today paper theirs with pictures of rock stars.

By 1918, at twenty-four, Prince Carol was head over heels for Zizi, despite the fact that members of royalty were prohibited from marrying native Romanians. He was so enthralled that he was willing to give up his future kingship, thumb his nose at the Romanian people and the hard-won legitimacy of the royal family. Or do I have it backward? Could he have so hated the vaunted legitimacy of the royal family that he wanted to thumb his nose at them by falling in love?

I peel off a sheet stuck to my thigh by perspiration, mulling over my own bohemian gesture. Romulus, for whom I've given up my own country, has suddenly fallen into a foul, contemptuous frame of mind. I could say that it's happening only for an evening, but I can tell the mood will return. This Eastern locale, which I thought I chose in a ballsy exertion of will, has turned into a stage set for failure.

Even British-born Missy, in an uncharacteristic lapse into bigotry, would call her adopted country—where I now lie stuck to the sheet in anguished doubt—"incomprehensible" and "licentious," an entity undecodable to Western eyes. "Being near the East, morality is lacking," was her facile defense for the several lovers she took.

Shortly after her marriage in 1893, she became addicted to the same drug of travel that has given me such an erotic charge. Eventually she filled the palace with one exotic "souvenir"—meaning lover—after another. Many of them, not incidentally, also furthered her brilliant political aims. This was a war against her own royal background.

Allegedly, Missy's lovers ran the gamut, before she became queen and after: from the melancholy Russian Grand Duke Boris Vladimirovich, a first cousin trapped in a loveless marriage, to the sickly financier and publisher Waldorf Astor, who despite Missy's passion may have never consummated their relationship.

The most lasting and intriguing lover was a local, with all the traits we associate with the Byzantine and the Latin: the hypnotically soft-spoken Prince Barbu Ştirbey, a dark-browed Boyar full of expressive glances and suave gestures. So many state secrets had Missy told him that he had to shrug off an offer to write his memoirs by saying he simply knew too much.

In Romania, everybody—from the ladies-in-waiting to the shoeshine boy on the street—talked about Missy's affairs, whether they were real or not. In the way subjects admire a virile king, Missy's powers of seduction and her sensual lifestyle only made her more popular with the people. She was, then, a phallic queen, a female sexual adventurer.

Sex can slay. Smarting from Romulus's cold, sadistic behavior, which culminated in his kicking me hard in bed when I tried to put my arms around him, my mind still insists on playing with the image of his sullen body. I torture myself with visceral snapshots of lips parted in a half-doze, a two-day growth of soft beard that he's too lazy to shave in the heat. Unable to sleep, I fantasize running a hand over the warm, indifferent body, or pass the time trying to reconstruct Missy around forty during World War I, a few years after becoming queen, when she entertained Ştirbey in her newly decorated Bizance bedroom, with its sham ec-clesiastical fixtures and Turkish tapestries. I envy her plans to use her rebellious, frustrated son Carol, the future king, as her mouthpiece. And it occurs to me that History, and my history, are part porn novels.

*

The Hohenzollerns came to the throne in the 1860s, after the Crimean War, as the result of a deal cut between Ion Brătianu, the powerful Romanian Boyar responsible for Romania's formation of two principalities into a nation, and Napoleon III. It was Brătianu who spirited the Prussian Carol I—whom Missy called *"der Onkel"*—into the country, even though Austria, Russia and Turkey threatened to occupy it if a foreign prince made a claim. Obviously, Brătianu was no psychologist. It never occurred to him that there was any danger in introducing the iron-willed Hohenzollerns to a world of fabled Oriental pleasures and Byzantine strategies. Did he really want to make Romania the place where West struggles against East, or where the will battles desire?

On the wall across from me in the dark, I can just make out Missy's picture. I printed it from the Internet as part of my own project of adapting to life here. It shows her in late 1893, at eighteen, in a gown choked in tulle and lace, blissfully clasping her firstborn, who's wearing a dress, to her bosom. The infant is Carol II, the first member of the royal family to be born in Romania and their first native speaker of its language. What a perfect excuse for blaming the dissolute habits he later developed on nearness to the Orient.

It's true, however, that something implacable about this Eastern place batters away at your defenses. I suppose I'll end up loving it if I can stick it out. Even hyper-British Missy ultimately became a fierce defender of her strange new culture. Gradually, she grew more and more at home in this Eastern place. Unblemished as her hands were by outdoor work, she had herself photographed in Romanian peasant drag. She and her visiting sister made bold visits on horseback to Gypsy camps. She took refuge in her affair with the Boyar Știrbey and in an intimate bond with her first Romanian son, Carol. Ecstatically, she began to envision the future with him on the throne and herself as the power behind it.

Marie's relationship with Carol titillates me partly for its perversity. Always headstrong about her own sexual experiments, she saw no harm in meddling with his. Behind my closed lids explodes a bright bucolic image of Arnold Mohrlen, the Swiss teacher whom Missy chose to educate her son. I can see Mohrlen and his pupil at the secluded pond they discovered in the woods near Cotroceni Palace, around 1909, when Carol was, say, fifteen and had become a long-limbed teenager, with a high, thick mop of blond hair and a sensuous, serious mouth. It might also be relevant to mention here the Eiffel Tower dimensions of his equipment, luridly referred to by Alice-Leone Moats in her shocker about the Prince's most notorious affair.

As Carol climbs naked from the pond, the tense, hazel-eyed professor gazes fixedly. Without Marie's seeming to take the slightest objection, tutor and student have become surprisingly intimate. The first consuming relationship outside family in the prince's young life has begun. Missy jokingly refers to them as "two old maids."

But it's less Mohrlen's homosexuality that disturbs the royal family than the discovery that he's a fervent democrat with socialist leanings. He's convinced that the era of kingships is coming to an end and sees in Carol a chance to fashion the first royal antimonarchist. Only three years later, Marie will blame her son's carousing in bars and cabarets on Mohrlen, never once guessing that Carol is the pouting production of her own philandering and overinvolvement.

A crack of light pierces the room, and the door opens tentatively. A disheveled Romulus glares down at me, panicked, probably, at the sudden thought of losing his meal ticket. "What's wrong with you?"

"Me? I'm thinking," I manage to croak out in a testy voice. I can't explain that I've been traveling into the past to get away from him, from the way he kicked me in bed, which is why my face must look so ghostly and blank.

Worry shrivels his. "Are you again taking those white pills?"

"No, *dragă.*"*

"You will sleep here?"

"I'm not sleeping, Romulus, I'm *thinking.*"

With a resigned shrug he leaves, closing the door. And in the ensuing darkness I admit how at home I am with the perplexed heart of a teenaged Carol cornered by a seductive, overinvolved mother, who was herself like a teenager, seeking to escape a prison of Germanic discipline. Disturbed by her affairs, spoiled rotten by her indulgences, young Carol would have had to be full of seething resentments and perverse impulses, flying into increasing rages at his mother's narcissistic pretensions.

At nineteen, he left the palace to get a taste of the streets his mother had yearned for when she was just his age. On Bulevardul Kiseleff he gaped at the women in tight-waisted dresses and enormous hats choked with feathers and flowers, as young, sometimes corseted, officers with waxed moustaches made X-rated comments about their private parts.

One day an expensive carriage whizzed by, showing just the hem of a skirt. "I had her last night," snickered a young dandy. It was only afterward that the fancy carriage was identified as that of the Patriarch of the Church. The young man was mistakenly whistling at his robe.

Carol was by now already a "deadbeat dad." An early affair with a high school student had led to a child, who was immediately placed in an orphanage by the embarrassed royal family. But the end of this early affair only pushed him more emphatically into bohemian circles, until he fell madly for the headstrong, deliciously plump Zizi Lambrino.

He couldn't have chosen a worse time. World War I was raging. The royal court was facing extinction at the hands of the Germans, and Russian-inspired Bolsheviks were threatening the political system. The Germans were hoping the whole mess would unseat the king and queen.

Wearily, I rise and tiptoe into the other bedroom, the only way to get to the bathroom. Sprawled naked on the bed, hair glued to his forehead, is my obsession, my reason for abandoning a worried mother and friends in New York. One naked leg is curled over a crumpled sheet, a pillow has fallen to the floor. I scan the room, littered with underwear and socks, the television now a fuzzy screen of static. What a perfectly pretty picture for the end result of passion. But as I think I've already indicated, passion is an emotion that rarely respects its own aftermath.

I suppose Prince Carol's was no exception to the rule. When strong-willed Zizi Lambrino with her maternal breasts held out arms in an invitation to ecstasy, he leapt. How could he help being attracted to her? In order to love, he must be sure his family would consider it an abomination. At the palace, his eyes must have shot cruel rays of irony as his mother railed against his lover. He was already planning a stupendously rebellious gesture that would result in his desertion from the army, a crime sometimes punishable by death.

In 1918, amid the chaos of World War I, Carol abandoned command of his regiment at Tîrgu Neamț to don civilian clothes and carry out a dangerous elopement into enemy territory. In Odessa, with the help of officers from the German army—enemies of Romania—he and Zizi were married. His father, Ferdinand, who'd become king in 1914 after the death of *der Onkel,* thought of a love of his own given up in youth for his country and was lenient. For the crime of desertion, he sentenced his son to only seventy-five days at the Horaiţa monastery near Bicaz. Pouting Zizi was sent home to Iaşi and put under a palace guard.

On the way to Carol's confinement comes that train I've often thought about, whose monotonous rhythms, even without codeine, lulled him into desperate imaginings of Zizi's distant body. By the time he met his distraught mother, who'd come to intervene, his eyes were glazed, as if drugged. To his brain inebriated by rebellion and passion, his mother seemed to have shrunk. Her judgments didn't matter at all.

Confined at Horaiţa, Carol fell into a manic depression characterized by suicidal feelings and flights of exhilaration. In other words, he was in love. In the meantime, the royal family concocted bizarre strategies worthy of the best Byzantine schemers to break up the romance for good. Zizi was detained by police and besieged with legal documents. Headstrong and determined, she held out. She knew that Carol's attachment to her had the contours of an addiction. It soared into and crashed out of worlds impregnable to the practical.

What, exactly, is it that sets the dogs to howling? What appetite? I stretch toward the window again and survey the empty street. Is it the wind or the moon that creates these unpredictable changes in activity? My eyes search the shadows outside with raw nerves, damaged by too much passion. It has pulled me into the firmament of an unknown future, drained me of all free will.

Unexpectedly the wind and the howling stop. In the stillness glows the future of an expanded Romania, thanks to Missy's behind-the-scenes efforts at Versailles after the armistice. Also thanks to her, Carol's right to succession is preserved; he's brought out of confinement and leads his regiment in a victory parade in Bucharest. Surrounded by policemen to keep her from rushing to him, Zizi watches the parade at the curb. She knows that in return for signing the papers agreeing to an annulment, she'll be granted permission to see him one more time.

That one time is enough, for some months later, Zizi announces to the world that she's pregnant; and Carol decides to renege on the annulment, recognize the child and marry her again. The decision drags the royal family into baser strategies, to the point that they attempt to bribe an old lover of his to reentice him. But only Zizi herself can release the prince from his obsession; and she does it unwittingly, by publishing a love letter in which he admits to being the father of her child. The indiscretion sways Carol to Missy's opinion of the commoner. Zizi is just too vulgar. He never sees her again.

Could it be morning already? The story of the "royal rapscallion" is dissolving into dawn light, which seems to have quieted the dogs again. To the screech of a garbage truck outside my window, Carol's hell-raising takes on clarity. It was just an unconscious parody of his mother's power with the means at hand: sexual conquest. It's part and parcel of his other revolts, all meant to mock the tenets of her royalty. So vicious is their oedipal drama that it rivals that of the incestuous Krupp-inspired characters in Visconti's *The Damned*. Not one phase of the "family romance" is repressed, not even Carol's obvious jealousy of his mother's lover Ştirbey. Later, as Romanian politics sink into chaos, Missy will plot with Carol's younger brother to dethrone him. Carol will squelch her completely in the political arena, but even then, his promiscuity will remain his most powerful weapon. In the end, a perhaps sordid victory is his: rumors about his sexual indiscretions overshadow the legends of his mother's accomplishments and goodwill. Even Barbara Cartland will eventually write a book about Carol's notorious love entanglements.

By mid-morning, as I walk with a chastened Romulus up Bulevardul Brătianu in search of breakfast, I can't help thinking that myths about flesh and the East have become my talismans. Carol was part of the process of Romania's Westernization; and Missy, the phallic queen, was, as Hannah Pakula reveals in her biography *The Last Romantic*, a Western queen set adrift in a libidinous Oriental adventure. Perhaps because of Missy, I can't keep from noticing the overt sensuality of this place, the marked sashay of its assuredly feminine and sloe-eyed women, often taller and always more slender than their male companions. Their long, lissome legs and elongated flat abdomens are like magnets to Romulus's eyes.

We stroll into a supermarket to buy *cascaval* and eggs. With a hint of last night's worry on his face, Romulus asks me what I'm thinking. I can't tell him that I'm still mulling over my own relationship to history and the temptations of the Hohenzollerns. Their struggle between duty and sensuality—which happened at a time when democracy in Europe was rising and the monarchy was getting drab.

For the first time since yesterday, I take a good look at my lover. He seems slight and depressed and rather inconsequential, but still encased in the shiny ectoplasm of my desire. I know our bedroom melodrama isn't over, just beginning its rebellious second act.

XV

The bitch with swinging black teats is trailing me. I'm sure she's about to bite. It's barely past seven in the morning, yet the heat is so intense my shirt is plastered against my back. I'm wheeling a gigantic Samsonite packed with books, shoes, manuscripts and gifts across the parking lot between our street and Piaţa Unirii, on my way to the plane to Paris.

The thundering sound of the wheels on the brick pavement is what frightened her. I remember seeing her looking depleted and nearly delirious under a parked car, nursing four pups that were fighting for the most swollen teat. As the noise of the suitcase ricocheted off the bricks, she decided to banish me from the lot. Now she's at my heels, the hanging tits stretching skin, fur missing in places from some skin infection, her eyes welling with bewildered misery, as her canines jut from a clenched, growling jaw.

I shake the suitcase to make more noise, hoping that will discourage her. She backs off, then lunges forward even more enraged. What a miserable biography this poor bitch must have. Obviously she's passed a horrible night in the unrelenting heat, her pups chomping hungrily at her belly. She herself was probably born under another parked car and from that time has known nothing but eating out of garbage cans or catching rats. Her posturing is just as useless and doomed to failure as that of Romulus, who's spent four nights refusing my sexual advances, after which I tried to sleep under the layers of smoke and the sound of TV action films, as he lit cigarette after cigarette, until I was driven again to the bed in my study. I've barely slept a wink all that time. Now he's dozing peacefully as long as he wants, while I drag my suitcase across this parking lot and am inches from being bitten by a sick, ferocious dog.

As soon as I get to the curb, the bitch retreats, satisfied that she's banished me from her territory. I can see her lumbering exhaustedly back to her pups, her back swayed, her tail dead-limp between her legs. I stand at the edge of the lot for a while, watching her exhausted gait under the blinding sun. Like her, Romulus was born in city squalor, with only a confused notion of who his parents were. And like her, he thinks that shows of bravado, pride are enough to fashion a life, to make a stab at dignity. With a surreal feeling, I imagine him coming from the outskirts of Bucharest into the city like some raw-boned animal, eyes blank and bewildered like hers, muscles twitching in exposure to want and danger.

By the time I get on the plane, he's recomposed in my imagination. Now he's coated with that charge of longing and excitement that makes me say yet again that I love him. This isn't an illusion, I tell myself, merely the clearer vision of distance. As flawed as our relationship is, I'm living out a basic homosexual dream. Current gay politics have covered up the fact that homosexuality is submission to a constant dilemma. The maleness toward which our sexuality is directed is—culturally at least—defined by heterosexuality. No one admits it anymore, but successful gay couples often play a constant game of switching. Each takes turns at playing "the man," while the other temporarily enjoys this sociological projection of masculinity. Those who don't do this seem to become denatured Bobbsey Twins, unmarried "sisters" living together. I've made a different choice, which some would call "unliberated." Everything attractive about Romulus stems from his heterosexuality, and of course, that's the very quality that prevents me from possessing him entirely. Well, maybe I'm on a more honest path of homosexual desire.

Paris explodes into something alien and overcharged as soon as I get off the plane. Like a dog's, my first experiences are fragrances carried by the milder, more humid air. It's like being transported into another world where perfume is abundant enough to be wasted. As the taxi enters the city limits, I gaze dazedly at the parade of shop windows, cafés and hair salons. In Bucharest, at the store in Piaţa Unirii, Romulus and I had found only a small selection of poor-quality, low-cost merchandise. A certain prudishness on my part that astonishes me makes these Parisian sights seem overluxurious and unnecessary.

At the Centre Pompidou, I walk across the concrete terrace beneath the stairs with Marianne Alphant, the woman who invited me, and Bernard Blistène, a witty, bright bon vivant, who's an official at the museum. In his unstructured, all-black Yamamoto suit he seems a mockery of the self-abnegating clergyman. I suppose he belongs to another order, art, but his appearance suggests a level of sophistication and irony that has no place in my new Romanian life, where somber, black-clad men are more likely to have long beards and faces preoccupied by the details of the liturgy.

Meeting us is my colleague for the presentation at the Centre Pompidou, which is supposed to treat the relationship among art, popular culture and homosexuality. He's the novelist Guillaume Dustan, considered one of the most outspoken gay radicals in France today. I've already read his novels, *Plus fort que moi* and *Je sors ce soir,* which are obsessive, minimalist evocations of gay male promiscuity. They never leave the confines of gay culture but try to subvert culture in general with their aggressive excesses. He's scowling and seems uninterested in me. It's as if he leaked resentment from every pore. I've enjoyed his novels and tell him so, but this doesn't penetrate his surly exterior, which I begin to realize is partly a cover for shyness.

In a state of some disorientation, I give my lecture, accusing certain lauded visual artists who were Situationists, and those who more recently are Conceptualists and Appropriationists, of severing the essential bond between art and pleasure—between eye and appetite. Focusing on Guy Debord's paranoid concept of the "Spectacle," that capitalist media show that keeps us "enthralled," these artists think that their job is to free us from our enslavement to the pageant of mediatic manipulation. In place of this, I call for a return to Georges Bataille and his belief that all cultural production is rooted in ancient traits and myths, in sacrifice, communal celebration and sexuality, behaviors that are not structured by anything rational or concertedly political. Those who've carried on this tradition of sexual celebration, I claim, are certain pre-Stonewall homosexual artists, whose immersion in popular culture and promiscuity pushed pleasure to the extreme, penetrated class and social barriers, and by means of parody subverted that "Spectacle" so bandied about these days. In the pansies' interest in drag, Hollywood and sex, I see a true movement toward a kind of orgiastic celebration that automatically challenges capitalist media production.

Reaction to my speech is slight, but when Dustan gets up to speak, offers an accusatory diatribe against the straight world and affirms his belief in barebacking (sex without condoms), the audience warms up. Here's an outsider with an accessible hostile agenda that seems to interface perfectly with straight guilt. The audience is delighted, apologetic.

The days after the museum drag on. I see some friends—the writer Benoît Duteurtre and his lover, Jean-Sébastien; my editor and my agent, François and Catherine Guérif; and my publicist Agnès Guéry-Plazy and her companion Gilles. I'm staying in Montparnasse, in a tiny apartment that belongs to Duteurtre and used to be a maid's chamber. Something is wrong with me. I have spent months in Paris in the past, but now its beauty seems sharpened by what Romulus doesn't have. I can't like it, can only gawk at it in curiosity as at some fetish from my past.

Jean-Sébastien gives me a tour of the Marais, Paris's gay ghetto. With glazed eyes, I watch men on the streets and in bars, who are supposed to be my brothers. Is my exile from the cultures of my past permanent?

I've promised to write an article for *The Village Voice* about my desire to live in Bucharest with Romulus, so I hole up for a couple of days.

"I'm back in the closet and loving it, in a country that still criminalizes homosexuality, with a lover who doesn't consider himself gay," I boast. "Here in Bucharest, Romania, where I've opted to spend several months with my Romanian partner, I am, it occurs to me, a willful sexual exile...."

Later in the article, I claim, "From the very beginning, our relationship has had an 'old-fashioned' dynamic. It's a 'don't-ask, don't-tell' aesthetic in which the growing solidarity between us is forbidden to be put into words. Since my friend isn't gay, it's understood he'll sometimes be sleeping with women. But when he's with me, the sex is hot, though the roles—who does what to whom—are rigidly enforced"

I end the article maintaining that "I've chosen to write my own script, which is a mixture of old values and experimental approaches. It's a risky, shadowy thriller that won't ever make a pilot for primetime television."

However, when I call Romulus, who has the only key to our apartment, to say I'm coming back pronto, my "risky, shadowy thriller" is deflated. He seems happily integrated into his own community minus me, in no hurry to get back to Bucharest. He's at his mother's in Sibiu, playing soccer, yet probably aware that he's supposed to be in Bucharest already, to meet me the next day with the key. Adamantly, I make his mother go to the soccer field to get him. He comes to the phone out of breath, sounding elated, relaxed and casual, like some American teenager called in from baseball. There are other people in the room, who seem to be having a good time. I think I hear a girl's voice. With a sinking heart, I ask him what bus he's leaving on. "Too late now," he chirps. "When soccer finishes, no more bus."

"You have our keys!"

"The old lady is there, this I am sure. She will let you in."

He's referring to the landlord's stoop-shouldered, fearful, poetry-reciting mother, who lives below us on the shadowy first floor, among the fading portraits of her family. She's tried to show her goodwill in a variety of ways, the last being a china plate holding two wrapped hard candies, left outside our door. In Paris, I've bought her some Belgian chocolates and planned to put them on the same plate in front of her door when I got back. But what if she's not home? I can see myself with my heavy suitcase banging on the front door, as the wild neighborhood watchdogs howl and bark. Or coming across the parking lot again with that cumbersome suitcase, as the bewildered bitch with the swinging black teats, resentful and confused, attacks.

"But the dogs!" I shout shrilly.

Was that a chuckle I heard? "Is the way you walk," he says. "They feel when you are afraid."

I'm infuriated. "I'm not any more afraid than you are! And the danger's real. Dozens of people a day get bitten in Bucharest."

"Only those who are coward," he teases.

I fly into a rage. "You were too fucking lazy to make another key. So you'd better get your ass on a bus and be there when I arrive tomorrow!"

"All right," he says, suddenly sounding submissive. It's almost as if he was hoping for my rage, sees it as a kind of mastery. "I will come."

As I hang up: a Technicolor tableau of Romulus on the soccer field, so real that I fall back on the bed, bedazzled. The image devours every other reality and reduces Paris to a shrunken figment. It's that state of transport Saint Ignatius believed could be achieved by rigorous meditation and the use of the imagination, when the Lord and the places touched by His steps surge up, blinding you with their three-dimensionality. Through belief and discipline, sacred scenes become real, palpable.

His shorts are green, his calf muscles so tensed that every sinew shows, his body crouched as he tries to block the black-and-white ball from another, bulkier outstretched leg. The calls and raucous laughter are sucked up by the funnel of heat above the playing field, with its coarse grass churned into the mud in places; I can smell the acrid sweat making bulged half-moons on his shirt under the arms, and see, rooted like some sacred figurehead at the edge of the field, an innocent blonde. Probably no more than seventeen, her forehead a smooth dome over a heart-shaped face, her smile placid but fearful.

That smile holds everything I need to know. It has a message for me. When he stops playing for a moment and strides breathlessly to the edge of the field to take her in his arms, I'm filled with a sadness I've never experienced before, a form of reverence whose meaning I search for in her half-trusting, frightened eyes.

The next morning the feeling stays with me all the way to the airport. As the plane takes off, I face the fact that I've condemned myself to a weird antechamber. In exchange for the impossible fantasy of loving a hustler, I've convinced myself that nothing else—not even Paris—matters. I'm thinking about the girl again, wondering what she could have to tell me. She knows, I suddenly realize, what it feels like to be desired by Romulus. To be the one he kisses on the mouth. But this knowledge feels so frightening.

XVI

He's meeting me at Unirii to help me with my bags. What a vivid fantasy striding toward me as if it were flesh and blood. Across the wide avenue swaggers a lower-class man, muscular, depressed. For some reason he looks astoundingly vertical, like those Futurist demigods they drew in the thirties. His lips, the corner of which holds a cigarette, are smiling at me. For a moment I don't feel any connection. It all seems too new, exciting, like my mother's repeated tale of not believing that blue-eyed treasure was hers when they first brought me to her in the hospital. Is he really coming to meet me?

He hoists the suitcase on one bulging shoulder, and we walk across the parking lot toward our street. He'd recognized me in the crowd, he jokes, by my walk. But this time the reference is jovial, even affectionate. The dogs bark, advance, but I feel inviolable. Without the slightest fear we stride to our door.

By the time we're sitting on the couch, drinking kiosk-bought bootleg scotch that tastes like metal and rubbing alcohol, I realize what's causing this strange sense of equilibrium. He's telling me how he got here the night before. Wanting to impress his parents with the hundred dollars I'd left for him, he took them to dinner at an expensive restaurant, then spent the rest on a leather jacket. He then had to hitchhike to Bucharest because he had no money for the bus. His week of misbehavior, coupled with my belligerent orders on the phone, is what has produced this sensual, vital mood in him that's giving me so much pleasure. He even sneaks a hand across the couch to clasp mine. He's responded, I realize, to a kind of authoritarianism. Disobeying me and being reprimanded is a gratifying ritual. He's actually a kind of masochist.

The next day I start some work that, preposterously, will play a huge role in my relationship with him. Because we're almost out of money, I've agreed to translate Céline Dion's co-written memoirs for the publisher William Morrow, in an impossibly short time—three weeks. The $10,000 that Morrow was offering made me accept the project, despite some embarrassment at having my name linked to such a frivolous enterprise. I told myself it would be taken as a prank by my more serious readers. But the text seems amazingly false, a mountain of unaware narcissism whose banality falls just short of camp.

Those who translate are familiar with the deeply intimate experience of working on a text; in many ways it becomes a merging with the consciousness of the author. Dion would complicate the project by requiring post-translation additions, and I would end up working at it ten to fourteen hours a day for about six weeks, not three, while editors at Morrow waited on pins and needles for each new section. Sheer immersion would entangle me in her lust for pop power, her sentimentalizing of her husband's relentless career ploys and her working-class sense of always being the little girl no matter how many crowds she swayed. Juxtaposed with the life I was leading here in Bucharest, Céline's life and her dreams would take on a hysterical absurdity. As the poor girl with the too-long incisors struggled to become "the greatest singer in the world," I was sinking into a proletarian fantasy in a country that the world seemed to have forgotten. I tried sharing some of the more absurd passages with Romulus for a good laugh, but he failed to see the humor.

Even so, the project adds a comic element to our playing house. There is Romulus, cooking a hot lunch while I pound away at my inane text about the queen of pop, my overworked eyes beginning to resemble fixed marbles. Occasionally, he chases me out of my seat, puts on my glasses and does a parody of my concentration, which seems deranged to him, and I take pictures of the imitation.

The heat wave has gotten worse. With nothing to do, Romulus immolates himself with cigarettes before the television in the sweltering bedroom, watching soccer and soft-core movies until he's nearly comatose. Every hour or so, I go in and lie facedown next to this smoking sarcophagus and put my head against his hip. Then he absentmindedly pets my head or back as if I were a dog. Tiptoeing into the bedroom late at night, I find him in a nonverbal state, and since I'm so worked up, I grab the key and go to the bar at the end of the street for a drink. The first time I did, a dirty, shaggy animal that probably served as the bar's unofficial watchdog followed me growlingly right up to the bar seat. I was wearing shorts, and at one point, I felt gums, whiskers and hot breath touching my leg. This seemed unremarkable to the barmaid, who merely asked me what I wanted to drink. After that, I carried dog biscuits and left a trail of them from the house to the bar, like something out of Hänsel and Gretel. The dog scarfed them up on the way, but barked belligerently whenever I went through the door.

In the meantime, I've discovered the correct phone number for the Romanian film critic Alex Leo Şerban, who's taken me for a fascinating walk through the more elegant neighborhoods of Bucharest. He's the first intellectual I've met in the city, and I'm astonished by the ways he's adapted to life here. He's a pure aesthete who speaks English and French fluently and leaves the country regularly for film festivals throughout Western Europe. Somehow, his wit and epicureanism are unabated by the squalor around him.

Through Alex, I learn to marvel at the fractured beauty of Bucharest, its crumbling homes that hint at Mediterranean and Oriental grandeur. I begin to understand that much of the city is a reference to other times, places and peoples: Rome, nineteenth-century France, the Greek Phanariots, Turkish sultans and French-educated Boyars; these displacements from the present gradually become a rich source of poetry and fancy for me, not confusion and fear.

Alex takes me to the offices of a magazine called *Dilema* that will eventually publish a satire I write. They are located in a little red-brick villa in a fashionable part of the city, on Aleea Vulpache, and I'll later learn that this was once the pied-à-terre of Carol's terminal mistress Lupescu. The Fascist Iron Guard turned it into a museum of decadence after she fled in 1940. They tried to display what they termed proof of her extravagant luxuries at the state's expense and her orgiastic behavior. Apparently, her royal assistant, "Puiu" Dimitrescu, who may have also been her clandestine lover, and who later plotted to murder her, took care of the decoration. Scandal sheets boasted of the decadence of the place; but Countess Waldeck, author of the gossipy, brilliantly written *Athene Palace,* said it would have made Madame Pompadour turn in her grave. According to Waldeck, it was dark, dismal and full of bric-a-brac, except for a few pieces of eighteenth-century china with pornographic scenes and some paintings rumored to have been stolen from the state museum. There wasn't much else—some detective novels in French, a few Elizabeth Arden cosmetics and "a staggering amount of alum," which Waldeck surmised served as that same "arcanum" employed by seventeenth-century ladies.

The night I invited Romulus, Şerban and Şerban's writer friend Mihai Chirilov to a restaurant, I learned about a new side of Romulus. He smelled and looked stunning in the Issey Miyake cologne I'd bought him at the airport and the iridescent shirt he'd so hated to put on for the French embassy. His gleaming hair and suave, decorous gestures seemed so elegant, impressing my new friends and filling me with yet a new ardor. I realized that I had little understanding of the manners of this until recently classless society, and that probably because everyone in Communist Romania had been given at least a high school education, there was somewhat less of a difference in culture among Romanians than among most Americans. Or maybe I wasn't equipped to perceive it.

Old World charm suddenly oozing from Romulus rekindled fantasies of a successful life with him in France; and when he got up to go to the rest room, Şerban leaned toward me and said, "I see why you like him."

I was all the more astounded when we got home and I asked Romulus what he thought of my new friends. "I do not like them at all," he said quite soberly. Then he launched into a complicated explanation of "that kind of person," which to my ears sounded distinctly paranoid. According to Romulus—who, it must be remembered, had gotten nowhere past a one-time failed chance to play professional soccer—anyone in Romania with a privileged journalism career who was allowed to travel regularly outside the country must have gotten where he was by unholy alliances. In a country that he felt functioned on corruption and bribes, the successful were the criminals. What compromises had Şerban made, he asked with cynical vulgarity, to have such a cushy life? As for the other fellow, Romulus accused him of being a hanger-on.

I consider myself a savvy judge of character and felt that Romulus was dead wrong. Şerban and his friend lacked the veiled glances and the false platitudes of climbers and opportunists. I'd liked them both immediately, found them candid and generous. In the future I would know I was right. They are intelligent, principled people.

Romulus opened the closet door to hang up the iridescent shirt, and my eyes fell on the underclass trappings of the rest of his wardrobe, which he'd chosen. Now I doubted the gracious worldliness I'd just been startled by. Despite the obvious failure of the former Communist system, he still had the classic Communist's distrust of individual accomplishment, the worker's resentment of hierarchy.

Romulus had a very different reaction to my only other intellectual contact in Bucharest, the renowned jazz pianist Johnny Răducanu, a dark graybeard in a Kangol hat, with devilishly ironic eyes. We met when a Romanian jazz singer I'd encountered in New York invited me to go out with her in Bucharest, then unceremoniously dumped me on him. What followed was a crazy ride through the city in sixty-eight-year-old Johnny's beat-up car, while he kept up a perpetual dialogue with the other cars in broken English: "Here I'm gonna turn left," he'd mumble at the windshield, "though we [meaning he and the other driver] know I'm not supposed to." Then he'd swerve in front of the car, which would miss him by a hair. "Wrong way," he'd say with a chuckle at the oncoming traffic, "so excuse my U-turn," which he'd grind right into as I covered my eyes with my hands.

At a private restaurant for artists run by the poet Iolanda Malamen, Johnny treated me to several Jack Daniel's and ordered some food for himself. First, though, he opened what looked like a pen but revealed a hypodermic needle. He unbuttoned his shirt near the navel and plunged it into his stomach with a comic leer. "It's insulin," he explained, "not dope."

A slew of details followed, stories of lost loves that entailed superhuman sacrifices. He couldn't have been more comfortable with me or about the idea of Romulus and me, and by the end of dinner, he claimed that he and I were locked for life in friendship. "Special connection I'm feeling," he said grinning, and gave me an awkward full-body hug. Tears rimmed his soft brown eyes. "Like you I'm a Jew."

But Johnny isn't a Jew. He's a Romani, or Gypsy, and the claim brought crinkles of smiles to his Romanian colleagues in the art world whom I later met in New York. It was then I learned from his autobiography that he was born Creţu Răducan, in Brăila, a cosmopolitan port city on the Danube with an Oriental feel. In Brăila's *mahalaua,* or slum, Johnny received an international education of the streets, hanging out with stevedores, sailors, gamblers, Greek barbers, Italians, Armenians and Gypsies. Or he'd go to Komnorofka, a ghastly suburb that teemed with destitute Russians and treacherous jailbirds; or to the borough of Brăiliţa, where upper-crust crooks sported spats and walking canes and drove fancy cars.

So well did he learn their swindles and pranks that he was well on the way to becoming a *golan,* or hooligan, according to his distraught mother. One of his more lucrative gigs was as a shill for a notorious con artist known as Nea Gicu', who'd perfected a three-card monte game similar to those that used to be seen often on the streets of New York. When onlookers saw the little boy winning an Omega watch, they'd rush to play the game, but a few blocks away, Johnny would be handing over the watch to his accomplice for five lei.

Johnny's stories fascinated me because they were proof of the world of Panaït Istrati, that illegitimate son of a Greek smuggler and a Romanian peasant, who was born in Brăila, too. Istrati's books about shepherds turned bandits, about vagabonds, and evil Greek Phanariots in fur-trimmed robes, caused a sensation in France in the 1920s because of their subversive political intent, which gleefully opposed rebellious underclass rip-off artists—bandits of the people—to the Turks and their avaricious Boyar puppets. Johnny was well aware of the legend of one of these figures, a Robin Hood icon called Terente, who hid in the moors near the Danube and once forced a Boyar to dance barefoot on hot embers while a Gypsy accompanied him on violin. Terente would sneak underwater across the Brăila port, breathing through a long reed, and one day Johnny watched the police fire cannons into the water in an attempt to catch him. He actually saw Terente in Bucharest, but only his head. It was on display in a morgue on a quay of the Dîmbovița, brought there by surgeons who wanted to figure out how its superb criminal brain functioned.

It was music that lured Johnny from the streets, after he sat down at an old piano in his house and started picking at the keys. Some time after, his impoverished family fled Brăila for Câmpulung, in Moldavia. The educated Germans and Jews he met there widened his cultural perspectives, and before long he was studying piano and then double bass in various academies. If he'd tried to convince me that he, too, was a Jew, he was probably thinking of this period in his life when he first had contact with cultured people who happened to be Jewish, and got it into his head that he could be like them.

There were setbacks, of course. Johnny's education at a music academy in Iaşi was interrupted when the Communists reformed the system, but he continued his studies at Cluj, in Transylvania, where he had to deal with some very civilized but very frigid Hungarians. After Cluj, the former street boy managed to get into the prestigious Ciprian Porumbescu music academy in Bucharest, where he studied double bass. He showed me a picture of himself at the time, when he was twenty-one, which I playfully told him stimulated my baser instincts. More chocolate than he is now, Johnny resembled a mulatto Elvis, with a shiny crown of brilliantined hair combed just like Elvis's, sultry eyes and cushiony, almost feminine lips made for landing.

At La Zisu, the best jazz club in Bucharest during the 1950s, Johnny would hang outside or behind stage, until he got his big break, when a pianist couldn't perform. From then on, his career skyrocketed. One of the first American jazz artists to visit Romania during the Communist era was Louis Armstrong, whose performance made Johnny burst into tears of awe. Later, Duke Ellington came and heard Johnny play. He dubbed him "Mr. Romanian Jazz."

During the Communist regime and after, Johnny performed throughout Western Europe and America, sharing the stage with jazz greats like Miles Davis and Thelonious Monk. The poet Nina Cassian taught him how to compose, and he created his own pieces. When he received an honorary diploma from the U.S. embassy in Bucharest that proclaimed him ambassador of American music in Eastern Europe, he had to translate the wording for the Securitate, who needed to make sure the content was approved by the regime.

Johnny had numerous opportunities to defect, but he kept coming back, believing that his success belonged to his people. Yet it almost seems that he was immune to the devastating setbacks others suffered under Communism. It's true that the most famous artists in Romania had special privileges. But his constant evasion of oppression and his steady nerves came more from what he'd learned on the streets of Brăila. Communism itself had quickly decayed into a con, and Johnny, a con artist from way back, knew how to outsmart it. Like Istrati, whose work is heavily influenced by Gypsy lore, he knew that rule-breaking and crime are a kind of revolution when the law itself is repressive and corrupt. His jokes and his driving, as well as his playful lies, are indications of the blissful and prankish psychosis in which he lives; he has long ago convinced himself that the world around him is of his own making. True, his impish eyes may now be deeply circled by years of struggle and show his conflicted emotions about the tragedies he escaped while others didn't, but they're still proof that subversion can triumph—as long as nobody takes you seriously.

From the beginning, Johnny and I had an instant rapport, unless, of course, I as well was the butt of a playful con. It amazed me that he claimed not only to be a Jew but to have the same musical tastes as I did, for outdated vocalists like the Hi-Lo's and Chris Connor. At his subsidized-for-artists apartment, we sang some of their songs while he played the piano; then we drove to the concert he was giving at a posh hotel, only to lose a headlight in a minor head-on after he made a wrong turn at that terrifying intersection where Bulevardul Kiseleff meets the Romanian Arc de Triomphe. He came back to the car grinning, of course, claiming that the other driver and the cop had recognized him and had let him off scot-free.

A few nights later, Johnny, Romulus and I dined at Bistro Athenee, in the same hotel where the writer Countess Waldeck spent several months in 1940 as an eyewitness of the Fascist takeover. In the 1970s the restaurant was a small knot of anti-Communist resistance in the hypersurveilled hotel, with a jazz club hidden in the cellar. The men's room was the only place that wasn't bugged. It was here, according to the painter Sorin Dumitrescu, that Johnny gave a jazz concert while perplexed tourists tiptoed in to relieve themselves and then didn't dare flush the toilet for fear of interrupting the music.

Romulus was at first awed by Johnny, then charmed and relaxed, but he was never resentful of the Gypsy who became a famous jazz musician. And Johnny laconically suggested that my relationship with him couldn't be compared to the heartbreaks he'd suffered because, after all, Romulus and I were just two men. He launched into a tale about the recent red tape he's had to endure in this country, where nothing seems to function and every hand is held out for a take. When he noticed my expression of fascination, his once plush lips, now thinned with age, curled in contempt. "For you is fun, a dream and an adventure," he spit. "But see how you like the party when you stay forever!"

By the time Céline Dion's autobiography was almost half translated, I needed a vacation. Work on a new first chapter had delayed the second half for a couple of weeks. Aside from the fact that I was exhausted, I was worried about Romulus, whose television marathons seemed symptomatic of a severe depression. When I suggested a car trip to Transylvania, which might include a visit to his family in Sibiu, he acted interested. But about a week before our trip, we were invited to dinner at the tiny apartment of Şerban and Chirilov, who wanted to thank me for taking them out to eat. Romulus refused, so I went alone, rather nervously. The directions were confusing, and I'd gotten lost before in the labyrinthine streets of Bucharest. Overreacting to Romulus's moodiness, I'd decided at the last minute to bring along with me the $800 I was saving. It was a bad-faith gesture, a giving in to a neurotic fantasy of Romulus's taking it and taking off because I was fraternizing with people he'd dubbed his social enemies. I folded the bills into a small chamois purse that was held to my waist under my shirt by an elastic belt.

Just as I'd expected, I got miserably lost on the way to their apartment, which is in a romantic, dilapidated neighborhood behind Bulevardul Bălcescu. At some point, a youth leaning against a building, who may have been a Roma, dashed toward me in response to my lost look and, lightly touching my shoulder, asked if I needed directions. Seeing that he'd been standing with a rowdy bunch, I coldly declined, said that I knew where I was going.

The fish dinner at Şerban and Chirilov's was delicious, and the wine plentiful. The conversation was relaxed and witty. I sprawled on the bed that served as a couch and regaled them with tales of my adventures with Romulus, how we'd met that night by the Danube in Budapest and my machinations in an attempt to get him to France or America. I spilled out comic stories of other sexual adventures as well. They seemed somewhat taken aback by my exhibitionism, slightly repelled by my obsessive sexuality and perverse, sloppy approach to living, but like the gentlemen they were, took the stories in stride. Somehow the myth of Mioriţa came into the conversation, and Şerban denied that it mythologized the character of the Romanian. He felt that the implied passivity and morbidity were clichés, which hid the resourcefulness, energy and ambition of his people.

I was halfway home from the dinner when the same youth leaning against the same building approached me again, tried to strike up a conversation, but as I remember, I got past him without letting him touch me. A block later, I felt for the lump of money under my shirt, and it was gone. I went back to Şerban and Chirilov's, and we turned the bed, and then the rest of the apartment, upside down, but it wasn't to be found. We emptied the wastebasket in the bathroom, where I'd gone to pee, on the chance that it had dropped into it. They were getting more and more disturbed, anguished. For them, $800 was a major fortune, its loss a tragedy. Finally Chirilov took a flashlight and we retraced my path on the street, searching minutely for the lost purse, looking in gutters and garbage cans. His sensitivity to my loss felt caring, mournful. He even ran to our apartment while I waited, to ask Romulus to see if the purse was there.

When I got home without the purse, Romulus's face was about to glow with dark irony. "I can't believe it," I said. "Alex and Mihai think the Gypsy took it."

"What Gypsy?"

"The one I passed on the way to their house. I swear he only touched my shoulder for a second. I didn't feel a thing. Alex and Mihai said that's how they do it. They have a very sharp knife or straight razor. They distract you for a second by touching you, then cut the elastic band and it's gone."

Romulus's angular face had a look of depressed fatalism. Was it pity or vengefulness? He lit up a cigarette and glanced away.

"Don't you know who take it? They."

"Romulus, that's ridiculous."

"I am sure," he said in a monotone. "They did not steal it. Probably it fell from your body at some time when you are there."

"That's what we thought. We looked all over for it!"

"Yes. Afterward. But first when you leave, they see it lying there. Sticking from under pillow on couch maybe. Inside they look, see how much money, cannot resist, make a decision."

"That isn't what happened!"

"You come back, they pretend to look all over. I have seen such thing before."

"Romulus, Mihai even went into the street with a flashlight to help me look for it."

"Yes," he said gravely. "Shame is what they are feeling then. You must not suspect that they cannot resist."

His face looked funereal, nearly tragic.

For a split second, I became part of his reality, believed it. Then sadness overwhelmed me, similar to the sadness I'd felt when I'd imagined the girl, sweet and bewildered, and her love for him, at the soccer field.

I knew what he was saying wasn't true, but understanding why he believed it was almost more than I could bear. Șerban and Chirilov were true gentlemen, anything but thieves, yet Romulus couldn't imagine a different mentality and stayed imprisoned in his past. Affection spread hopelessly through my chest like nausea. We were in bed, and I rolled toward him, held his face close to mine.

Two nights before we left for Transylvania, Romania played soccer against England in the European championships. I was still struggling with Céline, in cahoots with her, manufacturing a stilted, contradictory persona that pretended proof of her good nature and simplicity in the face of her monstrous ambition, her relentless need for attention.

I could hear uncharacteristic yelps and shouts coming from the bedroom all through the match. Romania's ath-

letic triumph was awakening Romulus from depression. The
television was roaring, I knocked but he refused to turn it
down. Around midnight, the door to my study burst open.
Romulus's eyes were ablaze. "We won," he said. Then he
strode over to my desk, hooked an arm under mine, lifting
me from the chair.

"Come with me!"

"Where?"

"Out on the street. With everybody in Bucharest."

Through the open window I heard the noise of cheering
and horns honking. The sweltering air was saturated with
it.

"I haven't finished!"

"Can't you do for me this once? This, finally, is my thing."
His eyes were imploring, needy. So I followed him down the
stairs, but my heart was pounding with fear. I was imagining
stampedes, riots and violence, that aggressive hysteria that
can push the citizens of the smallest countries into displays
of reckless power, making them feel invulnerable. And
as soon as we were out the door, we were swept into the
throngs—practically the entire city was outside.

I was ready for the worst, but it wasn't the chaotic row-
diness I'd imagined. Instead it was a sort of procession,
thousands walking as one in a heightened, ecstatic hypnosis.
This wasn't any Flacăra, either, one of those frenzied youth
festivals during the Ceauşescu years in which light, smoke,
music and patriotic poetry were staged to drive young
crowds into frenzies of patriotism. Instead it was a nearly
solemn celebration that felt almost mystical.

Chants that seemed a cross between hymn and anthem
echoed through the air. Small children rode on the shoulders
of adults. Hastily decorated cars cleaved the crowd as if it
were butter, sliding through to shouts of elation. I turned

to Romulus to ask for a translation, but he cautioned me, "Don't speak English. They will think you are, and God knows what they will do."

At Piaţa Universităţii, the crowd congealed into a trembling mass. Crowds coming from other directions choked the street. High above me, a small boy began climbing a telephone pole. Now he was hanging from the wires, fifty feet above the heads of the crowd, swinging slowly to and fro. Policemen parked in their cars at the curb watched him imperturbably. "They are afraid to act," Romulus explained in my ear excitedly. "The crowd will not tolerate them tonight."

What struck me, yet again, was a feeling of timelessness in the celebration, a primeval dignity I'd never associated with sports. I thought of those aimless people on the street, who'd always moved as if through a medium of gelatin. Now they'd been pulled toward a joyous focal point and infused with its optimism. A static, charged bliss reigned. There wasn't much movement in the enormous crowd, over which the boy swung from the wire like a pendulum. Everything had stopped at this high point of pleasure.

I turned to look at Romulus. A kind of justification had colored his face, and the muscles of his body bristled with dignity. He looked at me knowingly, as if to say, "You see?" But he was a sad warrior, with nowhere to go from here, a knight standing still in the face of doom.

XVII

I lurch out of the parking lot of the Bucharest Marriott, my feet struggling with the clutch pedal of our Dacia, the Romanian national car. A map is spread across the knees of Romulus, who has no license ever since that terrible accident that led to the operation on his neck vertebrae—the one that caused the scar I first noticed at our hotel in Budapest.

Since the night of the soccer game, we've settled into an easy, joyous intimacy. Romulus feels like a winner, or is it that he thinks I've finally found a way into his culture?

The entire city is in the midst of a road-renovation project as part of Romania's bid to join the European Union; potholes and frustrated drivers are everywhere. Romulus tunes in to some Romanian rap. Its thudding, polka-like beat and Turkish flourishes hammer at my temples, augmenting the jolts in the road, as history scuds by my window. We fly past the gorgeous villas of Bucharest with their Turkish-style gables, the monuments to defamed heroes, and the depressed pedestrians detoured from their fantasies. At his recommendation I'm going very, very fast. "Slow driving is so dangerous," he claims. "They go nuts and try to pass." Nimbly he inches his foot toward mine and bears down on it, gunning the engine. As if on cue, a white Toyota draws up to our fender, then squeezes in front of us just in time to miss an oncoming car.

"Wild dogs keep darting into the road!" I plead as an excuse to go slower.

"Just go, go!" he barks laughingly, slapping the dashboard in rhythm to the music, as the buildings blur past.

Once I hit the periphery of the city, cars are careening past us even more recklessly, especially on curves, the drivers expecting us to swerve onto the shoulder if a car is coming the other way. Romulus chortles at a near miss. Everybody is in a frantic hurry, probably hoping to catch a flying fragment of the new market. But unlike the others, we have no idea exactly where we're going, except north toward the Carpathians and his hometown of Sibiu. "Just go!" he keeps chanting like a joyous incantation.

Outside the city limits, buildings fade away into fields of thick-bladed grass, then slowly into soothing hills. The road meanders into sweet curves. We're driving through the Wallachian plain. Amputated oak trees line the road like driving casualties. Beyond them, fields of sheep stretch toward the hills; then suddenly there's the apparition of a barren landscape, the fat, grimy smokestacks of a chemical plant.

In many cases, these industrial messes stand where centuries-old villages used to be, before they were razed by Ceaușescu and the entire populations sent to work in factories. At the edge of cities are the dreary "blocks" like the one Romulus grew up in—ramshackle housing projects to which the displaced villagers were sent. To me they look destitute and lunar, but Romulus's eyes glisten with contentment, even security, when we drive past them.

"Just like where I live," he says with self-satisfied defeatism.

"Where are the trees?"

"Hmph, trees he wants! We got clubs."

Glancing at him from the corner of my eye, I try to imagine his *Blade Runner* life, picture him at night strolling through a squalid street illuminated by salmon-colored riot lamps, on the way to a club. "You like living there?"

"Was better before, during Communists. Now you got to find rent."

The car goes faster and faster at his urging, and the slide show of our trip speeds up. Sixteenth-century bucolic Romania keeps alternating with the scarred industrial present, as if the two were giving birth to each other. In their isolation the bloated chemical refineries and grimy steel mills look gothic, or like futuristic castles in a decadent science fiction film. Getting within a few feet of them fills me with a kind of daring. They've become the grim decor of my love affair.

I pull over and photograph a rusting factory, zigzagged with catwalks like a spiny juggernaut. It hovers in the haze of pollution it expels, a diabolical mirage. Among the other consequences of Ceauşescu's hysterical push toward total industrialization was an incident that occurred earlier in the year, when a hundred metric tons of cyanide leaked from a gold mine into the Lăpuş River, then flowed through Hungary and Yugoslavia before returning to Romania.

Among the blur of fences, trees and passing cars I feel my heart thumping: anything is possible. All that lies ahead is the future, new sights and new sensations.

My eye fastens on a sign that says "Bran Castle," in English, so I follow it by swerving onto a side road. At the end of the road looms a rocky hill topped by a colossal white castle with red-tiled roofs and four towers.

"Dracula!" Romulus gasps with bared teeth, diving toward my neck. I fend him off with my elbow, but he's right in a way. Billed as Dracula's Castle by the Romanian Tourist

Office, from 1395 to 1427 it belonged to Mircea the Wise, who was Dracula's, or Vlad Țepeș's, grandfather. Vlad himself may have hidden there from the Turks in 1462, but he spent only a short period. Staying much longer were other historical Romanians, including Queen Marie, into whose hands the castle had passed.

We trudge up the long, narrow path to the entrance, and a cloud obscures the summer sun. Because of the elevation it's much cooler here than in Bucharest. Wind erupts like a whip, and goose bumps pop out all over our exposed arms. Above us towers the castle, so high that we have to tilt our heads back to see its parapets. Sprouting from a bulbous rock formation, it has a convex, faceless look, clandestine and aggressive; it hides, in a sense, Romulus's larger historical past. Behind his own convex shutters, those hooded eyes, lie secrets of his culture, part of the mystery of my obsession.

We head immediately for a table selling hand-knit sweaters, buy one each for about seven dollars and pull the coarse wool over our shivering bodies. Then we climb an almost vertical staircase set into the rocks, at the top of which sits a homeless, bewildered parody of a guard dog with dirt-caked fur and cloudy, dismal eyes.

It's a gorgeous, gloomy castle, originally in the gothic style, to which architects over time have added harmonious Renaissance and Romantic elements. Inside the courtyard, paved with flagstones, I photograph Romulus standing at the fountain from which Dracula must have drunk and beside which Marie must have spent summers avoiding the heat of the city. With his slicked-back hair and dim, depressed eyes, he has a medieval look, that "ancient face" my friend Ursule Molinaro identified.

We edge up a narrow, curving staircase leading out of the courtyard, our nostrils stung by mildew. Romulus pries open a squat door in the wall. Before I can bat an eyelash, he's disappeared inside. I follow down a narrower stone staircase flanked by curving stone walls, which is so dark and steep I need to light a match. At the bottom are damp, windowless catacombs through which I creep nervously. Then I come to a dead end, a high, tiny window covered by a grating, and a gray stone room containing only a draped wooden coffin. Its top rattles and raises just a hair. Suddenly it opens, revealing Romulus sitting up in slow motion, looking more than apt for the role. I don't know it at the time, but later I'll find out why the prop is there. In the 1970s, Ceauşescu tried to make Bran Castle a principal attraction for tourists. Capitalizing on the Dracula myth, he hired actors to hide in cupboards and coffins, then scare tourists as they walked by. The plan was scuttled after an American woman was surprised by a stagy Dracula and succumbed to a stroke.

The castle may be vampire-free, but it has a Byzantine feeling, or should I say "adapted Byzantine," which is how the essayist Sacheverell Sitwell described it when he saw the way Marie had changed it into her concept of Transylvanian exoticism. Because there are no guides or guards, we've floated undisturbed from room to room as if we lived there. This has produced an unspoken intimacy between us, as if the implacable atmosphere were given us to play out our instincts. Finally we come to a white bedroom dominated by an eighteenth-century rosewood baldaquin bed in baroque style. It's enormous, with carved spiral posts. This is the very bed, I realize from my reading, where Marie sometimes slept on summer nights. The red rope surrounding it is easy enough to hop over. The bed creaks and groans as we land together on the mattress, and a dusty odor of frangipani reaches our nostrils. It puts me in an awed trance, as I wonder which of Marie's lovers was privileged enough to share this fragrance with her. Was it Ştirbey, her Russian cousin or someone unnamed? Even her severed heart, placed in a gold coffer, was once buried in a grotto near this castle, after it was moved from its original location in Balcic.

When we get back on the road, the sun is sparkling and the driving even more treacherous. Cars speed recklessly by as the lanes change from three to two and back. Wind howls through the trees, spitting loose leaves in gorgeous spirals against the windshield, as I grind into second, struggling up the steep, winding hills. "Turn here," Romulus says suddenly, pointing the way up a narrow road.

"What for?"

"They got the best *mititei* in whole world. Like this"—he spans his wrist with his fingers.

The stand with *mititei*—those juicy, oblong meatballs made of pork, lamb and/or other meats—is part of a larger souk on a steep, leafy roadside, teeming with Roma with sun-baked faces in flowered skirts, roving dogs, exhausted bus drivers and families. Next to the *mititei* stand are shops selling handwoven baskets and thick wool blankets covered on one side with a mat of long sheep's tresses still containing fragments of hay from the fields. A teenage boy with a soft face and enormous eyes wanders from table to table, holding an open fan of long butcher knives for sale. "Halloo!" shouts Romulus at an unshaven man stooped over a beer at one of the tables. He motions for us to sit down.

"This is bus driver," says Romulus, "when I come from Sibiu." The man wearily shakes my hand, then mumbles a few sentences.

"He say he fucking sick with this goddamn job," Romulus tells me with a flat respect in his voice. "You know his, what you call it, schedule? From Bucharest to Dej every day, six days a week, ten hours each way, sleep overnight in back of bus."

I mime sympathetic gestures, offer the man some of the *mititei* we're ordering. The servers cooking the meat on a charcoal grill are incongruously chic young women with gleaming painted lips, long pearly fingernails and shiny moussed hair. Romulus brings several meatballs over on a paper plate with dabs of mustard. I break one open; it's ultra-rare inside.

"Aren't these made of pork? You can't eat pork rare."

Romulus bites off the end of one. "Better this way."

"You can get trichinosis, you know, a disease."

Mouth full, Romulus shrugs me off with a wave of his hand. "Only in America. Meat is safe here." So I bite into one of the meatballs, which is fragrant with spices and tangy with fresh meats.

It's late in the afternoon when we reach nearby Braşov, a city founded by the Teutonic Knights in the 1200s. A calm elation has spread over us, created by the wild, trembling firs of the Carpathians and the crystal sharpness of the mountain air. Walking past the gothic Black Church, we survey the square, framed by buildings in cotton-candy colors like a Bavarian town's. While Romulus smokes, I gape at a dirty begging child holding a nearly comatose baby in a matted pink bunny suit. "Don't you know they rent those kids?" he says, hoping to nip some naive show of charity on my part. He makes a point of ignoring them and turns his head away, blows a few smoke rings toward the blue rim of mountains surrounding the city.

Exhausted from only a few hours of driving, I suggest we hire a taxi to see the town. Romulus signals a rust-encrusted Toyota and spends a few minutes bargaining with the unshaven driver, who's been hunched in the front seat over a scandal sheet. Thrilled at his catch, he gives us a royal tour, pointing out the remnants of the city walls and the oldest original portal, known as Caterina's Gate. Then his broken-down car putt-putts up a steep hill to the remains of the sixteenth-century citadel. Bad as my Romanian is, I realize that not everybody we encounter is speaking it. "Are they speaking a dialect of German?" I ask. Romulus and the taxi driver exchange a sly, cynical look. "Hungarian," spits Romulus, as if it were a curse word. They're part of the 1.7 million Hungarian ethnics who live in Romania, mostly here in Transylvania, who don't call this city Braşov, but Brassó; and tension between them and ethnic Romanians is legendary. Things are quiet now, but in the past there was constant struggle for ascendancy, climaxing during the last days of Carol II, when Hungary, at the behest of the Nazis, again took Transylvania for itself. Romulus, a Transylvanian, has an innate resentment of these Hungarians, aggravated by his difficult days in Budapest.

At my request, the driver takes us to a Roma settlement, built against a quarry. No one but them has claimed this site, because of the danger of falling rocks. According to the driver, the mayor wants to demolish their shantytown anyway, now that it's started to grow.

It's a bare-dirt encampment with shacks made out of anything at hand: corrugated fiberglass sheeting and car fenders, hastily sawed boards. As soon as we enter, in a cloud of whitish dust, a glowering man rushes toward the car, followed by three raggedy children holding sticks. Nonchalantly the driver swerves away from them and heads for a small incline to show us the outhouses: five tiny shacks, like miniature cottages in a fairy tale, with ramshackle doors and roofs painted bright pinks, greens and yellows.

On the way out, the same man tries running toward us again, a look of outraged dignity on his face. I'll understand his expression only too well when I read about Gypsy encampments set ablaze by town vigilantes in Isabel Fonseca's book *Bury Me Standing*. But thanks to Panaït Istrati, I already have a very noble image of the Gypsies, personified by his magnificent character Trăsnilă in *The Bandits*, a boldly heroic giant whose arms swing "like dangling posts" and crush the bones of the Boyar tyrants, and who is willing to die to preserve his identity.

The next morning we start out for a nearby ski resort, Poiana Braşov, which is not far from the city. Just outside town, bucolic Romania unveils abruptly. An adolescent farm boy stands with whittled staff in hand, herding goats against a background of all of Braşov on the next hill. We leave him behind and struggle up tortuously steep roads. Deep gorges spill away from the wheels of the car, and narrow curves clog with traffic. "Faster," Romulus keeps chanting, his hand caressing the back of my neck. Every nerve of my body feels open to sensation, and my eyes drink in the lush mountain landscape.

We pile into an aerial cable car, which begins its long ascent to the mountaintop. Gusts of wind send it gently swinging on the single cable from which it hangs. Below us are the ribbons of ski trails, snaking gracefully to the top. We get out near the summit, where the thin air mixes with my elation of being there. A much more agile, exhilarated Romulus scrambles upward and holds out a hand to hoist me to him. I struggle breathlessly up the steep incline until we reach the top. The view below sends my head spinning, but Romulus unzips his fly and takes a whiz, the stream arcing high into the sharp, cold air.

An hour later, we're still at the cable station, waiting to get down, eyes fixed on the car, which is suspended stock still halfway up the mountain. My pulse is racing. I'm shaking with panic. "It's broken. We'll be here until tomorrow morning. They're stuck."

"Always you worry. Probably turned off power for a while, to save money."

Forty-five minutes later the gears groan and the car jerks forward, swinging crazily as it advances toward us. Inside the car, there are paper cups and an empty wine bottle. Our driver is drunk. "You see," says Romulus, "they were just having party."

By now we know where we're going. I've bought Romulus a card for his cell phone and he's used it to call his mother, who's expecting to meet us at his apartment for dinner. But the route to Sibiu is roundabout and full of bumps as we try to cross westward in the Carpathians. Since we were considering going to Sibiu, we should have taken a more northwesterly route, instead of driving to Braşov. Not only that, but we've gone right past places I would have been thrilled to see, such as the castle district of Sinaia, where so many royal family dramas took place. We begin a zigzagging backtrack toward Sibiu, full of wrong turns and surprises. At first the road squeezes between steep mountains littered with loose boulders, which only makes the other drivers more frantic. They shoot past me on the curves, then screech back into their lane just in time to avoid a barreling truck. The dense firs block out the light, creating a greenish nighttime. My eyes are glued to the road unblinkingly, and so are Romulus's. His hand strays again to the back of my neck. "For a gay you are good driver." Then suddenly the line of cars in front of us comes to a halt.

The wait is endless and unfathomable, and I try to pattern myself after Romulus, who uncomplainingly fills the time with yawns and channel-switching on the radio, then lights a cigarette or unwraps a stick of gum. When a horse-drawn wagon lopes toward our front window, the Roma driver holding out an array of pencils and combs, he ignores him, not even bothering to tell him to go away.

At my urging we study the map again and find a series of rural roads leading back south and then to Sibiu, with fewer trucks and less traffic. We drive through a kaleidoscope of tiny, wistfully bucolic towns, each with its own way of slowing our progress to a near stop. In one, geese waddle forever across the road at each farmhouse. In another, we're halted by a procession of sheep; still another has lines of farmers carting hay, who nonchalantly hog half the road.

To my left outside one village stretches a vast field of alfalfa being plowed by a middle-aged peasant couple and a single ox. The dirty, sunburned face of the woman is framed by a blue kerchief. She's wearing a flowered skirt and a soiled red apron over thick woolen leggings. Unable to resist, I pull the car over to study her and her husband, who's wearing mud-caked blue overalls and high rubber boots. Placid focus ripples from their sunlit faces. They stop for a moment to stare unabashedly at us, then go back to work, unruffled by the attention. In their imperturbable eyes, I sense an equilibrium where the world of dreams and the imagination of myths are one with the world of waking and working. It's a mystical integrity rooted in the flow of life's energies, the very same state I futilely search for in love. What I don't understand yet is that this sense of wholeness flows into loss—and death as well.

Closer to Sibiu, the road is filled with anxious hitchhikers: couples and teenagers; businesswomen in high heels; old peasant grandmothers in boots, kerchiefs and aprons; an occasional nun. The rubber boots, leather vest and conical suede hat of a shepherd fascinate me, so I stop to pick him up. He overwhelms the car with a smell of lanolin, coming from his body like a thick cloud around his softly smiling face. He's nearly mute, and even Romulus makes no attempt to communicate with him. When Romulus's cell phone goes off and he seems to be discussing some off-color business involving pimping with a friend, our quiet passenger—who seems separated from us by several centuries—doesn't even flinch.

We let him out several miles down the road. He tries to press the equivalent of twelve cents into my hand to pay for the ride, but I refuse. The man gets red in the face, dismayed, Romulus explains, that I take him for a freeloader. He calms down only when I offer to take a picture of him as payment instead. He roots both rubber-booted feet on the road, cocks his conical-hatted head and lapses into that same expression I saw on the faces of the plowing peasants. It's simple but opaque, as if he were stubbornly present in an unconflicted way. I'll be thinking about it for the remainder of the trip, because now it has hit me: That attitude is still present in Romulus, if half lost.

We drive through Sibiu in early evening, and I'm fascinated by the caved-in beauty of some of the neighborhoods, collapsing elegantly under the weight of five hundred years. Like Braşov, this is a German town full of pastel buildings, stone-paved streets, crumbling walls and gothic and Renaissance churches. Preserved within it is the real presence of the late medieval, not a replica of it found in some of the restored towns of Western Europe. We're only passing through, however, headed for the edge of the city, to his apartment in the block, toward which my money has gone and which I've imagined so many times in fantasy.

It's almost just as I've imagined: smog-stained gray concrete buildings sprouting satellite dishes, children's voices echoing from the terraces, and near the parking lot, several steel rectangles used for hanging and beating rugs. Romulus's neurasthenic sensitivity, which I realize reminds me of a small-boned, intelligent dog's, has heightened. I can see his Adam's apple bob as he swallows nervously, and I assume he's wondering how I'll react to the place he calls home. His hard brown eyes, shiny as seeds, are opaque to my questioning glances. He leads me into a dirty lobby and then a very narrow elevator, so small that we're pressed against each other. It makes a terrifying racket, and we ascend to the ninth floor in pitch blackness; either the light's broken or there isn't any.

The elevator door screeches open just as the elevator comes to a jolting stop, which almost catapults us out of it. Before Romulus can use his key, the door to his apartment opens, revealing an adolescent blonde, shockingly similar to those I've concocted in my most paranoid fantasies.

"I thought you were never coming back," she says to him in a quiet, wounded voice, before fixing me with cold, guarded eyes that betray a hint of fear and translating the sentence into English. "I thought he was never coming back, mister."

In an abashed but somehow sadistic gesture, Romulus pushes her toward me. "My girlfriend, Elena." But she turns away and rushes to him, squashing her lips and body against his. I stand watching, taking in her oatmeal complexion and steel-blue eyes. Only the slightly bulbous nose I'd imagined is missing, but she's wearing the skin-tight jeans. She holds out a damp, limp hand to mine, her eyes dull and contemptuously suspicious, then picks up my bag and disappears with it into a bedroom, while Romulus, in a shaky voice tempered with bravado, whispers, "I hope you don't mind."

"Why didn't you tell me?"

"I'm thinking things going too well, you know. I'm going to tell you on Marie's bed at Bran. But something about your eyes."

"Take me to a hotel."

"As you wish, but now, please, tonight must be my guest. Whole family coming to meet you and..." His nerve fades and a real sign of fear creeps into his stance. "You are mad? But you saying you don't care about me and girls."

Mad isn't the word for it. A giant scimitar has crashed from heaven, severing me from the last few hours. Marie's alpine bedroom and the Gypsy huts, Poiana Braşov and the thrilling gorges are dissolving into nothingness, having never existed because everything I was feeling—elation, intimacy, fascination—was connected to my faith in our relationship and now seems like nothing more than my projection.

A coffin of steel compresses my throat in a feeling akin to withdrawal as I struggle to reply; but Elena reenters, sniffing at the bad vibes in the air. She studies me the way a person with animal phobias studies the details of an unknown dog, then shoots an accusatory glance at Romulus as her eyes narrow cynically.

"Come, come," he says, sweeping past her, forced joviality yet true hospitality in his voice. "I show to you the room. Is big but television don't work. If you prefer, you take my room."

Elena trails morosely behind as he leads me into a large unpainted bedroom, similar to one in a New York project, with a sagging couch bed and an enormous TV. Someone has turned the broken TV into an objet d'art, adding a symmetrical display of spotlessly clean empty liquor bottles and polished beer cans, plus a few giveaways, such as a button with Jim Carrey on it.

"I said, Take me to a hotel."

Romulus runs a nail-bitten hand through his hair as the girl studies him; he rubs one eye in anguish and shakes his head. "Please, please, Bruce, just a couple days, then we leave and everything forgotten." The word "forgotten" brings a flash of panic to the girl's eyes.

"You don't like it here?" she sneers, and marches out of the room again.

"You love her, don't you."

He fakes a short, supercilious laugh. "Hah. Me? No."

"And she knows about me?"

"Of course not, only one who knows something, that's Bogdan, 'cause he do similar in the past."

"I'll find the hotel myself." I pick up my bag.

"Please, please, Bruce. One night."

Elena has come in with a quart of beer and is pouring him a glass. He glowers at her until she extends the bottle toward me from a distance. "Want a drink?" she mumbles disingenuously as I shake my head.

A hollow bang reaches us from the hallway as the apartment door is pushed open and slammed against the wall. A powerful bass voice booms, "Romulus?" Then a man comes toward us grinning. He's massive and barrel-chested with generous features, a nearly shaven head and one earring, like a kind of friendly Bluto from *Popeye*. "Bruce!" he thunders, crushing my hand in his. "Ha, famous Bruce, I finally meet! This is famous Bruce? Bruce Willis, Bruce Springsteen or Bruce Lee?"

He's Bogdan, Romulus's bouncer-and-boxer brother, evident from the emblematic bandage over one brow, covering stitches. "So Bruce, Romania you like?"

"Sure, sure," I answer a little nervously. Then he's silent, having spoken all the words in English he knows.

He's followed moments later by a very incongruous girlfriend, an attractive, savvy-looking woman dressed much too chicly for the environment in a tight pricey silver blouse. Her makeup is Kabuki-thick, highlighted by a strange sharp brown outline of pencil around a heavily lipsticked mouth.

"I am Iris Dumitriu," she says suavely, in nearly perfect English. "How was the driving?"

Frantic for some connection, I latch on to her as we walk to the kitchen. She keeps her eyes, which seem metallic because of the fluorescent-green eye shadow, assiduously away from mine and reacts noncommittally to all my remarks. Is it because she knows something? Flatly she explains that she just got back from Japan two days ago, where she was working as a "dancer and hostess"—a term she pronounces in a precise, detached voice. The money was good, but she detested it and got tired of serving those "midgets" steamed towels and bowing to them. Now she and Bogdan plan to do nothing for the next couple of years. The $40,000 she brought back is quite a lot of money to have in Romania. A sense of satisfied anticipation flows coolly from her about her wealthy future, and it's evident that Bogdan, who couldn't be a more improbable partner for her, is excited about it, too.

The next to pound on the door is Floritchica, Romulus's grinning, portly forty-something mother. Her face is brown and shaped like an apple, her features sweet, elfin and sensual. "Bruce," she says, almost seductively, "speak no English I am sorry." With her is her youngest son, Renei, seventeen, lost and intense, dark like her. A quiet fascination shoots from his sloe eyes at the sight of me, and when he presses his hand to mine he is trembling with excitement. With a twinge of guilt I find myself wishing I'd met him instead of the jaded Romulus. Romulus catches the feeling in my eyes.

Whiskey and beer are flowing when Romulus's stepfather,

Silviu, a stocky blond with an exhausted, disillusioned look, arrives with the middle brother, Vlad, a handsome, grinning adolescent with clumsy, abrupt gestures. They've all gathered around me as if I were some exotic animal. Floritchica musters her spare command of English. "Tell me, Bruce, why you come to Romania?"

Uneasily, I launch into an explanation about an assignment in Budapest, but Romulus stops me right away by saying, "Bruce, in this place they will want to hear something short."

"To be with Romulus," I say, testing the limits. Everybody grins at the response except Elena, who sneaks her hand into Romulus's. Floritchica makes a remark to Romulus in Romanian and beams at me.

"She say you look like politician," he says. My eyes cloud as I think of Romania's long problem with corruption, but Romulus adds, "Is a compliment."

Floritchica has her youngest son translate to me that she'd like to make me dinner but has no money for it, so I slip the equivalent of twenty-five dollars into her hand. "Bruce, you speak *franceză*?" she asks. I nod.

"Merchi beaucoup, voush e formidable," she tells me, kissing me a little too lingeringly on the cheek.

When I walk down the hall to the bathroom, I see Romulus making up my bed, so I slip quickly into the bedroom and close the door. My eyes are stinging with resentment. It catches in my throat, making me cough, as if I were having an allergic reaction.

"Does she live here?"

He looks frightened, as if I were about to hit him. But then there's something else, like a curious erotic anticipation of punishment, which he deserves and desires. He nods almost ritualistically in an admission of guilt.

"How long?"

"Bruce, is nothing. One of girls I work with."

"You mean she's a whore?"

Relieved at the categorization, he nods again, almost eagerly. "You know, when I go to club, maybe there is foreigner looking for girl. So her I send." He makes a dismissive gesture with his hand, as if he were shooing away a fly.

"But she's your girlfriend, too."

Reluctantly he nods again. And suddenly, based on her obvious hostility to me, I have an insight. "She's the same one who was in Budapest, isn't she."

Again a reluctant nod. And as he sees my jaw stiffen, the color flood from my face at the thought of all the times I was probably paying for her, too, he adds quickly, "But really, Bruce, is nothing. She say she love me, but I do not love her. You say you don't care about the girls, now, suddenly, is something. I don't see why—"

Before he can finish, Elena has popped urgently into the room. Romulus is bending to tuck in a sheet in a futile effort to pretend business as usual. She enlaces his waist and yanks him toward her stubbornly, all the while looking at me in an invitation to take close note of the gesture. "I thought he was never coming back," she says to me accusingly.

In a kind of helpless schizophrenia, Romulus blocks out my presence and turns to take her in his arms. "Well, I back now," he tells her, and caresses her hair, "so shut up already." They kiss.

Surprised by the acidic nausea welling up in my throat, I leave the room, holding back angry tears by telling myself that the whole thing is ridiculous anyway. Strangely, the hurt is less uncomfortable than the enormous task of revision, like the deleting and reformatting of a hard drive. There is one benefit from this experience. None of these people, except perhaps Romulus, seems capable of carrying out the blackmail I've fantasized.

More guests have come to meet "the American." A sturdy, starkly handsome twenty-year-old named Mircea, with olive skin and pale green eyes framed by delicate eyebrows, holds out a gentlemanly hand and crushes mine. I notice fresh scabs over each knuckle. "This is bouncer at club, like me," explains Bogdan. The two sit back on the couch in a pose that couldn't exist in the States without the wrong interpretation. Bogdan has his arm around the junior bouncer, who has rested his head on Bogdan's shoulder. The image unleashes fantasies in me, part vengeful but mostly just horny. Meanwhile handsome Mircea is staring at me with eager urgency, curious about every gesture or emotion on my face, as I struggle to hide my suffering and keep my eyes away from his crotch.

Behind me, Iris, who is standing with Elena, holds out a camera. "Would you, Bruce?" It's a high-priced Nikon with an enormous lens, obviously one of the spoils of her stay in Japan.

The two girls—two whores, it occurs to me—laughingly pose in an erotic parody, clasping each other by the neck and touching tongues. Focusing the shot gives me a chance to study Elena's skin. Beneath the makeup, it's flawed by acne scars; also, her forehead is too convex, its bulge overshadowing otherwise regular features. I'm ashamed to admit to myself how much this pleases me.

The appearance of the camera leads to a round of picture-taking. Everybody wants to be photographed with Bruce. Mama encircles me with her short arms and pulls me against her body. She's soft and fragrant, having splashed on perfume for the occasion. For one picture, young Renei strikes a karate pose and gazes straight at me, as I stand with arms at my sides, grinning stiffly, at a loss as to what complementary gesture to make. In fact, I'm overcome by his large liquid eyes, upon which seem to float all his fears and dark imaginings. At my most mesmerized point the flash goes off, catching me in embarrassing sensual fascination. But Renei's hypersensitive glance isn't really directed at me; it's a limpid, swirling pond ready to suck in anything. His vulnerable face is starting to unsettle me; it takes all my strength not to keep staring.

During all this, only Romulus's stepfather Silviu sulks, in the background, sucking at his beer, refusing to be in any of the pictures. It's then that I remember the small gifts from America I packed for the possibility of meeting his family: Renei gets a black T-shirt from New York's East Village with the word "FUCK" repeated all over it, which he seems to adore; my "mother-in-law," a scented soap and a scarf; and for Bogdan, Vlad and Silviu, small light-intensive flashlights. But Silviu shakes his head when I hand him his gift.

"What's the problem?" I ask Romulus, who stays mute, looking embarrassed.

"Give to me American money," says Silviu with a sardonic grimace.

Affronted, I answer, "First give me the flashlight back."

He hands it to me, and I hand him thirty American dollars from my wallet, then pass ten each to the other members of the family.

Pocketing the money, Silviu says, "Ceauşescu good."

Renei tries to explain. "My father don't like capitalism, Bruce. He old-fashioned. Saying under Ceauşescu he not worry, everything paid for. Now, he only make maybe sixty dollar a month as construction worker. And during summer, even less because construction stop and he need to work as security guard. He don't like capitalism, he don't like America."

Surreptitiously, I study Silviu's blond face, which must have been very handsome once upon a time, but now projects palpable depression and distrust, especially when he glances at his wife.

The last to arrive is Iris's father, Mr. Dumitriu, a man in his sixties who lives on the floor above. He's frowsy, unshaven and alcoholic-looking, with bitter blue eyes ringed by gray circles. He tells me frankly that he's a bankrupt jeweler. With passable English, he tries to draw me into conversation about exactly what's ruining the economy of Romania.

"The greed of certain people, Bruce, pull this country to its knees."

"But aren't there greedy people in every country, Mr. Dumitriu?"

"Ah, but here we are cursed with special problem."

"What is that?"

"Why, the Jews, of course."

"Hmm." I take an overlarge gulp of whiskey.

"You are thinking," he says, searching my face, "that I live in the past. That Jews are gone now. That this happened before war."

"Look, Mr. Dumitriu, even before the war, it wasn't the Jews that—"

He interrupts me. "You know, of course, there are only couple thousand of these robbers left in this country. So where did they go, while us rest are under the yoke of the Communists? They go to Israel, after cursing us with Communism, which they were instrumental to bringing. Then off they go merrily, leaving us in misery."

Knowing that it's futile, I'm drawn in anyway, and my voice has gotten shrill. "You know why there weren't many Jews left here after the war, don't you? And the others had to leave because the Communists persecuted them. Ceaușescu was actually in the business of *selling* Jews to Israel! But even if what you're saying made any sense, which it doesn't, it really doesn't, well...they're gone now."

"Oh, in this you are wrong, my friend. These few Jews still hold all the powerful positions, and we are slaves to them, penniless."

"I'm Jewish."

"And I know."

Iris intervenes. "Shut up, Papa. Leave the man alone."

Mr. Dumitriu stands shakily and bows formally, irony distorting his smile. "Very nice to meet you, Mr. Bruce. That isn't very Jewish name." Then he walks out the door, leaving me to ponder uneasily who told him I was Jewish and why.

Mama calls from the kitchen. *"Masă!"** In the room where I'll sleep, she and Elena have set up a large folding table, groaning with an enormous dinner of roast chicken, *sarmale*, tzatziki, a plate of scallions, roast potatoes, tomatoes and several bottles of red wine. Beamingly she ushers us to the table and forces me to sit at the head. A toast is raised in my honor before the pack begins to devour the succulent food. Iris elegantly raises a whole scallion to her lipsticked mouth, nibbling on the white head, hardly touching the robust plate before her. By this time, things are a blur. Everybody, including me, is drunk. They've decided that after dinner Bruce and the family must visit the local disco where Bogdan and his friend work as bouncers and where Romulus, I now understand, pimps. The table is hurriedly dismantled.

Elena appears, changed for the club, having gone all-out as a pointed defense tactic. She's refreshed her lips with bright pink and added a thick new coat of foundation. Blue eye shadow and a false birthmark near her mouth complete the transformation. A cell phone is stuck in the waistband of her skintight gold Lurex slacks, and she's wearing those platform

shoes I concocted in my fantasies, probably based on shoes
I'd seen on the prostitutes in Budapest. She snakes her body
against Romulus, all the while throwing me a brash snarl.

Since it's Tuesday night, the disco's virtually empty, the
dance floor occupied by Romulus, Elena, Floritchica and
Romulus's brother Vlad. House music rattles my drunken
brain as I watch Elena shimmying backward, raising her
blouse to reveal naked breasts, and Romulus gyrating with
unzipped pants that have been lowered to show his pubic
hair. Vlad is shirtless, undulating seductively at his mother,
whose chubby arms are raised, her fingers snapping with
jubilation, her jarring smile like a proud mother's at a sporting event. For me, it's a surreal scene, a cartoon evocation of
my worst fantasies. Despite the nearly naked exhibition on
the dance floor, all the smiles indicate that everyone finds the
entertainment wholesome. Every other song, the DJ, a friend
of Romulus's, booms through the loudspeaker that the selection is dedicated to Bruce. I try to show my appreciation by
grinning at the DJ booth and waving a stiff hand.

Back at Romulus's apartment, I struggle to the bathroom
and vomit, and when I notice that trails of the stuff have
landed on my arms, I strip for a shower. But it's ice cold. It
turns out that the hot water in the block is turned off every
night at eleven until the next morning. So I sponge off the
mess with a cold washcloth and head for bed.

Moments after I switch off the light, I hear bare feet pad-
ding toward me. Hovering above me in the dark is the face
of Elena, still as stony-looking but with its mouth fixed in a
sympathetic smile.

"Bruce," she says, "are you sad?"

"What do you care?'

Taken aback, she answers confusedly, "You mustn't be sad,
Bruce. You will find somebody."

Whatever Romulus has told her, she obviously feels reassured enough to make this awkward gesture of largesse, so a vengeful recklessness takes over me. "Then why don't you send Romulus's brother Renei in here?"

The vulgar remark doesn't have the shock effect I was expecting. Instead she answers, "We all know you like Romulus's brother. But we cannot tell him that, we wouldn't know how."

"Don't worry about it," I mutter, and turn my humiliated face toward the wall.

XVIII

Sleep doesn't come. After an hour or so of spinning, the room is coated with fuzzy particles, like a low-resolution print. The hot night air is palpable, encasing me in a form of paralysis. A dull realization has surfaced, signaling the end of my fantasy life. With tonight's revelations, the mechanism of my imagination has been shattered. All those narratives of sex and fear, fueled by lack of knowledge, have been deflated. There's no more secret Romulus to explore, no treacherous family to fear, no more invented girlfriend to star in paranoid scenarios of betrayal. I've seen them all in flesh and blood. Crushing boredom, worse than the lacerating pain of passion, lowers against me; inspiration is over.

What strikes me more than my loss is the banality of reality, always unavoidable. It's reduced my adventure to a humdrum story, no more interesting than the story of any other masochistic relationship. When I think about it, Romulus's neglecting to mention there was a girl means little. He'd told me from the start there'd be girls in his life, and I'd agreed. But in order for my passion—that great machine of creation—to continue its fantasy production, she had to remain at a more remote level. Now not even the codeine I was taking can bring back the bright, fearful world that was fueled by my own self-deception.

Should I go back to New York? I've already drained that location of meaning. All trajectories promise only drops through ashen chutes to dust piles. I can't think about movement of any kind.

Unable to sleep, I turn on the light and from my bag take the large monograph on the Romanian sculptor Brancusi that I'd brought with me to read. I thumb through the pages haphazardly, looking at the smooth ovoid shapes. His sculptures strike me as puzzles. There's a stillness and passivity to them, just as on the faces of the peasants I saw; yet enigmatically, they hint of living, uninterrupted pulses deep inside. All of his figures—bodies, heads and birds—are purposely incomplete, cryptic synecdoches for entities and natural processes.

The streamlined pieces in reflective bronze or marble draw my eyes to them again and again, looking for signs of life. Their allure is too much like what I've been enduring: drawn over and over toward a beautiful blank form, which I suspected held some warm, embracing vitality deep within.

The most elliptically shaped remind me of something else, too. They produce the same effect as that new trance that came over me in the countryside before Sibiu, similar to but even better than the opioids. What was it? A hypnotic fascination on seeing those light-shredding firs; the ancient, indifferent rock formations; but most of all, the sun-streaked meadows and peasants' faces caught in conflict-free congress with Nature...

Brancusi himself, I learn, was one of these poor peasants, from the hamlet of Hobiţa in the region of Oltenia. At the age of seven, in the late nineteenth century, he climbed the hills of the Carpathians with shepherd staff in hand; and according to the author of this monograph, Ionel Jianou, he never lost his cosmic connection to natural processes, even when he moved to Paris, reached by a marathon hike almost all the way from Romania.

Like his sculptures, his biography reveals only a tantalizing surface. It has been shaped into an aesthetic gesture shrouded in mystery, which lets sensual elements peek out coyly. True, there's a worldly, decadent period near the turn of the twentieth century, when he's young, experimenting with café society and hashish and women and orgies with his friend, the relentlessly degenerate Modigliani; but a traumatic love affair with a very perverse heiress, an American—possibly Peggy Guggenheim—turns sour, setting him on a path of renunciation that leads to an interest in Eastern philosophy and primitive art.

Later in life, Milarepa's Tibetan Book of the Dead becomes his Bible, and he becomes a virtual hermit, hidden in his studio in Montparnasse, executing the same forms over and over. Alienated from anything that seems contrived, he uses direct carving, like a peasant, instead of models, believing that each piece of stone or wood holds some spirit he must release.

His studio is a shrine in which the precise arrangement of sculptures takes on occult value. As he grows older, dressed in the all-white costume of the Romanian peasant, he makes an eccentric white-bearded figure on the streets of Paris.

White: for purity and mourning. With shepherd's flute tucked into his waistband, he leads a white dog to cafés and movies and even glittering social events. In his studio, covered in white dust from his work with marble, he cooks the organs of animals in a clay oven he built himself, serves his white dog milk from a white washbasin and makes everything by hand; and he even sets his own leg in white plaster when he breaks it at an isolated country retreat.

Noguchi became his apprentice in 1927. Brancusi told

him that the saw he used had to cut only with its own weight, regardless of how long it took, that the marks left by the axe blade had to remain as tangible signs of the contact between man and matter. All this contributes to Ionel Jianou's theory that Brancusi succeeded in expressing the simple, spiritual yet cryptic world of the Romanian peasant—a pagan, mystical world, intimately linked to the earth, to matter.

The story chips away at my brain like a mason's tool hollowing an aperture in a sealed room—especially when I study the many incarnations of *The Kiss*. Pictures and reproductions of this work have been so well distributed that it has the banal familiarity of a Mona Lisa. Earlier versions depict an embracing couple as a single block of stone, fused eternally in hermetic union. The bodies of the two lovers in *The Kiss* have melted together. I can hardly make out the woman's boyish breast because it fits so well into the concave curve of the man's chest. It's as if the two were one androgynous object, a neutered union that has sacrificed some of its dynamic tension.

In all these sculptures, the lovers are eye to eye, fixated on each other; but they're so close that they're beyond the focus of their sight. They can't see each other and don't need to. In some, their eyes are even fused together, forming one obscene, bulging cleft circle, like a fertilized ovule, or even a female pubis and its slit.

Love is stone. Is that the message—that in deep love there's no psychology, only unity, design?

Reading on about Brancusi's life, I begin to see the sculptures as indicative of his bachelor state. The last half of his life was spent in nearly total isolation. The kiss may be a remembered one that represented a missed opportunity and led to forty years of artistic creation. Brancusi's fantasies of union in stone seem pre-oedipal and infantile, attempts to reproduce the undifferentiated bliss of the child and the breast. Eyes, ears and noses have all but disappeared, buried in their closeness or perhaps not even yet born from the stone. The moment of the kiss is eternal, like suspension in the womb. So static has the moment become that it represents what we all must miss—security, pleasure. Even so, I can guess the truth: his life is a story of disillusionment with the Other and with love.

The book confuses me, and I put it down. The lack of psychological content in these forms, the elimination of a nose in some...the blankness of the eyes...seem to portray what I'm feeling, a loss of differentiation and identity...both damaged by the foolish expense of desire. In Brancusi, at least, the lovers are equal and eternal, and in fact, one of these sculptures was made as the headstone for a tomb. But what about me? My kiss is ephemeral, it would be embracing thin air.

There is, however, another feature: his spiritualization of matter. He may have failed in human love, but he found vitality and comfort in some hidden life force, which was rooted in Romania. According to the critic Jean Cassou, who wrote the introduction to this monograph in the 1960s, Romania "still maintains an essentially prehistoric appearance. It remains at the stage of the primitive herdsman, of gods and fables." At such a stage, "the spirit retains its natural quality. It is an elemental spirit, a spirit of the mountains, rivers and forests, a rural consciousness, the verb of all creation." Brancusi may have been irrevocably disappointed in love, but perhaps he was able to relocate desire on the cosmic plane.

I think I saw such union with matter in the faces of the peasants, but I didn't realize then why it was so compelling. Even stranger, I could swear I've glimpsed it inside Romulus, a corrupted hustler. A kind of trance; something fatalistic referring to the myth of Miorița, the shepherd's ecstatic union with death. It could be that all this obsessive behavior on my part has merely been an attempt to link myself to it.

If so, there's no reason to put up any fight. What good would it do? I take another look at the soft irony of Romulus's preposterous TV installation, with its symmetrical arrangement of Budweiser cans and empty gin bottles around the big, broken television. Then I head quietly for the bathroom, hearing on the way, as I near Romulus's bedroom, a bed creaking, and moaning endearments in Romanian, which pass through me, not affecting my mood, as if they were the sound of wind rustling and the bleating of Miorița.

XIX

The next day, in the calm of shock, I stick to my resolve to find a hotel while we're in Sibiu. Romulus takes me to the Împăratul Romanilor (Roman Emperor) Hotel, an eighteenth-century building that once hosted Brahms and Liszt. It's on Nicolae Bălcescu Street near the beautiful Piaţa Mare, and it's only thirty dollars a night. The lobby is so overcrowded with real and fake antiques that it looks like a shop. My room is Empire style, with a walnut bed and a woven spread in burgundy and ivory colors, which match the rug.

I head right for the marble-floored bathroom, but the water filling the tub is ice cold. It takes several calls to reception for the truth to come out. First I'm told to leave it running for a long time, then to wait an hour, but finally they admit that the boiler is out of order. So I endure an ice-cold sponge bath and fall into a doze on the firm mattress.

Warm and more sweet-tempered than I've ever seen him, Romulus, with chastened eyes, sits patiently by the bed, waiting for my nap to be over. He's left a sulking Elena at home and wants to show me the city, of which he's proud. But when I awake, in a mini-fit of ill temper, I tell him I plan to spend the day alone. Real disappointment floods his eyes, and in his face I catch another glimpse of that soft, pastoral fatalism I'm beginning to understand he's hiding. Quickly it's replaced by the usual cynical pallor as he dryly agrees to my request, asking only that I stop at his mother's place with him first, since she's counting on seeing me.

She lives on the ground floor of a much smaller building than Romulus's. It's the same two-room apartment that Romulus endured with his father and three brothers during adolescence and where his father sleeps in the kitchen by the gas stove, just as he did in the apartment in Vîlcea. There are a couple of lurid tapestries on the wall, a waterfall and a forest scene; and over a bookcase, a black-and-white first communion photo of Romulus at seven, looking oversensitive and optimistic. The room is shabby yet scrupulously neat, with even the couch pillows arranged in a geometric design.

But we've walked in on a disturbing scene. Renei, the youngest, is marching in circles around the small, freshly vacuumed room, mumbling to himself and swatting at the air. Floritchica, distraught and pale, is sitting on the couch and wringing her hands as she stares at him. When I ask what's wrong, Romulus in English and Mama in French offer a disjointed explanation. It seems that Renei has been having mental attacks, characterized by racing thoughts, which come close to being aural hallucinations. His mind shouts at him; he can't stop thinking or pacing, has bouts of agoraphobia or suddenly is struck mute, and the only way he can break these spells is by turning over a table or kicking a hole in the wall.

I can read the process in his eyes, which focus and unfocus repeatedly, showing an awareness of my presence by warm, friendly glances, then abruptly spacing out, after which the eyes turn blank and the pacing and tortured mumbling start again.

It's a pathetic sight. The muscles in his young body twitch as if at the beginning of an epileptic attack, then relax again just as suddenly. There's something luminous about his gingery skin and swimmingly anguished face that projects a heroic vulnerability. Because he's so transparent, what he's feeling flows toward me in unimpeded waves, engulfing me in its torment. Eventually he's exhausted by the whole process, which I'm told has been going on all night, and I'm left wondering whether his condition has something to do with overstimulation from my visit. He struggles to the bed in the tiny kitchen, and when we check on him a few moments later is asleep.

Romulus says that the doctors have diagnosed it as a panic disorder. But Floritchica can't afford the antidepressants that were prescribed, and after a month, Renei stopped taking them. I try to gather my wits, wonder whether I should offer money for antidepressants; but when I whisperingly suggest it to Romulus, he counsels me not to by saying, "This is too much bigger for you to take on, Bruce. Better to do nothing."

I study Romulus's face with a sad sense of astonishment, realizing that one of his greatest talents is his ability to project composure. During our months together, while I believed intimacy was developing, he never mentioned this problem with his brother. How much is he hiding beneath those hooded eyes and laconic, coarse replies? Have I, all along, been totally unaware of the endurances of the person I've claimed to love? All at once, I catch a glimpse in him of the same neurasthenic sensitivity that flowed torturously from his brother. It makes me shudder.

Eyes moist, Mama pulls herself together and tiptoes into the kitchen to get the whistling teakettle. She brings it out and serves us tea with tiny anise cookies. She's like Renei, in that there's a vulnerability to her soft gestures; but as her ringed, alert eyes testify, there's also a kind of cunning.

"Vous savez, Bruce," she tells me in French, *"je mène une vie de chien."* I lead a dog's life.

"Pourquoi?" I ask, putting a sympathetic look into my eyes.

It seems she's just had a terrible argument with her husband, who refused to turn the thirty dollars I gave him—half a month's salary—over to her for housekeeping expenses. Instead, he'd disappeared for the entire night, didn't show up for his job as a security guard and came home at seven in the morning stewed and defeated, his clothing reeking of vomit. Then he left again. An image of his weary, accusing mouth, his lax, disillusioned stoop, flashes into my brain, filling me, for some reason I can't quite grasp, with anguish. But Floritchica has already mutated into a girlish, slightly flirtatious manner, shamelessly complimenting my blue-green eyes and my hands, which she says look like a writer's. Do I, she asks coyly, ever intend to write a book about them, believing, like almost every impoverished person I've met, that the story of her life would make a bestseller.

The conversation drifts to other matters, and by asking where her children are, I realize that none of them holds a regular job. Bogdan's occasional boxing and bouncing are now supplemented by his girlfriend's windfall, though no one as much as says so. Renei went to mechanic's school for a month but was thrown out when he hurled a wrench at a car window during a panic attack and now shares his father's sixty-dollar check, seldom leaving the house because of his bouts of agoraphobia. Vlad seems to pick up a buck as a runner for some substance, although whether this means he's a gofer for a local pharmacy or delivers illicit drugs never becomes clear.

As Romulus slips into a doze, I'm startled to find Floritchica hissing conspiratorially at me and signaling me to follow. She stands, and I find myself praying that we're not heading for the adjoining bedroom. But she leads me to the tiny kitchen, where I'm aghast to see her shaking exhausted Renei awake. In a severe whisper she commands him to do something, and I can make out that he's crossly refusing. Finally he sits up on the paltry kitchen cot with a sigh and reluctantly says, "My mother want me to say to you that she got something she going to tell you. She got a note in English that neighbor who studied in America helping her to write. Okay, Bruce?" and he falls back on the cot to stare at the ceiling, exhausted eyes pouring out misery.

With a sigh of satisfaction Floritchica sits on the edge of the cot and takes out a folded piece of paper. She begins to recite what is written on it in a singsong voice that betrays little knowledge of the meaning of each word:

"'Dear Bruce, I ask to you from bottom of heart please help me. Romulus he give me nothing. I will lose apartment in two months. Renei is so sick mentally. I don't know what do. I need seven thousand dollars to buy new apartment. Please, please, you must help me. Do not tell to Romulus I ask to you this.'"

Like a schoolgirl satisfied with a difficult recitation, she looks up from the note with a soft, foolish smile, her eyes sparkling with naive anticipation.

My heart thumps with embarrassment, and I try to avoid her gaze; but the room is so small, I manage only to fix my eyes on the handle of the refrigerator door, right below my waist.

"Please, Bruce."

I clear my throat several times, and in a strained, alien voice say, "Umm, I haven't really got that much money."

Floritchica gives me a doubtful look, like a motherly reprimand. "Is so much money for you?"

"I'm, uh, just a writer."

"*A writer?* So much money they make!"

"Look, Floritchica, I don't have much money. But I'll make a deal with you. I'm thinking maybe I'll write a book about us, I mean about me and Romulus and all of this. Now if I do that and I make, say, more than thirty thousand dollars, I'll give you your seven."

I can't believe what's just popped out of my mouth. But it seems to satisfy Floritchica. She stands up from the cot with a new energy, her eyes mirroring her imagined future. "Come," she says, "we have more tea." But first she shakes Renei to attention again and gives him another sentence to translate for me. "She say she need money for her own medicine, Bruce. Twenty dollars." I hand her the equivalent in Romanian money and she beams at me. As I walk back to the other room, Renei's voice reaches me in a ghostly moan. "Bruce, I am sorry!"

Romulus is sitting on the couch, playing with the settings on his sports watch. For a moment I think that he's set this up, but when his eyes narrow with suspicion at his mother, who avoids his glance nervously, I know he hasn't. "Hey, I've gotta go," I tell him in an abrupt, impatient voice. The urgency in my tone startles him into a standing position. Mama, on the other hand, seems weirdly trouble-free. She enlaces me again with her plump arms and pulls me to her breast for a warm, tear-stained good-bye.

As we walk toward a phone booth to call a taxi, I say, "Your old lady asked me for money."

Romulus takes a drag from his cigarette and exhales callously into the air. "My old lady," he says. "Well, I am not surprise, she can be real bitch. You not going to give her any, are you?"

*

That evening, Romulus insists on assembling a more civil Elena, a temporarily recovered Renei and me for a trip to a local club. We walk across the square to a squat, pistachio-colored medieval building and down a narrow, winding staircase in near darkness. Here in the cellar, to my amazement, is a goth disco. In windowless rooms, beneath vaulted brick ceilings, gyrate young Romanians with long, vampirish dyed-black hair, wrists sporting studded black leather bracelets and eyes circled in mascara. The techno goth music shrieks through the cavernous rooms as one young dancer, who seems caught in a trance, stands alone in the center of the floor, moving his upper body in big, careening circles. The others look on soberly as if they were participants in an occult rite. We drink huge steins of German beer until all of us are having trouble keeping our balance and I suggest it's time for me to go back to the hotel.

From my walnut bed, the high ceiling of the room looks mobile, hovering threateningly above me like the broad black expanse of a prehistoric bird. In the sweltering heat, an unenthusiastic breeze swells the heavy curtains. I half dream about swimming helplessly in some unfathomable night, a black ocean, distressed because my identity has floated away from me like a life preserver; I reach out for it, grabbing only handfuls of black. A sharp, precise knock on the door startles me fully awake.

Romulus has appeared, to spend the night in the hotel with me. When I grill him about what Elena may be thinking or whether or not they've had a fight, he shrugs off my questions. "This is of no importance."

In the darkness, he strips to his bikini underwear, crawls into bed and rolls toward me. The sensation of his body spirals me away from all resolve, and realizations and vows of the last thirty-six hours slip through my hands like wriggling fish. Sensation returns, a drug taking hold of my entire brain; but when I begin to caress his hard body, it feels dead, and a phrase from the novel *Là-bas* by J.-K. Huysmans spills into my mind: "He clasped a corpse, a body so cold that it froze him...." Although my hands keep moving down his lean, velvety chest to the coils of his abdomen, the refrigerator feeling is overwhelming, and I can't help asking what the matter is.

"Just go, go," he says, pushing my hand farther downward to his crotch, though his body keeps its rigidity with the arms straight at the side, like the victim of a ritual sacrifice.

XX

Cîntă cucul lăngă noi
Si ne iubeam pe zăvoi
Să fi murit amăndoi

Nearby the cuckoo cried
As we loved by the riverside
It's there we should have died

—FOLKSONG OFTEN
SUNG BY BRANCUSI

The heat wave, like an episode of shock, is over, too intense to be remembered exactly. Here in the mountains, a mild chill pings the air with promise and cures the past like a tonic. The girl Elena and Mama's request for a new apartment seem like a lost chapter, an interruption of fantasy—the kind felt by a junkie suddenly shaken awake, before he sinks once more into a fainting, timeless rush. Romulus and I are back together, approaching our seventh month together.

He is sitting next to me in the Dacia as we head north, sighing with relief at this new escape, glad to leave Elena and his problem-ridden family far behind. She'd been shrill and hysterical all morning, bursting into tears when he returned from the hotel, then begging and threatening when he announced his intention to continue with the trip. It dawned on him that my demands were far less difficult than hers to satisfy. His good-bye to her was cold.

Now, slowly, he's working to reestablish our complicity, sneaking a hand out from time to time to slap me playfully on the thigh. For him, being with me is like bachelorhood, since he has no template for considering himself gay. He's convinced himself that we share an ideal camaraderie that just happens to involve some inconvenient requests for sex—no big deal.

"You know, you are only friend I have in whole life?" he says to me as we drive past the fantastic homes of a wealthy Roma enclave, their pagoda-like aluminum gables glinting in the sun. The word "friend" lacerates me only slightly, like a paper cut that I try to medicate by answering, "You're my friend, too, and more."

For the last twenty minutes we've been caught behind an open truck of chestnut-colored horses, a situation I can't get used to. Seven of them are crowded on a flatbed protected only by a four-foot-high railing, phosphorescent diesel smoke spewing around them. As the truck careens around curves, they struggle for balance, falling one against the other, their dark eyes bulging with fright. Finally, the truck turns off and I barrel up the mountain road, even passing the white van ahead of us. At Romulus's insistence, I've learned some new skills of navigation, closer to those of the other drivers.

We zoom along for about twenty minutes until another open flatbed appears before us—it, too, carrying some live cargo. As we near it, I realize what it is: a peasant funeral. Dressed in their Sunday best, a family is crouching on the open platform, around a black coffin that has been draped with a black cloth. About twenty miles farther on, the cortege mercifully turns off; I press the pedal to the floor again.

We'd planned to leave this morning, but a late rising, complications from Elena and the decision to have lunch in Sibiu delayed our trip to four p.m. Our destination, which we hope to reach shortly after nightfall, is the region of Maramureş, near the Ukrainian border, one of the last untouched places on the continent of Europe. It's an area where farmers still toil the land with oxen and where some villagers still observe pre-Christian rites.

About sixty miles outside Sibiu, we're caught in the town of Alba Iulia in the midst of an animal fair. In a field, peasants are examining oxen, horses, goats and donkeys for sale. A long line of animals in pairs, reminiscent of those brought onto Noah's Ark, have clogged the highway. Three hours later, in an urban traffic jam, my throat is strangled by an acrid odor. We're nearing Turda, the glass-making town with the lead-ridden air. Surrounded by palpable, bluish-gray wisps of pollution, poorly fed factory workers line the road, waving glass vases and tumblers in the air at us as we pass, hoping to sell them for a few dollars. Within minutes, my head is pounding from—I assume—the toxic chemicals. Although no one has ever said Elena is from Turda, I remember my fantasy of a blonde being from that locale. Forever after, I'll associate my memory of Elena with this polluted town and its vaporized-metal odor.

After Turda, the air freshens and the houses become more suburban. Large storks' nests sit atop some of the telephone poles. Romulus has regressed into full bachelorhood rather annoyingly, pointing out anything on the road that looks female and making macho, predatory comments. I'm getting worried. Night's arriving, and the sky has darkened threateningly. Then, slowly, a few fat drops spatter the windshield.

I gun the engine, hoping that we're driving out of the

storm. When I reach eighty miles per hour, I have to come to a screeching stop in front of an enormous flock of sheep, which are claiming the entire highway. With curly tresses reaching almost to the pavement like astrakhans and led by a donkey saddled with one of their pelts, they're ambling down the road, oblivious of the cars in front of and behind them. Each of their beady eyes above pointed snouts is fixed and still, in an expression that reminds me of our hitchhiker's cryptic calm.

It's almost ten p.m. as we drive across the edge of the city of Cluj-Napoca. Then a stagy thunderstorm begins to follow us up and down the steep curves, strewing the road with slippery leaves and coating our windshield like vibrating gelatin. Forks of lightning burst through the sky, some so close I'm afraid they'll hit the car. We pass an old peasant woman who's already drenched to the bone, rivulets of water spilling from the folds of her kerchief onto her face. I try to slow down, to give her a ride, but the car behind me honks threateningly, signaling that it can't stop so suddenly on the slippery road. Going is rough. I've slowed down to about fifteen miles per hour.

It takes about three more hours to reach the town of Gherla, only thirty miles away. At a crossroads stands a frail girl, her body like a bowed sail against the oncoming rain. "It's a whore," says Romulus.

"You mean she's so desperate for a trick she's willing to stay out in this storm?"

"Hmm, hmm. Or maybe her people don't come to pick her up. Now she caught."

I shudder at the girl's situation, but Romulus adds, "Her pussy must be so wet now, because of rain."

"How can you think of such a thing when she's suffering like that?"

Romulus shoots me a contemptuous sneer. "Is normal. You think has not happened to me?"

After one a.m., between Dej and Baia Mare, as we descend a chain of mountains, the situation worsens. Bolts of lightning seem to land right on the pavement, illuminating the car in blinding explosions. Great gusts of wind try to nudge us off the road. Our leaf-coated tires begin to slide down hills, sending us across the road sideways. We make wide U's around fallen branches. From time to time, I pull over to the side of the road, wait to get back my nerve. Because we can see almost nothing, an endorphin-filled calm has invaded the car. Both of us stare without blinking through the spiraling sheets of rain caught in our headlights. This is a state of total alertness, the calm that strikes people faced with dire danger. Strangely, it forges a complicity between Romulus and me, emphasized by the touch of his rough hand on my neck.

As we ascend a narrow slope about thirty miles from Baia Mare, we come upon a dead body in the road. It's lying nose-down on the pavement in the rain, and no one has even bothered to cover it up. A few feet ahead we squeeze by a police van and the car of the driver who probably hit it. The sight comes as a shock to me, which I'm able to put out of my mind almost immediately; but from the corner of my eye, I can see that Romulus is quietly sulking. An hour later, all my senses are fixed on the red taillights in front of us, the only clue to the location of the road. "I cannot get feeling of dead body out of mind," Romulus blurts out, then launches into a potential scenario of peasant children waiting anxiously by the fire, only to discover that their father has been killed on the highway.

The story shames me, reveals my ruthless ability to forget traumatic images that stand in the way of my goals. I haven't been thinking about the dead body at all, just about getting to the end of the trip. Romulus is, I realize, more faceted than I've been conveniently supposing. He has to be hiding some delicate, even humanist, quality.

The minutes roll on excruciatingly slowly, ticked away by the successive bolts of lightning. Our vehicle, dark and isolated on the brink of danger, transports us beyond time and context into some rippling, associative sea. My mind lapses into reflections and revises my opinion of remarks he's made. "Her pussy must be so wet now, because of rain...." The words came from some close identification with the girl, her abject isolation. His words are predatory, yet they intimately share the vocabulary of the prey. Imperceptibly, his secret allegiances, which make up what one might call character, are surfacing. For the first time I can really see him in his context of poverty and urban want. As the car is illuminated by another bolt of lightning, I glance at him with a flash of understanding; telepathically he returns the look, as if sealing a new pact. An image of him as vulnerable, even sentimental, begins to gel, and a kind of anguish spreads through me—panic about dumping those assumptions to which I'd been so attached.

In this eruption of Nature, I think of Brancusi. His spiritual journey has, perhaps, something to tell me. Early versions of *The Kiss* show the lovers bound together in an infantile fantasy in stone—the rest of the world pushed into another realm. But between 1935 and 1938, *The Kiss* expands into a memorial for those who died in World War I. It takes the form of a gate, an enormous archway that is part of an ensemble celebrating love, in a park in the town of Tîrgu Jiu. To transform *The Kiss* into *The Gate of the Kiss*, the two lovers had to be moved far apart in a gesture of objectivity, forming an arch, which created an entrance that let in the whole world. Brancusi described *The Gate of the Kiss* as a "fragment of a temple of love," and the critic Sidney Geist said the gate was "love and community, upheld by sexual energy." He didn't see the fact that Brancusi created variations of this image over and over during a forty-year period as obsessional, but merely as "reverie" that attains the cosmic, something "outside of chronological time."

It took forty years for Brancusi's kiss to invite us inside. But when it did, it opened itself up to the universe. The cleft circle of its two joined eyes, once blind, now gazed out at us. By some miracle, Brancusi had turned obsessive love into agape, a love of life's energies.

Just as dawn is peeking over a hillside, the storm dies abruptly. The hills and curves smooth out as we near Baia Mare, and in the gradually increasing light, everything turns limpid. I want to touch the moist air. It's clear and viscous, the way water gets when okra is boiled. Beyond an odd formation of wet haystacks piled into perfect cones like some witch's charm is a tile-roofed brick barn with ornately carved wooden doors. Through its open window I can see a cow's full udder and haunches; and the tree beside it, split lengthwise by last night's lightning, is spectral, vulnerable, like Romulus's face now.

An ancient wooden Orthodox church with a steep shingled steeple looms from a grassy hillside. It's a style of architecture that's been termed "Maramureş gothic" by historians because of its high, sloping roofs and razor-thin steeples. Huge, wet fields, some dotted with sheep hovering in the morning mist, swallow the landscape.

The sheep lead us to the outskirts of Baia Mare, a mining and metal-processing city remade in an insipid image of the new global market. Again, a strange metallic odor in the air, but not nearly as bad as in Turda. We find a white, suburban-looking hotel and fall on our beds without unpacking. Images of the rain-swept road are still pulsing behind my eyelids as I sink into a black sleep.

XXI

That evening, after a late dinner, we decide to check out what's left of the shrunken old quarter, where everything is already closed for the night. All we can find is a bar tended by two grinning teenagers in Scottish kilts. It's a novelty act. One of them has even bleached his hair blond. With dignified curiosity, they circle us while we sip our single malts. As usual, we form an eerie twosome—an overfed middle-aged American talking in hooded, wheedling tones to a petite, hawk-nosed Romanian hustler with sharp, distrustful eyes, hollow cheeks and pointed teeth. What do they think of us? The question dissolves into the second single malt.

Out on the street, an aggressive chill has claimed the air. It feels more like September than July. A young stray dog starts to follow us, acting as if we're familiar. When we slow down, he lingers; when we speed up, he gallops by our side. This isn't the abject ferocity of the poor bitch in Bucharest, but youthful optimism; and before long it begins to touch me. The shivering animal's body is thin and dirty, his brown-and-black fur scruffy, but his eyes are eager, full of good nature. "I feel sorry for him," I say.

"Not me, a dozen of those I brought to home in Sibiu. I feed them, then give to friends."

"Why is that a reason not to feel sorry for him?"

Romulus shrugs, and when we pass a kiosk, I suggest

we buy the pup a can of pork pâté. It doesn't occur to me that we have no can opener. Romulus stomps on the can with a stone lodged under his thick platform shoe. Finally it pops open, pâté oozing out like lava. But our canine friend, frightened by the noise and the aggressive gesture of Romulus's stamping, has disappeared. We leave the can right there on the sidewalk in front of a respectable-looking home, in case the dog decides to come back. I can imagine a woman hurrying from her house to work the next morning, stepping into the mess with one of her high heels.

"Don't you know what she do?" says Romulus. "Eat it. And if I didn't have you taking care of me, maybe me, too."

I know what he meant, but I quip, "You're saying she'd eat you, too?"

"No! My meat is too bitter."

The next morning is exceedingly clear, tingeing the mountains surrounding the city a deep purple. Still traumatized by the drive here, we bribe a good-looking, golden-eyed taxi driver, all in blue, an ex-peasant who used to work in the nearby mines, to take us to the villages on the other side of nearby Mount Gutîi. His name is Emil, and his car is a puttering twenty-year-old Dacia with a floorboard as riddled with holes as a sieve. We pass a smelting plant spewing smoke from a thirty-story chimney and jerk up the winding single-lane road, until we're lost in thick forest, then caught in a cul-de-sac. It's a clearing with a strange totem pole rising in the center, carved with cryptic, constantly reversing pictographs. Emil motions for us to get out of the car and draw nearer. Pointing at the weird structure, he says, "Brancusi, the column."

It's not, of course, as he thinks, Brancusi's legendary *Endless Column,* cast in iron in a foundry at Turda and

standing in the park in Tîrgu Jiu with *The Gate of the Kiss.*
It's just a New Age totem by a local artist, who like Brancusi
is inspired by schematic images of Nature: suns, plants, birds
in flight. It also reminds me of pictures of those wooden
"death poles" in Brancusi's province of Oltenia—long, thin
columns, carved with the angles he later reproduced, sometimes topped by a bird, that mark individual graves, like
Jacob's ladders transporting the soul to heaven.

Back in the car, Emil begins chattering in a mixture of
pidgin English and Romanian. To quell any suspicion,
Romulus has him convinced that I'm a writer doing research
for an American magazine and that he's my paid guide. The
corners of Emil's lips are white with froth, so excited is he
about my being from New York. His most pressing concern
is the women there, whether they're as hot and easy to tum-
ble as those in Romania. "Not really," I tell him, thinking
of the many long-limbed, almond-eyed women I've seen in
this country. Most of them seem to have a savvy knowledge
of their sexual power as well as a fatalistic attitude about
some of its consequences.

Emil pushes the subject to a daringly off-color level
until the three of us are talking about pussy and ass with
the clichéd enthusiasm of working-class guys. For him and
Romulus, it's obviously a preferred topic, and I get my kicks
from the atmosphere of male arousal. Emil's hand keeps
brushing against the crotch of his vivid blue trousers. He's
fallen into a casual, barroom mood, and after each dirty
joke, pinches my arm.

Farther up the mountain, thick fog suddenly enfolds us.
We're driving at the edge of a precipice, but at times it feels
as if our right wheels are hanging off. All of this is subjective,
since visibility has been reduced to zero. This doesn't faze
Emil, who only increases his speed. He puts a tape in his

cassette player. A raucous rendition of boom-boom party songs by Nicu Noval hammers away at my anxiety. We scud through the dense fog as he begins describing some of the wilder parties, culminating in orgies, that he's attended. Romulus's eyes twinkle with perverse pleasure at my fear of falling off the mountain, as if he knew all along that both our existences were only a sick joke.

Just as the ironic delight on his face seems to be the last image of my life, the fog lifts like a pulled-back stage drop. The limpid, glossy mountain light returns, wrapping us in a thrilling cocoon. We're on the other side of the mountain, approaching the village of Mara, on a single road lined by large, ornately carved roofed gates that look like variations of *The Gate of the Kiss*. Behind them are the steep brown-shingled roofs of farmhouses. Now we really are in the heart of Maramureș, which is called *țară lemnului renghiat,* or "land of ornate wood carving," by Romanians.

Over Nicu Noval's partying baritone, our driver explains that a villager's status used to be determined by how elaborate his gate was. My eyes fix on the most humble—two mangled, moss-covered tree trunks to which have been affixed a mass of branches, like an upright harrow, behind which chickens scurry and a ferocious dog barks. It's part of a long line of gates of varying size and quality. In fact, the entire village, delineated by a row of gates, is laid out before us on this one main road. All is silent, and we're the only motorized vehicle. Nothing passes us except a flatbed being pulled by two oxen. Even the faces of those few people I see working in the fields look detached and beyond context. "Is because even Romans could not penetrate these mountains," Romulus explains.

The most elaborate gate in town is a massive structure covered with rosettes, geometric designs and vaguely anthropomorphic shapes. Detached from house and barn, offering merely a façade to the road, like the others it serves no function besides the symbolic. Gates here represent the threshold between the inner world—and inner life—of the peasant, situated in his home, and the outside world. Later I'll read that the gates also have a deeper spiritual meaning. They represent the threshold between this life and the world beyond death, a religious affirmation that life and death are easily connected.

Surprisingly, the cryptic ornaments carved into the gates are derived from pre-Christian Thraco-Dacian, Greek and even Persian cults, which found their way into Romania over tens of centuries of migration and whose imagery hasn't yet been swept away by the cleansing tide of money. But today, what were simplified images of natural mysteries have lost most of their occult power, becoming merely aesthetic designs. The rosettes once paid homage to the cult of the Sun. The childlike stalks with branches are artifacts of the Tree of Life, whose constant burgeoning eventually reaches heaven; and the unfolding spiral is no different from the shape of the universe, which curls upward and back into itself in an infinite series.

Later the French writer Benoît Duteurtre, looking at pictures I took, will claim that the gates of Maramureş look African; and scholars of Brancusi, such as the astute Edith Balas, maintain that Brancusi's influence comes from both Africa and the Romanian peasant, and that both these cultures preserved an essential relationship to matter by escaping the merchandising influence of Mediterranean civilization. This is, then, an aboriginal geometry, uncorrupted by the greed for objects that began with the Industrial Revolution and continued through late capitalism.

Brancusi's goal was to reconnect with these elemental

forms of matter. He dreamed of sculpting through all the subsequent significations to their fundamental core. The capacity was in his blood and articulated the lonely, exultant years he spent as a shepherd as well as the isolated latter part of his life. But if, in some modernist project, he could strip down matter until it revealed its form beyond the trappings of technology, it was because his fellow peasants had been doing it that same way for thousands of years.

Past the elaborate gate is a fence of long, slender twigs woven in a zigzag pattern along vertical stakes. It's another specialty of this region, which is still living in the "epoch of wood"—the ability to make wooden structures without the use of nails. Behind the woven fence stands an old man in a conical hat, padded vest and rubber boots, his blue eyes clouded by cataracts. He's using a thick, whittled branch to scrape mud from a trough carved from a log. So fixed is he on his task that he seems hypnotized, aware of our gawking presence but finding little meaning in it. This reminds me of descriptions of Brancusi working patiently from the core of a meditative trance in his studio tucked away from the hubbub of Paris.

Behind the old man is his low-slung house with its drooping shingled roof, the walls constructed according to the *Blockbau* system of interlocking beams at the corners, like an American log cabin. With the last of the mud scraped, he peers up at us, but not very closely, taking a cue from our curious faces to invite us inside.

The interior produces a visceral shock. It's an intensely blue room with clay walls, as minimal as and much cruder than a Shaker house. Everything except the hundred-year-old wood stove, his only source of heat, could have existed in the sixteenth century. There are two stools, which, like the bench, bowls and spoons, have been hand-carved by the old man himself. One stool, a backless pedestal like the mushroom-shaped structures around *The Table of Silence* that is part of Brancusi's installation in Tîrgu Jiu, still shows the sloping marks of the axe. It reminds me that for Brancusi there was very little division between the practical and the aesthetic. He was as much an artisan as an artist, and his stools sometimes served as pedestals for his art or as art themselves.

The old man points to a large sunken structure with a chimney, made from the same clay as the walls, which he says he uses as a bread-baking oven. It's almost identical to the clay oven that Brancusi built in his Paris atelier, which can be seen in a reconstruction of the room at the Centre Pompidou. Running along the top of two walls in the old man's vivid blue room are crinkled paper illustrations of Eastern Orthodox saints. Hanging from horizontal poles above the narrow bed, which is covered with a handwoven sheep's-wool blanket like those I saw at the *mititei* stop, are rugs, evidently the most valuable of his earthly possessions.

In this house without electricity or running water, there isn't any distraction, such as a book. Certainly, back-breaking labor beginning at five a.m. and illiteracy preclude leisure activities; but it's clear from the man's placid, slightly arrogant face that he has no need for pleasure or meaning outside work, rest or prayer.

"I'd go crazy here," Romulus whispers in my ear. "There's no television." And then he adds, "I never told to you, but here just like my grandfather's."

It hits me. If Romulus's family's village hadn't been razed to build a factory and his family exiled to a city, he might still be here or someplace like it, in mute preoccupation with the forces of Nature. My hunch is confirmed when the old man, who's been making a show of ignoring me, fixes him with indulgent, almost tender eyes, then slyly mumbles a phrase in Romanian. Romulus blushes, almost hanging his head.

"What did he say to you?" I ask, as we're walking back to the taxi.

Romulus tries to shrug it off, but the blush returns to his face. "He bless me."

Yet not even the blessing of the old man can save Romulus—and perhaps the old man himself—from that great shift toward the West and its materialistic values that was accelerated by the fall of Communism. It's a shift that will continue as the European Union pushes eastward, until perhaps even the old man or his son finds its tentacles at his doorstep, questioning his children's health and education, suggesting better ways to till his field, frowning at his unlicensed plum brandy or grinningly promoting cartoon versions of his seasonal rituals, as designed by an ethnographer in Bucharest.

In the village of Hărnicești, we pull alongside a graveyard and climb the steep hill on foot. The corroded metal crosses are hand-lettered. Women with grimy hands, in kerchiefs and long woolen socks, rake leaves and clip branches. Their faces are set in a perpetual half-smile that reminds me of the best times I've been high. Is it the smile of Christian piety, a satisfied pantheism or merely isolation from modern distractions? Obviously, they believe they owe a certain humility to the mystery of death, and to both living and inanimate things. Their gestures betray an eerie lack of ambivalence, without any tendency to irony or struggle. Next to them, Romulus in his cheap club-kid platforms with dollar signs in his squinting eyes and me in my East Village black jacket and jowls set in intellectual ambivalence must look like the picture of degeneration.

We move away and climb to the top of the hill to look at the sharp-angled wooden church, probably similar to those Brancusi's grandfather, a church builder, used to carpenter in Oltenia. Its outdoor religious paintings and wooden cross have been draped with crisp white embroidered cotton shawls. I pick up a green apple that has fallen onto a weed-choked grave and bite into it. Romulus points to the name of the deceased on the rusting metal cross and tells me to thank that lady for feeding me.

In Giuleşti, we pass a farmhouse flying a black flag that Romulus says is a sign of a recent death. Just as when we saw the dead body in the road, his eyes brim with hushed respect. Two doors away is a tree whose branches have been adorned with upside-down pots, pans and pails in bright colors. Emil winks at the tree and makes a remark to Romulus in Romanian. "He say we must hurry past," says Romulus.

"How come?"

"The pails mean there is girl looking for husband."

The black flag, pails and even the conical haystacks are elements of the peasants' rich mystical life, most of which predate Christianity. In fact, the region is fraught with the notion that talismans and charms connect the user with hidden forces, that everyday occurrences—the crowing of a cock, a raven flying overhead—hold signs about the future, portending good or ill luck. These spiritual tools keep the mind focused on the authority of natural processes; but in more sophisticated settings, they degenerate into superstitions and prejudices that can open the mind to manipulative mythologies, such as those that were projected onto Lupescu, Carol's mistress, merely for being Jewish. Later, in New York, I'll read about the Romanian mystic Carmen

Harra, who lives in Queens and counsels people about color energy, bedecking herself in all kinds of magical precious stones. This will confirm my conception of Romania as a well of occult belief that enriches art and literature but that also provides fodder for irrational constructions—going so far as to have interfaced at one time with Fascism. For better or for worse, the joke between Romulus and Emil about the pail-covered tree has betrayed their folkish link to each other, and puts me on watch for Romulus's peasant qualities. He's spent his whole life waiting for luck, looking for signs of it with a kind of fatalism; and he supplements this fatalism with the best skills of a shrewd hunter and gatherer, picking up booty like me.

Farther down the road in Giuleşti, we gawk at the biggest gate, a rustic Arc de Triomphe. The massive structure is supported by thick columns decorated with the Tree of Life, rosettes, star petals and crosses enclosed in circles. Its large main doors, meant to give passage to horses or oxen, have semicircles cut out of the top, under which is a line of little fleurs-de-lis. On the right, a newer-looking door under an archway is meant for less majestic traffic—that of humans. Although the gate looks overdecorated, there's nothing oppressive about it, perhaps because of its pleasing proportions. I doubt it was designed from blueprint; it probably grew from the dimensions of the wood that was available. As Brancusi said, "Measurements are harmful." He thought that all measurements had already been taken by Nature. The question he never answered is whether Nature is not only balanced but also avaricious, the source of a primal appetite that leads inevitably to the greed and commerce that, in my world, will destroy Nature itself.

Back in our taxi, we have to wait several minutes as another farmer lumbers down the road. This one is wearing mud-caked pants with an improvised slit for a fly, and a bedraggled peaked hat. Wooden staff in hand, he leads a horse with a frayed canvas bridle, pulling a wooden cart piled with twigs, obviously his only source for cooking and heating. Surprisingly, this man stares us down, a determined, wily stare full of stubborn presence. There's also a tinge of Romulus's accusatory look, a challenge to my polluting presence.

We drive back toward Mara, feeling elated. Romulus's usual catlike crouch has softened into a kind of proud relaxation, revealing his satisfaction with my finding something interesting about his country. A few miles down the road, we pick up a hitchhiker, a gangly blond farmer with a strong-boned face, tired eyes and one hand wrapped in a thick white bandage. Two weeks ago, he lost a finger while sawing a tree. He managed to get to the hospital in Baia Mare on horseback without bleeding to death. However, the lost finger, which he forgot to collect, arrived after him, too late to be grafted on.

At the foot of a mountain, Emil spots a husky peasant woman selling mushrooms by the side of the road. Having made more than three days' pay chauffeuring us, he decides to treat himself. The mushrooms are laid out in rust, white and brown piles on a blanket, and the woman has a stubborn look of pride on her face. Emil strides toward her like a gladiator ready for combat, but she fixes his face with shrewd, narrowed eyes and a sly, toothless smile. She demands 200,000 lei, about six dollars, for a large grocery-sized bag full of the mushrooms, and Emil shows how absurd he considers the price by turning his back to her and moving toward the car. The woman shrugs imperturbably, waits until his hand is on the door handle and calls out a lower price. The pantomime recurs several times, until Emil has talked her down to 30,000 lei, about a dollar. As the woman is scooping the mushrooms into a bag, the mood between the two mutates abruptly. Raucous chuckles pass between them, a rascally twinkle bouncing off both sets of eyes. Then Emil climbs into the car and tosses the bag onto the backseat with a macho flourish, and we head back up the mountain, which is now fog-free.

After dropping the hitchhiker at the hospital clinic, Emil takes us back to our hotel. He's hoping, he admits, that we're planning to stay for a while and that we'll use him as chauffeur every day. But when Romulus explains that we expect to leave early the next morning, Emil's face sinks into a disappointed frown and he hugs us farewell like a brother. The gesture produces a sentimental feeling in me. "He was cute. I hope we run into him again."

"Don't bet. Every day paper has story about somebody poisoned by wild mushrooms."

The drive back to Bucharest the next day is accomplished in only nine hours, once we determine a much more efficient route. During it, I try to broach the subject of our relationship by telling Romulus, "I think I'm learning to love you in a different way." He puts a finger to his pursed lips, like a sorcerer worried about releasing someone from a spell. He turns up the radio, which blasts more Romanian rap. We pull into a wild, honking traffic jam in Bucharest just as the sun is setting, and get the car back to the Marriott fifteen minutes before the rental place closes.

Romulus admits that this is the hotel where he once had a bellboy connection. He'd bring three girls to the casino to find tricks, and the bellboy would lend them his room for the purpose in return for forty percent of the take. The story clothes the ostentatious curving staircase, crystal chandeliers and respectable gleaming floor with a lack of authenticity, as our rental agent, a genteel, chubby woman with carefully manicured nails and a sensibly chic suit, fastidiously figures the charges by hand. She looks up only for a moment to call our attention to a lavish wedding party moving up the staircase. "It's gorgeous, isn't it," she gushes, pointing to the bourgeois-looking older groom and young white-clad bride. "She's too fucking young," Romulus blurts out in English, adding, as the agent gasps and pales, "Must be for the money."

The uncouth remark makes the pen in her fingers slip, and she breaks a glued-on nail. Gazing at the padded bill, I feel like lecturing her with a maxim of Brancusi's: "Beauty is absolute equity."

XXII

Carol is in the hands of an attractive, redheaded little
Jewess of the most scandalous reputation.

—MISSY

Lu-pes-cu. The name rolls off my tongue in all its contorted
sensuality. Ever since I read the biography of Carol's last,
permanent mistress, it has become an emblem of all the
delicious peaks and deadly troughs of passion I've been
enduring.

Lupescu: the woman who thought love could rule the
world. If there's anything more improbable than the union
of a Jewish intellectual from New York and a Romanian
street hustler, it has to be the shocking liaison between
Prince Carol—a member of the royal Hohenzollerns and
the future king of Romania—and Lupescu, a Jewish shop-
keeper's daughter with a promiscuous past.

Maybe it's grandiose of me to inject a relationship that
changed the political destiny of a country into my own
abject narrative. But sitting in my mother's well-appointed
living room as I wait for her gay home health aide to arrange
a week's worth of pills, it occurs to me that history follows a
trail of sputtering desire, often calling on a delusional pair of
lovers to generate the sparks. Its greatest dupes are those who
think this time will be different; but if it weren't for us, the
world would suffer from a dismal lack of stories.

I can picture Lupescu in 1925, in Bucharest, mincing toward a military parade ground in a black crêpe Chanel dress with a shockingly green waistband and knife-pleated skirt. She has put all her bets on an impossible prize, a romance with royalty. Prince Carol will be at the parade ground. She's determined that he'll notice her.

Today Lupescu could easily be mistaken for any high-end Parisian drag queen; but in 1925, her Cupid's-bow mouth, pancake-white face and flaming red hair were a repository for male fantasy. No matter that the black crêpe Chanel was last year's Paris fashion—all she could muster from her small nest egg as the ex-wife of a petty officer. Libido is no impotent tool. It zooms past every limitation.

Lupescu was, according to the history books, a poisonous femme fatale, one of bohemia's grasping opportunists. Born in the Moldovan town of Herța to a father whom writers portray with the clichéd, hook-nosed images of the Jew, she decided early in life that the only barrier to identity was a lack of imagination. For this I'm rather fond of her. Like me, she actually believed that identity could be transformed—or at least defined—by the power of love. Incredibly, she accomplished her fantastic goals, going from demimonde flirt to the most powerful woman in Romania.

As Mom, Lupescu's contemporary, now confined to a walker, hobbles into the living room, I try to picture her in 1925 in a similar flapper-style Chanel dress. If only she hadn't thrown out all her old clothes; I'd probably be rummaging through her closet this very moment.

As always, my own fatal lady has put on makeup in my honor. In an exhausted, powdered face discolored by a poor heart and many medications, her vivid blue eyes scrutinize me hawkishly. She's trying to pinpoint any flaws in my grooming or the dark circles under my eyes as proof of her position that it's time to forget about that Romanian boy and stay home. From the kitchen wafts a mixture of odors of the welcome feast she's been preparing: a large pot roast, potato pancakes, a marble layer cake and other high-calorie treats. Alert to any foolish waste of money, she inspects the gift for her that I've unrolled on the floor: a brown-and-white-striped woolen blanket with its long, matted sheep's wool and fragments of twigs from the fields. I'm rather proud of the import, having smuggled it past U.S. Customs. At any rate, discussing it provides a welcome distraction from one of the reasons for my visit. Mom's ninety-two-year-old sister, my aunt Lil, is in intensive care. Mom's curtness about Lil's illness is a cover for her distress. It lurks behind her few words on the subject in a kind of agony. Strangely, grief comes out as anger in her case; sensing her raw nerves, I'm walking on tiptoe.

Blanket rolled and plastic-bagged, Mom announces the task we're to complete. She wants me to help her go through all the family scrapbooks and put them in order under her command. It's a daunting task. Aside from the seven albums of photos documenting family life from the '30s through the '90s, there are twelve scrapbooks containing curling news clippings that my father fastidiously collected whenever he or my mother made the papers. Hundreds are about her, starting with her promotion to head of Syracuse University's research library in the early '30s and running through the '50s, '60s, '70s and '80s as she climbed the ranks as a Democratic politician and community activist.

Using a brass-tipped cane to imperially point out objects and shelves, Mom directs me to haul and rearrange the heavy, dust-laden albums. Her face betrays no sentimentality about the lost prizes of the past, only a stern, managerial authority about getting them all in order.

We stack the albums on the kitchen table, and I open the one on top, leaf through the brownish crumbling pages. Mom's trajectory is a mini-version of Queen Marie's—from innocent country girl to power-wielding politician. It starts with the minor PTA presidencies of a bored housewife, then gradually blossoms into all-consuming directorships in the state Democratic Party and the National Council of Jewish Women. There are exhausting campaigns for board of education or state assembly and a short stint as the county's election commissioner, followed by directorship of the Jewish Community Center. By the 1970s appears a long bio in *Who's Who of American Women*; and as with Queen Marie, the images of her harden with age and accomplishment. She goes from a beaming, busty white-gloved fifties housewife holding a plate of cookies at a bake sale into an authoritative, overweight matron at an election headquarters, with a sober steel trap of an expression.

I can't help thinking of Lupescu's very different journey. The pictures in biographies show the expensively gowned self-styled Madame Pompadour rapidly mutating into an overweight, middle-aged harpy with the squinting eyes of a bookkeeper, the king's chief advisor and dominatrix. Yet as her torso swells, she never abandons her designer gowns and rather vulgar glamour, often photographed at casinos or in the back of limousines.

Essentially, my mother's roots and hers don't differ by much. Neither does their need for power and influence. Lupescu, however, had a taste for adventure and luxury, and played with fire at a time when her life was constantly in jeopardy. Mom's greatest needs were for security and respectability. She always played by the rules.

Tanklike images of Mom in seal coat and lampshade hats begin to dominate by the early '60s, when she'd reached her heaviest weight and my father had made enough money to dress her in furs. There's something implacable, forbidding and all-knowing about her during this stage, a painful contrast to the frail image across from me now with shriveled arms and stooped back. I look up at her with a pleading expression of exhaustion, hoping that she'll say we can put off the rest of this task until tomorrow. But Mom's not the type to let a job overwhelm her. A running joke between my brother and me is that she'll jump out of the coffin to dig her own plot at the graveyard, just to demonstrate how it should be done.

Near the end of one album, a clipping startles me. Five very handsome teenaged hoodlums with Elvis haircuts, one of whom has the dazed look of a blond Billy Budd, are being booked at the police station for sixteen shocking thefts in one night. The article says that my dad, their court-appointed lawyer, later got them off the hook by pointing out a loophole in their arrest.

The article brings up the subject of my deceased father again, a self-made lawyer who worked well with clients who were criminals because he'd come close to that life himself. During a dismal, violent upbringing in Buffalo, he was expelled so many times from high school that he didn't graduate until he was twenty-one. His nose was broken twice in fights or boxing matches; and even well into his seventies, he never lost his rough-and-ready style. Valentino-swarthy with a brooding, sensitive face, he could have attracted me when he was young, but by the time I was born he was in his mid-forties, his plush lips pursed by responsibility, his wild eyes tamed by Mom into a staid, capable, care-ridden stare.

As I've already mentioned, he was Mom's only defiant gesture. Her parents thought he was a ruffian and a no-account. Far below her respectable exterior, she has to be hiding libidinal tastes similar to my own. This isn't, of course, any reflection on her judgment. Despite her family's opposition, the marriage was an ideal one for more than fifty years. Dad was successfully rehabilitated, instead of dragging her backward into a morass of poverty and crime. When it comes to my bad-boy attachments, I can't say the same. Romulus, Mom divines, is a loser, unlikely ever to leave the elements in which he flounders or add any income to mine. I'm only thankful she has the bowdlerized version of his identity. Otherwise she'd cut me out of her will.

To tell the truth, Mom's middle-class respectability irks me. Why can't she understand that the con artist doesn't always come from a street milieu? As trenchant example, the very mayor of Syracuse who named a building after her in the 1970s was subsequently fingered and sent to jail for graft. As a newly self-proclaimed expert on the Hohenzollerns, I can tell her that kings, queens and princes can be more devious than any hustler from the streets. Their betrayals and subterfuges are no less slimy, just more epic because of their positions.

It's becoming more and more obvious that History, that whore, provides a favored backdrop for my infatuation with a street hustler. I may be draining my bank account for a shady junior pimp who spends my money on a string of girlfriends, but Carol II—a king, for God's sake—threw away his future for a sauntering tart.

Slipping discreetly toward my open suitcase, I remove one of the fifteen bottles of codeine I smuggled in with the Romanian blanket. I've been swallowing the pills since my arrival to assuage the anxiety about this trip. Although my pupils may be pinpoints, Mom's eyes aren't good enough to see. I can't imagine another way of dealing with Aunt Lil's illness or Mom's bad mood; and I know I must keep my own problems undercover. How to explain to my mother that I've left Romulus just a few days after being confronted with my female rival? The understanding is that he's gone back to Sibiu to wait for me, and Elena must be working her strategies at this very moment. No matter that we parted in friendship and warmth. History has shown me the wily ways of the courtesan, as well as that figure's untenable position, her or his lack of choices.

In the twenties and thirties, scandal sheets poured a kaleidoscope of fancy about the seductress Lupescu into the minds of readers. It's almost as if the Jewess born to very little future had been asked to oversee the dreams and fears of an entire nation. Her father's name was Wolff, a sure sign of his ethnicity; but he married a good-looking Viennese who'd already renounced her Judaism for the Roman Catholic faith. Before the wedding, he was baptized as an Orthodox Christian, ostensibly to satisfy her. It was shortly after this that he Latinized "Wolff" into "Lupescu," a reference to the same mammal.

Jews weren't allowed to own businesses in Romania in those days. Nor could they attend the same schools as non-Jewish Romanians. But her father's new identity allowed Elena Lupescu to get an education at the respectable but mediocre Pitar Moş convent in Bucharest. Years later, it was magically transformed into the high-class convent of Notre Dame de Sion, and a story was embroidered about Lupescu as a little girl meeting teenaged Prince Carol, when her mother took her to have tea with the poet queen Carmen Sylva. Historians are quick to deflate the fantasy by saying that Lupescu never met the queen in her entire life. Still, it's hard for me to let go of the sunburst of red-gold hair on the terrace of the royal country house in Sinaia. It outshines reality and makes it seem sham, like a world devoid of fantasies about Romulus.

Meeting the queen is one of the many stories told by the poor, disenfranchised Elena Lupescu in flight from a second-class identity. Just as Coco Chanel reworked her biography to hide her beginnings as a convent orphan, Lupescu allegedly went to absurd lengths to construct a respectable, aristocratic past. Her biographers mock her for changing her writing from the artless, even hand of a schoolgirl to the sweeping, pointed script she'd seen in the writing of royalty. But such scholars are only betraying their own snobbery and pretentious outrage at the usurped legitimacy of the ruling class.

With a cloth, I wipe each album carefully, while Mom irritatedly points out specks or spots I've missed. In my hands is the record of her struggles from Yiddish-speaking immigrant in a provincial upstate village to the Syracuse *Post-Standard*'s "All-Time Woman of Achievement." She is, in a sense, another answer to Lupescu's dilemma of disenfranchisement—living proof that discipline, patience and drudgery can bring at least a few of the social awards Lupescu desperately desired. But Mom's stolid march toward social acceptance provides little food for fancy and consequently has very little to do with my story. It could never be thought of as fiction.

Albums finally dusted, loose clippings reglued, I follow Mom's meticulous directions for putting them away. So detailed are they that it begins to feel as if she's seeking to control my body systems. She tells me when to lift an album, when to put it down and how to center it on the shelf. I start believing that she's hoping to decide when I inhale or exhale, even the changing circumference of my pupil dilation. Riding with me to the shopping mall an hour later, she insists on even more stringent control. I've known the route since childhood but still must drive as her robot. Like a drill sergeant, Mom calls out signs and lights, announces precisely how many feet from a turn to signal and stops short of putting her own foot on the brake. When I explode uncontrollably, she looks at me with false white-gloved astonishment, claiming innocence as to what could possibly have caused my bullish, tasteless behavior.

It's dawned on me slowly that all this insanity is merely the result of oedipal tension, which has increased tellingly since the death of my father. Something about my body unlocks impulses that frighten and annoy Mom. I know it's true, because our closeness flourishes on the telephone without a hitch; it's only when we're in the same room that she becomes irritated and resorts to obsessive critiques. "Why do you walk like that?" she might say, in imitation of Romulus. "There's a strange spot on your forehead. I sure hope it's nothing serious." "You never used to have jowls. It must be the drinking." Or, "That shirt makes you look even fatter. Why don't you go and change."

As I dart into traffic at Mom's myopic order, nearly causing an accident, I consider the fact that an analogous reaction occurs whenever Romulus and I have close physical contact. It's been stupid of me never to acknowledge the incestuous parameters of a relationship with someone young enough to be my son. There's no problem during genital contact, but what is that strange fidgeting on his part before we go to sleep? What is the sense of embarrassment he projects when we're seated side by side at the movies? Certainly, it has some parallel to what happens between Mom and me, a squeamish sense of being trapped in an uncomfortable intergenerational physical intimacy, saddled with the body of the one from whom one expects protection. A fear that such intimacy threatens to breach taboos about desire. I'd almost call it a kind of incestuous repulsion.

While Mom's directions continue to reduce the world to her miniature golf course, I retreat into thoughts about Lupescu's strategies for distancing herself from her own oedipal dilemmas. Unlike me, she devised a drastic escape from the magnetic pull of family romance. She reinvented her past, thereby shedding the mantle of generation. "Dad? Oh, he was interested in chemistry," she'd tell the few aristocratic visitors whom she could get to curtsy or kiss her hand after she became the consort of the prince about to become king. It was a revision of her father's ownership of a small notions shop in the city of Iaşi. This in itself was a miracle, since Jews normally couldn't own businesses. In fact, by the middle of World War I, few people of any kind were able to make a living in Iaşi. A large percentage were dying of infection or starvation.

The grotesque deprivations of life in wartime only exacerbated Lupescu's taste for glamour. I can understand this principle completely: the worse the conditions, the more urgent the need for fantasy. Disadvantaged people penalized by normal rules often flourish in chaos. I like to think of her trudging through the frozen streets in the winter of 1916–1917, the coldest in half a century, past houses stripped bare by renegade soldiers or emptied by robbers. She must have passed some of the thousands of war refugees swarming the streets, many half dead from typhoid or smallpox, others clattering by as corpses in horse-drawn carts.

Within this setting of want, the fledgling temptress managed to hook a lieutenant in Prince Carol's regiment named Tîmpeanu. The name was close enough to the Romanian word *tîmpit,* or "idiot," to lead to jokes among the soldiers about his stupidity in marrying her. The relationship was, as predicted, short-lived because of Lupescu's promiscuity. A few years after the war ended, the gay divorcée moved to Bucharest.

Mom hobbles through a shop at the mall, instructing me to hold up bargain dresses for her perusal. She scowls at the prices, standing straighter than usual in the face of curious onlookers. They're surprised to see such a decrepit lady on the loose and in control of her own life. If such judges of others—including the historians who sort out villains and heroes—could live one day in the life of the people they portrayed, I bet they'd rearrange their score sheets. They might even find a way to reinterpret Lupescu as something other than a poisonous femme fatale or Jewish scourge.

It was the street life of Calea Victoriei and Bulevardul Kiseleff in Bucharest that finally granted Lupescu's desire to escape the stigma of Jewishness. Among the promenading dandies and ostentatious women, she was able to walk right past the locus of her most visceral fantasy, the palace. Or she hung from a balcony overlooking the street in an apartment that belonged to three former school chums and coyly called down to the young cruisers below, sifting through the crowd of eligible men for one who might have a distant connection to the prince.

By 1925, gossip had it that Carol was already tired of his three-year marriage to Princess Helen of Greece. The whole affair had been arranged by Missy as a way of making Carol forget about Zizi Lambrino. Publicly, Missy patted herself on the back for having turned her son's life around. "I fought a mighty battle for you to put you back on the straight road," she loftily admonished in a letter that has become a public document. "Now it lies before you to walk straight upon it."

The marriage that Missy had brokered between her son

and Princess Helen was also supposed to strengthen the royal network that controlled the Balkans. Unfortunately, the two young people couldn't have been more ill-matched. Within a year of the wedding, Helen loudly declared herself appalled by Carol's pop taste, his poorly cut uniforms and his lack of interest in interior decorating. His table manners were a source of constant irritation as well; but he countered all her criticisms with the remark that he found her refinements deadly boring. In fact, even Missy mocked the princess's regal propriety and coolness, her perfect hairdos and overly cultured conversation. It was common knowledge that after the birth of their son, the married couple had begun to sleep separately.

If Carol needed a model for infidelity, his mother was, as always, a convenient case. By now, Missy had dropped all subterfuge in her affair with Barbo Știrbey. They carried on right in front of the palace staff.

Marie's affair with Știrbey had never stopped piquing Carol's resentment, but there were other reasons for his increasing rage against his mother and her consort. The fact that Știrbey and the other Liberals in the government dictated policy with the help of Missy infuriated him. All of it smelled of corruption and went against his youthful fantasies of populism and democracy, instilled in him by his homosexual tutor Mohrlen.

The time would come, however, when Carol would far outdo both his mother's infidelities and her reliance on camarillas. If what happens next titillates me, it's probably because I know how much my infatuation with Romulus irks my mother. Like Carol's, it's a descent from her notion of respectability, despite the chances she took in marrying my problem-ridden father.

*

Back at the house, I help Mom try on the royal-blue budget dress she purchased. It brings out her intense blue eyes, still sparkling with their enormous energy. An argument follows over my suggestion that we now have cocktails. Mom finally agrees to a small glass of wine. I pour a larger one for myself and surreptitiously use it to swallow another two tablets of codeine.

The wine soothes Mom's concealed worries about her sister. Her attempts to control my every move vanish. A sweet Mom takes the fore, eagerly asking me about my trip to Maramureş, the houses, peasants and animals I saw. Astonishingly, admiration for my love of adventure and travel are beginning to leak slyly from her often critical features. A strange absorption floods her face like a remembrance. She left her Russian shtetl at two, so she can't be reacting to memories; but my descriptions must still strike her as familiar, like something hidden in a collective unconscious imported from rural Russia.

She listens with rapt curiosity to my tale of driving through the storm and encountering the dead body on the road, and marvels at my courage in facing the slippery peaks of the Carpathians. It's no use reminding her that she's just subjected our two-mile suburban drive to minuscule, fearful scrutiny. Between us, the tale of Maramureş takes on heroic proportions and puts me in a time warp. Mom and I travel back to those preadolescent days when she delighted at my high marks or gave a sympathetic ear to childish anecdotes. Near the end of the story, we're sitting on the couch with my arm clasping her close enough for me to smell the 1920s perfume she discreetly put on in my honor. Mitsouko, by Guerlain.

Our relationship seems to function on weirdly autonomous levels. Mom's love floats out of reach repeatedly, replaced by resentment and criticism. Or is it fear of the intimacy and the physical feelings it inspires? But when her love returns, it has an overwhelming sweetness. If only I could find the place where she stores this raptness; with a snap of my fingers I'd make it manifest always.

Magic substances seem to accomplish something similar after dinner as I wash dishes. Stimulating my endorphins, the codeine accompanies a review of how far I've come with Romulus. During our first times together in Budapest, he'd leave his passport near the bed whenever he went out, assuming I needed proof he was coming back. But at least friendship and familiarity between us have long ago stopped that behavior. I wonder if he leaves his passport on the table for Elena when he goes out, say, to buy a liter of beer. Maybe not. Then she'd know what day I returned. He'd excuse himself to buy a pack of cigarettes and take the passport with him.

I also wonder what Romulus would make of the other Elena—Lupescu—given what he confessed to me one day near the end of our second stay at the Gellért in Budapest. I'd asked him somewhat fearfully whether he was having a good time. He answered that no amount of luxury could erase the fact that he had no future in Hungary. He could never be happy in such a hostile country. Then how did Lupescu carve out such a sparkling future in a country that resented and held back her people? Could it be that he lacks Lupescu's relentless drive? Or perhaps he's too genuine a person and would find her creative subterfuges distasteful.

*

In 1925, under the flickering projection of the silent film *Die Nibelungen,* Lupescu's face in its layers of powder and paint looked like a Kabuki mask. It was positioned directly across from Crown Prince Carol, who'd attended the film with his family. The event was a fund-raiser for the Carol I Foundation, meant to support Romania's college students. Apparently, that overly made-up face stoked his heart to the point that he decided to meet her.

The chance for the two actually to speak seems to have been arranged by a notorious womanizer named Tăutu, who lived in a leopardskin-strewn house in Bucharest and may have been an ardent admirer of Lupescu's Austrian, possibly promiscuous mother. When Carol asked to be hooked up with the hot redhead Lupescu, Tăutu threw a party to which both were invited. Yet when Tăutu realized that the prince was seriously interested, he freaked out. He knew Lupescu was playing for keeps when the enamored Carol offered to drive her home and she simpered, "But what would the neighbors think?" So at the next party, Tăutu tried to soil her reputation by faking an affair with her, calling her a slut and throwing a nightgown in her face. The plan backfired when the quick-thinking Lupescu innocently asked if there might be any gentleman in the room who could protect a lady's honor. Carol stepped forward, and the two were never separated again.

Accomplishing a real defamation of Lupescu required greater leaps of the imagination. At the beginning of the affair, she and Carol never appeared in public together. Even afterward, she kept in the background and lived a life of near isolation. The legitimate members of the nobility had abandoned the court to avoid her, and she feared the public because of several threats to her life. She spent most of her time during Carol's reign traveling from her small house on

Aleea Vulpache to the palace late at night, where she may have entered through an underground passageway and never got the chance to meet Queen Marie.

All this was happening as Fascism took flower in Romania and as Lupescu's lover, now the king, began making more and more concessions to it. It's no wonder that such a mystery figure as Lupescu became a canvas for projections of Fascistic fear. If she'd been more visible, demonizing her might have proved more difficult. But for the Romanian public of the time, she was the living embodiment of Jewishness, sexuality and government intrigue. It was a common rumor that she influenced the king not only in his personal life but in affairs of state as well. No matter how indirect this interference might have been, people were eager to see it as conspiratorial and manipulative, adjectives that the people of one of the most plot-ridden countries in the world associated with Jews. She was hated not just by the Gentiles of Romania, but also by the Jews of the country, most of whom thought of her as an embarrassingly bad example. Politicians tiptoed around her or schemed against her, and the aristocracy snubbed her as an arriviste. The Iron Guard, Romania's Fascists, tried to convince the world she was a supernatural Jewish demon. But no critic has come up with any hard proof of her being an éminence grise. The historian Paul D. Quinlan doesn't think she even really was. According to him, Lupescu's most important role consisted in providing home-cooked *mămăligă,* telling dirty jokes she'd learned from the barracks in Iaşi, playing cards, entertaining commoners and offering regular nooky.

Even so, most later historians were no kinder to the sensual Jewess than her contemporaries were; under a more objective guise, they perpetrated, in my opinion, myths forged by the Fascists. Alice-Leone Moats, her supposed intimate friend, went so far as to accuse her of single-handedly keeping Romania "in a constant state of turmoil for nearly fifteen years." Though her lover the king has recently been forgiven for his capitulation to the Nazis, Lupescu remains a stain of ill repute in almost every history book, and her remains were recently removed from the tomb she once shared with the king and reburied in a commoner's grave.

Mom gets ready to read about Lupescu in bed, and I spread out at the foot to keep her company, unwilling to let go while she's in such a loving mood. Off go the shoes from her swollen, once hardworking feet, and on goes the pale turquoise budget nightgown I've seen her put on for close to twenty-five years. With a hand knobby from arthritis she sweetly pats my back. Love, I've decided, flows unpredictably, ignoring arguments and the lessons of historians.

What fascinates me most about the tales of Lupescu is their marriage of evil and love. What were the feelings of the Jewess behind the king in the 1930s, as her lover issued one anti-Semitic edict after another? My own experience has shown me the possibility, if not the thrill, in loving someone whose actions should be condemned. After all, my mother and most of my friends consider Romulus dangerous, a destructive leech; and I can't come up with convincing opposing arguments.

It's not merely a question of love going on at the same time as contradictory resentment and disapproval, but it has something to do with the different levels our emotions inhabit, our efficiency at quarantining our sense of morality from passions that release our endorphins. The schizoid, unexplainable switches between Mom and me are proof, I suppose. It's as if everything has its separate chamber: outrage, desire, tenderness and fear. But in Lupescu's obsessive alliance, I see an even more fascinating feature: the notion that even in the most repugnant conditions, love is the sought-after paradise; it just has to be right.

XXIII

That night something about my current situation came out in a nightmare. I dreamed that my face fell off, right at the jaw hinges beneath my sideburns. It was only for a moment, and I pushed it back up. I wasn't aware it had happened, but my mother and others in the room noticed. It was supposed to be an allergic reaction to eating something like "cassava" seeds, an echo of the way Romulus crunches into one sunflower seed after another.

The next morning, Aunt Lil, my mother's sister, died. After a short, simple funeral, I headed for New York, where, in ironic counterpoint to the dream I'd just had about the loss of my face and lower jaw, I was supposed to give a reading at the Romanian Cultural Center. My friend Leonard Schwartz, the poet, had arranged it, and I was planning to read an excerpt of this book.

At the Center, I was met by a cultural attaché, Carmen Firan, who intrigued me on sight. Not only was she multilingual and highly educated like Ursule Molinaro, but whole facets of her intellect seemed dedicated to sensuality. Almost undulating in chic linen pants and a silk top, she graciously invited me into her office for a drink. When I asked if I could smoke, her beautiful face with its elfin nose crinkled into a smile. She nodded eagerly, making a sassy quip about Americans' fear of pleasure. Her cultured femininity was something with which I am completely unfamiliar, except perhaps from one or two Italian movies. It was coupled with a breezy lack of artifice and a subtle elegance, that union of allure and intelligence that some American feminists once claimed was impossible. Later I would discover that she's also a very gifted writer, and would collaborate with her and her husband on some of their texts. But that night I felt like an awed country bumpkin, recognizing that my absorption in the underclass life of Romulus had deprived me of contact with educated Romanians.

Before a crowd of mostly Romanian listeners, Firan sauntered to the front of the room to announce the evening's program. She'd pulled together a dissonant variety of American and Romanian writers. I would have to go first.

No one was expecting to hear what poured forth: the story of a Romanian rentboy, abject passion and problematic sex. I could feel the silence in the room, which I interpreted as a kind of rapt repulsion. Later, two Romanian men approached me to compliment me on the story. Incredibly, both had reworked it in their minds as being about a female prostitute. One of them told me he understood my interest in Romanian women but cautioned me to be careful with the hookers. Then he told an urban myth, about a client who wakes up with a kidney missing. Only Nina Cassian, the lauded Romanian poetess in exile, who had also come to read, seemed to have heard my story for what it was and enjoyed it. Later, though, she would flinch when I mentioned it, asking with a curious patriotism why everyone who writes about Romania always writes about prostitutes.

Cassian's reading, which came directly after mine, produced a bizarre reaction. Hardly had she started when a woman with tired eyes, dressed in a stretched-out, faded sweatshirt, began to protest. "I denounce you," she told Cassian before the whole audience, explaining it was for the patriotic poems Cassian had written during the Ceauşescu regime. The outburst led to a comic scene, in which supporters of Cassian stood to denounce the denouncing woman. After Cassian had finally managed to read her lyrical, linguistically rich poem, Firan glided to the front of the room to restore order and introduce the next reader, whom, she told the disruptive woman, she was presenting "with your permission," all the while shooting daggers at her with her eyes.

Cassian herself seems never to have forgiven me for my salty story. She granted me only one rendezvous with her afterward, when she was ill. It was then that she told me that Johnny Răducanu isn't really Jewish. It was also then that she expressed her disappointment about my subject matter, and we've not had a conversation since.

Not only did the tantalizing Carmen Firan show enthusiasm for my story, she became bit by bit my source for literary and topical information about Romania. Today I'm still intrigued by her intelligence, clear wit and sensuality. They seem part of the dream, or trance, connected with Nature that I experienced in her country—in such contradiction to the historical agonies Romanians have endured.

The flight back to Romania by way of Frankfurt on Lufthansa exposed me to other American exiles with whom I could compare myself. The plane was three-quarters full of African-Americans, who approached one another like members of a cult, all obsessed with the culture of Germany. In their eyes I saw a perverse audacity in favoring a country once known for its racism. Yet I realized that spending time there was also an escape from American stereotypes about them, a new and intriguing freedom. I saw similar features in my own exile. Very few tourists from the United States choose Romania. In being there, I was unconsciously deriving a feeling of a unique status.

Before leaving Bucharest this time, I'd made sure both Romulus and I had keys. Traumatized by his eleventh-hour standout when I'd been in Paris, I now wanted him to come back on his own terms. I tried to tell myself he'd return when he was ready, and if not, that was the way it was supposed to be. But behind this bravado were very real fears. I hadn't gotten to the point of projecting assurance in the streets of Bucharest; my body movements were still unmistakably American, and on almost every expedition without Romulus I'd run into some small problem, such as being charged triple for a purchase. New Yorker though I was, I was still intimidated by this city full of want, disappointment and trauma.

Just as I'd feared, the taxi driver from the airport vastly overcharged me. And once he'd dropped me off at Piaţa Unirii, I had to face the same poor bitch who guarded the territory around the apartment on Mihnea Vodă. It was the middle of July and the city was still baking in one of the worst heat waves of the century. Romulus, naturally, was nowhere to be found.

This time, as planned, I took a different strategy. When I called him on his cell phone I found him at the soccer field in Sibiu, just as before. I told him about the death of my aunt, to whom I'd been very close as a child. The news produced a kind of embarrassment, evidenced by a dull "Oh" on the other end of the line. I wasn't surprised. Having learned to silence himself about his own sufferings, he was distinctly inarticulate about others'. Implicit also in the silence was his reluctance to take the role of comforter. So I told him he could come whenever he wanted. "Tomorrow," he promised. Knowing his imprecision regarding time, I readied myself for a few days on my own. During them I would be isolated. My only friends here were Alex Leo Şerban, who was away for the rest of the summer, covering some film festivals in Western Europe, and Johnny Răducanu, who was on tour.

But these days alone—which stretched to about eight— were rather astonishing, especially when I was altering my endorphins late at night with codeine. On those nights, I gave in to obsessive thoughts, using the codeine again as a sacrament to produce visions of where Romulus might be or what he might be doing. Like Saint Ignatius doing his spiritual exercises, I tried to picture, smell, taste every detail of my meditation: the blurred movement of a leg on a soccer field, an apartment in the block and an unmade bed, hair falling limp over the tops of the cheekbones of a sleeping face in the heat. And then, of course, Elena. Telepathy took over again on those nights. I stayed in bed immersed in the images on the inside of my eyelids until way past noon. Then, rising with a codeine hangover mixed with the fear that Elena was gaining ground, I would tell myself that it was too late to start work on the second half of the Céline Dion translation, and set out to wander the city.

Each afternoon, I strolled along the bridge over the Dîmboviţa, still reduced to mud and dead fish in the heat, then across the massive canyon of Piaţa Unirii, where, like other pedestrians, I shrunk to a molecule against this crossroads the size of Times Square. And like everyone else, I would let my sight be pulled along by the perspective straight to the façade of Ceauşescu's monstrous palace, the House of the People, a building as large as a village.

On some days, I'd make a stop at the delicatessen that fills the bottom triangular space of the Bulevard Hotel, where you stand in line to order meat or cheese, then stand in line to pay for it, then stand in line a third time with your receipt to pick up your purchase. Or I'd stop to visit the gloomy interior of the Church of Saint Ioan Botează torul and stare at the silver icons and hanging Oriental lamps, which sent pallid shafts of light through dusty air. I'd watch the robed, bearded priest behind the altar hearing the confession of a woman kneeling before him, her head draped in a black cloth. I'd be amazed by the posture of old, impoverished Orthodox Christian women, staring as if in a trance, their bodies as still and stiff as anesthetized subjects, tilted obliquely in some ancient attitude of piety, as pain welled from their rapt, frozen faces. Spooked, I'd hurry outside through the ornately carved wooden doors, to the curses of a beggar that seemed to devour the air, and stare dumbly at the little girl selling stockings and listen to her monotonous chant.

I was in a mystical country full of people who believed they were in direct contact with the sacrament—unlike Roman Catholics, who experience it only vicariously, through the great bureaucracy of the Church. And I'd wonder if that expression of endurance and resignation I saw so often on the face of Romulus had its roots in the religion of his people. This was a mentality with which I was completely unfamiliar. I'd sense it as I climbed Mitropoliei Hill to the seventeenth-century Patriarchal Cathedral, the headquarters of the entire Romanian Orthodox Church. The beggars along that hill had all perfected stances of aesthetic agony, sad performances that seemed a kind of art. The entrance to the church was decorated with a fresco depicting the blessed ascending to heaven as the evil fall to torment. But inside is where I always lingered to stare at the little cadaver of Saint Dumitru under glass, the body concealed by a brocade cloth with a carefully hemmed hole revealing one wrist.

But of all the churches where I passed my afternoons, fleeing visceral visions of Romulus from the night before,

Stavropoleos, not far from Strada Lipscani, was my favorite. It was built in 1724 by Greek monks, designed by Constantin Brăncoveanu; and its ornate columns, Moorish archways and gold-leaf icons give it an occult, anachronistic feel, especially since a gleaming, glass-walled skyscraper has been erected not far from it. Visiting it was like a drug experience with the power to take me beyond my life's context, in the sense of where I was and who I am. There I always had the pleasurable feeling of doing something arcane and not allowed.

One day, as I sat reading Panaït Istrati's *The Bandits* in the park in front of the Atheneum, a boy of about eleven started yanking at my sleeve. He'd been watching me pop one mint after another into my mouth and was pointing imperially at the bulge the candy box made in my pants pocket.

"Candy!" he commanded, tipping the ash from the cigarette he was smoking into my lap, his face close enough to mine to spray it with a few droplets of saliva.

"Why?" I answered teasingly. "Why should I?"

"'Cause you good man is all," he answered imperturbably, stroking the outline of the candy box through my pants in a gesture that could have been misinterpreted. He was barefoot. One toe was missing a nail, and both feet were covered in grime.

I took the box out and opened it, not noticing the three other boys lined up next to me on the park bench. Two jumped quickly into a line to be served, and with exaggerated yelps of joy, each popped two or three mints into his mouth, then shot out his hand for more.

Only half a minute later, when the box was empty, did I notice the fourth boy, in a tattered T-shirt, still sitting patiently on the bench. He must have been about thirteen, but he had the calm, resigned look of someone much older.

"You're not fast enough," I joked, and with that, he slid off the bench until he was just a head above my knees. I thought he'd been sitting with his legs tucked under him. I hadn't realized he had none.

"No more candy," I said apologetically, coloring with embarrassment, as he eyed me gently from a shrewd, weathered face and answered, "Money."

All four pairs of eyes were glued to my hand as I reached into my pocket for my wallet. And when I opened it and held it high above their heads, the first child, who'd tugged my sleeve so insistently, leapt into the air to get a glimpse of what was inside. I held it higher and plucked out a 10,000-lei note, worth about thirty cents, then swooped it into the outstretched hand of the boy without legs, who snatched it away as if it were priceless.

"Money, money, money," chanted the others in a chorus I'd swear was harmonized and on pitch. Other people in the park had begun to stare. The curiosity on their faces was colored with squeamishness.

One by one I plucked out three more 10,000-lei notes, handing them to the others. Their streetwise stances melted into boyish gawkiness; they scrambled onto the bench and my lap, pushing and pulling at one another for the closest place.

"What you reading, mister?"

"Panaït Istrati." Three pairs of eyes went blank, but those of the boy without legs, to my amazement, lit up with recognition.

"Good," he said.

"Why you read?" asked the ringleader, the one who'd pulled my sleeve.

"Reading's good," I answered. "And besides, I write some books."

The boy's eyes clouded with confusion. "What you do?"

I pantomimed the act of typing, then pointed at the book.

"You make much money!" announced the smallest boy, who was about eight.

"Not really." His eyes dulled with disappointment.

"Bad." The three other boys echoed him. "Bad, bad," they chanted. But the legless boy, who I now noticed was sitting on a single skate, was studying my hands with absorption, as if they held the secret of what I did for a living.

"Mister," said the ringleader, yanking the smallest from my lap, "you buy us groceries now."

I gave him a doubtful look, and all of them lapsed into a mawkish whine. The ringleader had forced tears into his eyes, not the spontaneous tears of a child but a willful, stagy look. "Mister," he repeated, "you buy us groceries."

"Oh, all right, why the hell not."

The four boys sprang off the bench, the legless one landing with a splat on his skate. With an enormous push of his thin arms, he zoomed forward, the bottom of his body scraping and scattering leaves on the ground. The others ran joyously behind him as I struggled to catch up, suddenly elated by their yelps, while other people in the park gaped, their faces shrinking in repulsion. Every look showed disgust mixed with fear, but behind these I thought I glimpsed envy, even guilt.

The boys led me across the park and several blocks into a neighborhood I'd never explored. The legless one on the skate sped on and off the sidewalk, swooping in great arcs past cars. The reactions of pedestrians and motorists were always the same, a defensive annoyance at the sight of the boys, then amazement at seeing me hurry along beside them, which quickly mutated into a look of shame. As we ran, I got a good look at the boys. The ringleader really did look like a miniature adult, pants rolled halfway up his shins over bare feet, a cigarette spewing ashes from one hand, brown shiny hair and a little lemon of a face. His mouth was screwed up in determination and his eyes shot boastful aggression. The two smallest ones must have been brothers about a year apart. The eight-year-old's pipe-cleaner arms stuck out from a grimy tank top safety-pinned to baggy pants in lieu of a belt. He had dirty ears and a full, gleamingly wet mouth. His older brother was wearing shorts, out of which poked two heavily scabbed knees, and laceless sneakers whose toes had been painted Day-Glo lime. He was holding a stick that he loved rattling on garbage cans and car hoods, causing irate explosions on every block as car owners, shopkeepers and stoop-sitters cursed, sometimes darting out into the street after him, until they saw me and retreated in confusion.

The legless skater was dark, with piercing, all-comprehending black eyes, a face that seemed immune to suffering—or so familiar with it that it poured off in rivulets and was never absorbed. Behind this ruthless manner I sensed unusual intelligence, private and unreachable.

As we hurried through the streets, all my preoccupations melted away. I knew what I was doing was ridiculous, that I was caught in a sentimental fantasy, but the boys' rowdy mood sailed me along, and waves of pleasure welled up. We rattled into a supermarket, and the cashiers, produce man and manager snapped back their heads in perplexed indignation. But the nine-year-old had already grabbed a cart and sent it wheeling toward me, so I took it and we started down the first aisle.

The legless skater zigzagged ahead of us from one side of the aisle to the other, pitching anything he could reach toward the ringleader, who tossed it into the cart. When we were halfway through the store, and the cart contained a hodgepodge of steaks, bananas, half-gallon Cokes, ice cream, potato chips and chicken wings, the manager marched over and began shouting down at the legless boy, pointing one insistent finger toward the door. The boys all looked pleadingly toward me, so I tapped the manager on the shoulder.

"Excuse me, but these boys are with me. We're shopping. Is that allowed?"

Having obviously understood my English, the man retreated grumbling, while the produce man snatched a melon from the arms of the smallest boy. We headed for the checkout and I paid, about forty dollars in all.

Outside on the street, the boys were exultant. The ringleader had opened the half-gallon of Coke and was chugging it in big gulps, while the two smallest leapt toward it, trying to wrest it from his hands. The legless boy, unruffled, sat at the curb, grocery bags looped around his shoulders, watching me with gentle eyes. Then the ringleader passed the Coke to the youngest, who almost dropped it on the street.

"Mister. Taxi?"

Before I could answer, the boys had waylaid one at a red light, and as the driver tried to lock all his doors, they piled inside. I handed the driver a large bill and he sped away cursing, while the boys pressed their faces to the windows and waved good-bye.

Fantasies pulsed through my mind, a hundred times more romantic than any I'd ever felt for Romulus. Love suddenly seemed so easy in the context of the four black holes I'd just encountered. Receiving such an unguarded response to giving was a new experience. I was planning to come back to the park every day at the same time. The boys would become my adopted charges. They'd learn reading, English, responsibility. By the time I got back to the apartment, I'd constructed our farmhouse in Maramureş, big feather beds with sheep's-hair blankets, piled with exuberant little bodies at bedtime before a blazing fire, honest work with the peasants starting at dawn.

Excitedly, I called Romulus to tell him about the experience. He answered his cell phone sounding guilty, his breath almost erotic, as he savored the inevitability of a lecture about not having come back yet. Instead I told him my story, which poured out ingenuously, full of high-blown resolutions, inspiration, thrill.

Incredibly, he listened quietly, then sighed and said, "You are crazy."

"You're just like all the others," I spat. "They were all staring at me like I was nuts. No wonder why those kids—"

"Hmm, hmm." He clucked. "Where do you think boys go in taxi?"

"Home, I guess."

"And who they give groceries to?"

"Their parents?"

"Yes, or maybe boss they work for."

"What boss?"

"The boys must work for parents or maybe friend of parents. Or maybe even somebody who organizes beggars. You see, Bruce, this is probably parents' only way to make money. What you think they do if you take boys to the country?"

"I never thought of that."

"There is worse to think of, you know. Maybe parents hear about rich American. They see great chance for a lot of money."

"How?"

"By saying you molest boys, for example. Then blackmail you."

"Romulus, you're so fucking cynical."

"You think so?" It was a tone I'd never heard before. Paternal, absolutely serious. "Bruce, how many people watching in park? And how many people you pass on the street? And how many of those people even have money for bread? So they see you, handing out money like candy. You look...decadent. They become angry thinking, If only I had small amount of money he uses to be generous. Then maybe I could feed my children."

"Is that why everybody was staring at me like that?"

"Hmm, hmm. You think all the time they have no heart. But they cannot help the children and they must make themselves into steel. And for this they feel sick inside, you know? They feel ashamed when they look at what you doing. So they say fuck him, he stupid, a stupid, rich American. And maybe if there is way to get your money, like call you a child molester, then why not."

"But the boys wouldn't do that. They'd say it wasn't true."

"Tsk, tsk, and who listen to them? They are slave of parents or whoever they work for. You want to count on them?"

I had no answer, of course. My bubble had been pricked. And with its deflation, the world and its narrow, predictable parameters rushed back in. "When are you coming?" I asked, sinking back to where I'd started, greeting all my frustrations with a weary, defeated embrace.

"Soon, soon. Tomorrow."

"Whenever, Romulus. I'm here."

And there I was, half filling a glass with the bootleg scotch I'd picked up at a nearby kiosk, watching a TV comedy in a language I didn't understand, then sitting alone on the terrace to watch the gathering of the dogs at dusk, as a small group of neighbors—who according to Romulus were part of the vast group of inhabitants who had nothing to give—handed out their treats. Among the pack of dogs I saw the bitch, whose teats looked smaller than they had a month ago, but whose eyes still welled with misery. To my amazement, she stopped still in her tracks and sniffed the air, then jerked her head in the direction of my terrace and barked.

That evening, already drunk, I toured the clubs of the old city around the Curtea Veche, wandering from one disco to another. The majority were filled with students, but one of them, Cireașăul, had a more traditional feel. It was here that the svelte painted ladies with their minuscule miniskirts danced for their pasha-like black-suited boyfriends, who sat on bar stools watching them gyrate. And it was here that I met a group of rapscallions whom I'd regret knowing.

Their alpha, Răzvan, was a spindly half-Roma of nineteen with lips set in a perpetual slur and nervous, twitchy fingers. There was something unmistakably rentboy about him. What I didn't know at the time was that young Romanian males rarely hustle in their own country. Maybe he'd developed the manner while traveling the last few years, and maybe, at least unconsciously, he found something familiar and johnlike in me. But that night and four others when I hooked up with him and his posse, a ragtag bunch of undereducated, sluggish hangers-on, sex never came up, only alcohol and money. On my dollar we staggered drunkenly from club to club or met up with contacts selling bootleg CDs. I don't know why I hung out with them, except to blot out a feeling of aimlessness; but in no time at all, I was one of their homeys, privy to their cruising plans and vagrant money-making schemes, owner of a growing CD collection that had all the current pop Romanian hits. I suppose I'd been debased by my loneliness. I was getting my revenge against Romulus by parodying his idea of a "good time," the kind I suspected he was having as he lingered in Sibiu and didn't come back.

That's how he found me, drunken, idle and playing Romanian disco, in an unkempt apartment filled with six adolescent street boys. As usual, his reaction was poker-faced and mildly sardonic, as he tossed his gym bag on the bed and popped open a beer for himself. How idiotic I'd been in thinking I could show him I could misbehave. He felt right at home with the atmosphere I'd concocted; and on that very first night, the boys invited him to the clubs. Stunned at the stupidity of my own maneuvers, I demurred when they told me to come along. Because I didn't have the heart to watch Romulus cruise, I made up a weak excuse about work I had to finish. I spent Romulus's first night home all alone, with only the white pills to comfort me.

Céline Dion came back into my life the next morning, while Romulus slept off his night out. Despite the extensive revisions, she was no less saccharine than a month ago. With the Hachette French–English dictionary on my hard drive, the *Petit Robert* CD in my disk drive and some websites about Québécois expressions, I began to tool along. However, the platitudes were endless, and I began to run out of fresh synonyms. I felt as if I'd been plunged into a swamp of banality whose shores would never be sighted. When, oh, when will it end, was all I could think, as I swam with Céline through the waters of her pregnancy or pumped up her schoolgirl astonishment at the worship of the crowds. To his credit, Romulus continued with the hot lunches, dragging himself out of bed at noon to start his kitchen duties, then lumbering back to bed for another serving of afternoon television. There was little else to do. As for his other "spousal" duties, they were diminishing. When it came to our sex life, the heat was winning.

By late afternoon, when I'd laid twenty or so pages of
Céline to rest, I was a poached trout in the ninety-plus
degrees, rivulets of sweat running down my temples and feet
swollen from sitting. Sometimes I'd be wearing the bizarre
personal-air-conditioner collar you can buy at Sharper
Image, and with my glazed eyes and furrowed forehead I
must have looked to Romulus like the Creature from the
Black Lagoon. I'd find him sprawled on the unmade bed in
his bikini underpants, limbs limp in the airless atmosphere,
a cigarette dangling from his lips. Only a sadist would have
tried to make him have sex in these conditions, so I usually
contented myself with lying by his side, using the tip of a
finger to trace sweat-filled hollows in the indentation of a
muscle.

At times I wondered whether I'd put the fatuous, selfdeceiving, publicity-hungry Céline between us on purpose.
After all, she would have been more than half finished if
I'd worked during his absence. Whether this was the case I
still don't know. But ever since Romulus had set me straight
about the street boys, I'd begun to see him in a different,
disillusioned light.

The feeling bled from Dion's hollow hypocrisy and pooled
into the story of King Carol II, polluting Romulus almost
as if incidentally. But then again, it seemed to come from
Romulus himself. His body had lost its cathectic charge.

I remember the evening I strayed into the bedroom just
as a Romanian show resembling *Hard Copy* was starting on
TV. It was a low-budget show, shot mostly with a handheld
camera, and two of the sequences struck me as particularly
tasteless. The question presented for our consideration was:
What do crazy people think? To answer it, the inquiring
reporters went to a state-run mental institution and interviewed some schizophrenics. Their nearly empty, locked

rooms were disturbing enough, but soon it was clear that the sequence was being presented as comedy. One of the punch lines entailed a middle-aged psychotic's telling the reporter, "The government is in the trees over there," while the camera panned to the trees with their leaves blowing in the wind. Given Romania's recent history of bugged telephones and state-registered typewriters, I considered the possibility of its being historical satire. But no, Romulus's chuckle revealed the setup as purely *Laugh-In*.

The second sequence was about a provincial man the reporter called a "hermaphrodite." He was nothing more than a lonely, effeminate middle-aged homosexual who had become something of a small-town mascot. The camera tracked him trying on a dress in a shop and camping it up à la Dolores Del Rio to some scratchy cha-cha music. He shared some fantasies about the romantic benefits of being a woman, but there was absolutely nothing transsexual about him. He was simply a poverty-stricken gay guy who'd never been able to leave his hometown. Obviously, the archaic mentality of the ridicule repulsed me, and I tried to chalk it up to some naive ideas about homosexuality in Romania; but Romulus was truly entertained, and when I tried to interpret the sequence from a Western gay rights perspective, he silenced me with a few caustic remarks.

I had an anguished identification with those outsiders. As Romulus lay there in the sweltering, shuttered room, swatting mosquitoes, lighting up cigarette after cigarette to the inane blare of the television, I was struck more and more by his "collaboration" with corruption. He was "morally bankrupt," I decided melodramatically, without wondering why I'd never thought so before. Like any newcomer to a culture who suddenly meets with disappointment, I rationalized it into universal qualities. In the oppressive heat, as if under a new spell, I reconstructed Romulus within the context of Romania's dark past, reminding myself of all the underhanded and debased situations to which he could have been subjected in his youth. I thought again of those Flacăra (Flame) festivals I'd read about, organized by Ceauşescu's court poet, Adrian Păunescu, in which cheap special effects drove the young into patriotic frenzies; or of the Falcons— children aged five to seven—tools of Ceauşescu who were encouraged to renounce their parents. Suddenly all the possible cheats and betrayals liable to happen to someone who bonds with a hustler became apparent. Ironically, they were the same risks and dangers I'd found so delicious and looked to for meaning just a few months earlier.

My discomfort came to a head one evening at a favorite traditional restaurant specializing in game and known as Burebista Vânătoresc. It's a faux-Tudor place with hunting tools and peasant crafts on the walls. As soon as we entered that evening, I became oversensitive to the brutal, baronial atmosphere. The antlers and boar heads on the walls felt menacing, and I shunned walking over the bearskin rug on the way to our table. Boar, deer and even bear were on the menu, as well as pheasant, partridge and other small game, but I stuck to beef, except for an appetizer of *salami de Sibiu,* which, traditionally, is made from horse meat. Romulus ordered venison, and as he sat shredding it, the odor of singed flesh filled me with a foolish foreboding. We were playing a game with a folksong coming from nearby speakers. He would give me a literal translation, and I'd try to make it rhyme, sticking as close to the original meaning as I could:

Romulus:
Yesterday I buy you earrings
Today they are gone
Yesterday I buy you a ring
Today it is gone

Me:
Yesterday I bought you earrings
Why do they keep disappearing?
Yesterday I bought you rings
Flown away like they had wings

And then, it continued:
Yesterday I brought you love
You misplaced it like a glove
Yesterday you took my heart
Used it up like any tart

Yesterday I pledged my life
You have cut it with a knife
Yesterday I said, "I do"
Then you tore my heart in two

Chorus:
Now you sit out of hearing
All our love is disappearing
It was sold for just a pence
Life for me has lost its sense

Romulus nonchalantly tapped along to the song about a
maiden selling out her suitor's favors, and laughed good-
naturedly at my split-second rhymes—as a feeling crept
over me. What was it? Something that was a metaphor for

drug withdrawal, endorphins detaching from a previously rosy focus. It wasn't withdrawal from codeine, which I'd swallowed less than an hour earlier, but it reminded me of something Cocteau had said during an opium cure. He'd compared opium to winter, with its crystalline perfection, and the cure he was undergoing to the disruptive advent of spring.

I could feel an analogous breaking up of structures inside me, as if the frozen lock of my obsessions were thawing, unfastening. My positioning blurred and slowly melted, forming a new composition. And in this swirling, Romulus, Lupescu, my mother slowly rotated into a lack of relationship. I was falling out of love.

Once again it was the end of inspiration, and for that very reason, it couldn't be borne. By the time we were walking back to Mihnea Vodă, I was regluing the pieces together. But such an obsession can't be reconstructed perfectly. Now there were cracks that hadn't been there before.

Home we trudged, a faulty couple. It could be that most relationships follow a similar course. The thought didn't keep me from feeling that the world had come apart. I walked beside Romulus in silence.

"Are you thinking again, *dragă*?" Callous as he sometimes seemed, Romulus was always hypersensitive to these withdrawals. "Are you thinking about your Lupescu and your Queen Marie?"

"Hmm, hmm," I lied.

Intellectual flights away from him made him just as nervous, so he said, "Why are you so interested in them?"

"The subject," I said in a dead voice. "I'm interested in betrayal."

Romulus expelled air from his pursed lips, the way Frenchmen, as well as Romanians, do when they find a matter trivial. That seemed to be the end of the subject; yet later that night in bed, he got spooked again by my silence.

"Tell me about Lupescu," he said. "The Jew."

"Well, what do you know about her?"

"Not so much, *dragă*," he answered in that abashed, almost feminine tone of sweetness he would lapse into when he found me distant. "I know that whole country fell apart when she fucking the king. But why, why you are so interested in these things?"

"It just amazes me," I answered, "the fucked-up things some people will do for love."

XXIV

Lupescu's relationship with King Carol did, in truth, throw a moral pall over Romania. From the beginning it depended on a web of deceit. Its contours resembled those of a state crime, in the sense that each falsehood led to problems of national proportion. It stretched from Lupescu and Carol to Queen Marie and Ştirbey, as well as to other heads of government; but no one has ever been able to unravel everything that happened.

Psychologically, the story is a lesson in the constellation of ruin and danger that can grow from the node of a single obsession. Most interesting was Carol's ability to sustain this dangerous focus year after year. For the decade of his kingship, beginning in 1930, Romania was ruled by a hypnotized man. He was oblivious of the building repercussions of his passion and seems to have suffered none of my lapses, holding to obsession's final course.

That night in bed, Romulus and I were up almost until dawn as I spun the story of the self-destructive royal love affair. He'd never had much interest in history, but little by little, my soap opera became familiar. Neither of us spoke of the ways in which it began to enlace our own. Our airless room seemed saturated with Lupescu's Guerlain scent, and among the shadows marched an increasingly frantic King Carol, his boots treading impatiently on a carpet of green moss.

In 1925, at the age of thirty-one, Carol was already a long-time compulsive sexual adventurer when his nervous, proper wife, Princess Helen, urged him to retreat to Sinaia for the summer. There, at the castle of Foişor, early supper with Helen, prepared to her specifications, had become a wordless event. More annoying was the seating arrangement. The couple's young son was placed close to his mother, almost in her lap, while Carol was exiled to the other end, possibly to protect his wife from the sight of his table manners. Even after dinner, he would come no closer. Husband and wife slept in separate bedrooms. It had reached the point that her body bristled with disgust on those few occasions when he touched her.

After a formal array of Greek-style courses while the candlelight concealed Carol's expressions of increasing boredom, he would excuse himself to go outside for a smoke. It was here that the crunching of the green moss began, as his long legs strode toward his Bugatti. From the upstairs bedroom Helen could hear the awful roar of the motor as he gunned it and took off. The car sped angrily along the mountain roads, spewing exhaust and spinning leaves, waking the peasants who'd been asleep since sundown. Then, in a small clearing, it came to a screeching halt in front of a dowdy chalet known as Villa Gianni, which held only one guest.

With glazed eyes and dry mouth, Carol stepped from the car. Scooping up a handful of pebbles, he began throwing them, one by one, against a second-floor window. Behind the window sat a woman in near darkness, penetrated only by stray gleams of her red hair. At the sound of the pebbles she'd rise from her chair and quietly unlock the door. As she heard the heavy tramp of Carol's boots ascending, she'd settle back once more, arranging the hem of her skirt exactly halfway down her kneecap and thrusting her shoulders back to raise her breasts. Her face would compose into a welcoming look with just a hint of feeling neglected, and quickly she'd take a vial from her purse and touch perfume to each ear.

What happens when forbidden arms open wide? It's a moment of great violence when the world is crushed and all other connections severed. Children, mothers, governments, promises crumble into dust. Rage and rebellion take their hidden positions within the whirlwind of affect—gloating at the secret release of their power. From the dust arises a new order, simple and tyrannical. If thoughts about his wife's suffering or the impossibility of marrying a commoner came to Carol, they drowned in the fragrant white flesh beside him. The flesh blotted out every concern until dawn, when he'd hurry to the waiting Bugatti, already spotted by the locals, and drive back to Foişor.

One evening, Princess Helen made the mistake of bringing up his nighttime outings. Carol retorted by claiming they were the only recourse for a man wedded to frigid flesh. This time the dinner was shaken by imprecations. The breath of accusations disturbed the clean outline of the candle flames. The table was pounded so hard that the crystal trembled. When a plate was broken and the child started to howl, Helen decided to take matters into her own hands. With stilted calm she summoned the bewildered servants and had Prince Carol locked inside his room.

An impatient hand appeared at the second-story casement, pushing it open in one thrust. Carol climbed out onto the terrace and, without a moment's thought, leapt off to the ground. With one ankle fractured, he hopped cursing toward the Bugatti. Moments later the handful of pebbles rattled against the window of the chalet again. Lupescu must have been confused by the sound of the desperate struggle up the stairs, the curses muttered under breath. But the twisted ankle was just another boon for her as she fell to playing dismayed lover and overconcerned nurse.

The ravings of lovers fill pages and pages, but the beloved, the focus of all this energy and power, has almost no voice and never explains what it is to be loved in this way. Passion swirls around her, illuminating her flesh, but does she ever feel that she's just its tool, at its mercy? Are, then, the deceits and strategies of the beloved something that can be judged? Or are they merely the pitiful attempts at self-determination of a molecule caught in an atomic blast?

Nobody will know what Lupescu was thinking as she packed for a trip to Paris late that fall. It will never be discovered whether her mind was racked with scruples and fears or dulled by opportunism and cold with strategy. As she carefully folded a sheer black nightgown embroidered with pearls into its black silk case, her face was little more than a heavily powdered mask. She spoke to no one as she walked with her luggage to the nearby station, kohled eyes hidden by a large black picture hat. She picked up a first-class ticket reserved for her under a false name.

The day before, in an effort to wrench Carol from Lupescu's grasp, his mother and father had sent him as the Romanian emissary to the funeral of Queen Alexandra in London. The Liberals were also behind the plan, hoping that it would lead to a situation in which Carol would have to give up his right to the throne. But the day after Carol left was the day Lupescu boarded car L17 on the Orient Express for Paris. In the first-class compartment that had been reserved for her alone, she removed the picture hat and placed it on the overhead rack. Only X-ray eyes could have seen what might or might not have been in the chamois bag balanced on her knee, beneath the layers of lingerie, the silk stockings, the

Poiret gown and the bottle of Mitsouko. Was there really an envelope holding a letter with instructions from Brătianu, the leader of the Liberals? Did it contain a fat roll of new bills from him as well?

London was the first sign that the world was crumbling around the future king of Romania. Paparazzi followed Carol everywhere, exaggerating the details of his affair with the Titian-haired Jewess. Each drink he took was said to be proof of his decadent lifestyle. Each woman he looked at confirmed his reputation as an orgiast willing to jump off balconies for a taste of female flesh. But barely any of it penetrated his cocoon of desire. In his mind, this protected him like a ring of fire, repelling those who approached. Even the British royal family, to whom he was related by blood, made a wide detour around him, shocked by the stories that the tabloids carried and squeamish about his life of lust.

After the funeral, Romanian ministers were waiting for Carol in Paris; but as they greeted him at the train station, he shoved them aside. Standing at a distance was a veiled woman in black, a perfect symbol for doom. She was, I must emphasize, a symbol, barely a person. In a sense, she didn't exist. She was merely a geometric focal point, a target in a whirling vortex. All very well, you may say, for the story, but what was going on inside the mind of the actual person of flesh and blood? No matter that a thousand shrewd considerations may have caused Lupescu to decide to have this affair. Once she'd entered it, the narrative became unintelligible. You can call her scheming or innocent. All of the terms reveal their inadequacy, like profane words used to describe a supernal event. Plans for the future, hates and dislikes, even intellectual preferences are sucked away in its maelstrom. If Lupescu was a woman of qualities before she began her affair with the prince, she was shorn of everything but his desire as soon as she fell into his arms. And at the station in Paris, she was little more than a black thundercloud, enveloping a man and the entire future of Romania.

Shortly afterward, under pressure, Carol renounced his right to royal succession in favor of his mistress. The affair banned him from Romania and his family. But in 1930, three years after his father's death, he would return to seize the kingship in a coup, with Lupescu in tow.

Meanwhile, he had spent several years in exile and had taken a commoner's name. He and his paramour went to Italy, then Monte Carlo, Nice and Cannes. Then on to Biarritz and back to Paris—anywhere that would sustain the fantasy. The affair carried on, outside time, with no reference to anything else. It was a glorious escape from the strictures of the palace. But everything was waiting, like a world in suspension. Soon it would rematerialize, and Carol would be trapped.

XXV

I'm not a Jew-hater," Romulus told me. "Only when they think they're better than us." It was after I'd finished recounting the story of Lupescu and Carol, and we lay staring at each other as dawn light seeped into the room. Both of us knew that the story had produced the unexpected: an implicit comment about him and the difficulty of being the object of an obsession. Suddenly we found ourselves bumped into another phase, one that allowed us to question where we thought this irrational eight months were leading. Now it wasn't any secret that no future remained for him in this sealed-off room or that abandoning my culture, friends and literary connections in New York was having a negative effect on mine.

These feelings went unspoken, however, on both our parts. I decided to look at them as a passing phase. Romulus, in addition, must have been subject to great inertia. Having stumbled into this relationship without ever having set the terms, he approached it the way a hunter-gatherer exploits a meadow. This uniform landscape without any shade, which he'd come upon just by chance, was getting depleted. Still, there were fruits to collect.

Lacking better plans, we went back to our routine, with me under even greater pressure to get Céline done. Meanwhile she continued to send last-minute additions to harried editors. The absolute deadline for the text was July 29, three days before Romulus's twenty-fifth birthday, which was five days before mine. Holding up the fantasy of a rapprochement with the celebration of our birthdays, I fixed my eyes on the light at the end of the tunnel. Romulus went back to his abject lounging. Thanks to my wanderings before his return, he now had some buddies for carousing. Nearly every night Razvan and his dim-witted clique would come calling for him, chug a few of my beers and sweep him away, after I declined their invitations to come along.

My translating schedule had increased to sixteen-hour days. It turned me into a zombie with a fixed stare. Romulus grew gradually more repulsed at my preoccupied face, my puffy eyes with their frozen focus and my lack of conversation. It was the first time he'd seen anyone involved in intellectual toil. It confirmed his suspicions that a life of the mind was boring and unattractive.

Incredibly, the heat wave had not abated. It had hit 104 degrees for the past two days, and the television was full of more accounts of people collapsing on the streets. Romulus was tortured less by the heat than by the mosquitoes that found their way into our bedroom. As I sat peering at the computer screen in my study, my Sharper Image personal air conditioner looped over the back of my neck, I'd hear regular explosions of Romanian curses as he slapped at the insects. For some reason, the mosquitoes avoided my meatier body, concentrating on multiple assaults directed at his spare physique.

One day he came into my study with a triumphant smile, displaying a clear-plastic object filled with some viscous liquid and attached to an electric plug. It was, he told me, a fantastic invention. All you had to do was plug it in, and it released an invisible, odorless mist that killed the little buggers. I watched him plug it into the bedroom outlet, which produced a very low hissing sound. The noise aroused my American paranoia, making me wonder what the FDA would think of the device. Twenty years before, I'd had the same reaction as an underpaid English teacher in Paris, after a summer diet made up almost exclusively of red-colored Moroccan *merguez*, which looked fresher to me than the brown-colored sausages. When I later found out that the red *merguez* was colored with Red Dye #2, which the FDA had recently outlawed in the United States as carcinogenic, I spent the next few months morbidly wondering whether I was going to get the big C. As Romulus lay back on the bed with a self-satisfied yawn, I pulled the mosquito-killer from the outlet to see if it had a label with the list of ingredients.

"What you do?!" he shouted in outrage. "I am meat for every mosquito! You want they eat me to the bone?"

"It's a poison, Romulus, and the room's all closed up."

"Ah, Mr. Cleaning"—he meant Mr. Clean—"who devours half of pharmacies in Bucharest. Suddenly you are worried about your body?" He leapt from the bed and wrested the object from my hand; and at that moment, our ancient model of a phone jangled. I left Romulus to replug the mosquito killer and ran to answer it. It was a call about Ursule Molinaro, one of my closest friends and my closest literary colleague. I found out she had died.

I came back to our bedroom, which was a cauldron of cigarette smoke, and listened to the hissing of the mosquito killer. Romulus was back in position on the bed, looking at me with a defensive, triumphant smile. In the dimness of the closed room, his face looked sinister. The light got lost in the hollows of his cheeks, giving him a spectral air. "My friend Ursule died," I said in a monotone. He blinked once, and his face, with its long beak, took on the rigidity of a bird's. "How this happen?" he responded, for lack of anything better to say.

"She was pretty old, no one knew how old. And she'd been imprisoned during the War. She swore she'd never go into any institution again, but she fell. Her landlord called an ambulance. Against her will, they took her to a ward. I guess she almost lost her mind there. And when she got back, she refused to take her heart medication and died pretty soon after."

"I hate the people who give up on life," he said coldly. I knew I couldn't get anything else from him, so I left the room.

For Romulus's birthday, we planned a trip to the Black Sea. About twenty-five miles south of Constant¸a is a small resort, called Olimp, which was still state-run, next to a privileged seaside community for the Romanian *nomenklatura,* known as Neptun. It was here that I'd booked us a five-day stay beginning July 29, when the final translation was due. To get there I'd bought very reasonably priced first-class train tickets.

As the translation dragged on and on, the deadline began to look impossible. I spent gruesome nights in the heat, often working until past dawn. Then I'd throw myself onto the small bed in the study for two or three hours and go to work again. I was boycotting our bedroom with the primary excuse that I feared the mosquito repellent in the air. Romulus at first made a show of jubilation at having such a large room all to himself. But beneath the crowing, he was truly distressed, confused by the enormous amount of time and energy required by a translation when he himself, orally at least, had so effortlessly mastered his several foreign languages. He was frightened, I now realize, by my withdrawal, not just because it threatened a future without easy money but because he'd covertly developed the habit of looking to me for his self-esteem. I was, it turns out, the only male who'd taken any interest in him, including fathers. He would refer to me as his only friend, ever. Without admitting it to either of us, he'd become intensely attached to me, secretly flattered by the unerring attention of someone whom he thought was superior to him in many ways. As he often put it playfully when we were joking: "You are too good for me."

The question, then, I suppose, is why he didn't buckle down and show me some support when I needed it, get behind the task in spirit that was keeping us both with food and an apartment. The answer is that a whole segment of communication skills was missing. He had no vocabulary for gratitude and no way of comforting me. All of it threatened his machismo, opened the Pandora's box of his neediness and vulnerability. In some strange way, he felt he owed me so much that it couldn't be mentioned. There was no way to pay it back, so it was better to pretend it hadn't happened. Consequently, I was left on my own to wrestle with the translation, the heat and grief over the recent deaths of my Aunt Lil and my friend Ursule Molinaro.

However, something about how he was feeling would come out each night, around dawn, when I'd collapsed onto my bed with swollen eyes, behind whose lids annoyingly lingered the afterimage of the phrases over which I'd been poring. Then the door to our apartment would open as Romulus returned from his carousing. I'd hear him walk toward the bedroom and hesitate, whereupon he'd backtrack to the study door and enter on tiptoe. I'd see his pale, intoxicated face hovering in the dark above my bed, his body slightly stooped from the knowledge of the futility of trying to have a good time.

"You wish to come in bedroom?" he'd whisper in an abashed voice.

"No."

He'd go back to his room and leave the door open, and soon I'd see the colored reflections of the television screen, without which he couldn't fall asleep.

Three days before our trip, he approached me meekly with the news that a good friend of his, Ursu, was having a big birthday bash in Sibiu. He was wondering whether he could go there by bus for the party if he promised to get back to Bucharest the night before we left. Drugged by exhaustion and pessimistic about the future of our relationship, I acquiesced coolly and handed him the money for his trip. If he didn't return in time to use our first-class tickets, I told myself in a fantasy of revenge, that was it.

Fate reacted cruelly to his departure. Hours after he left, the refrigerator stopped working. The milk rapidly curdled and meat warmed in the heat, so I had to throw them out. If there was any possibility of meeting my translation deadline, it meant working every moment until we left. There was no time to go to a restaurant. I had to be content with trying to live for the next two days on a few quarts of warm fruit juice and some yogurt that was rapidly acidifying in the heat.

As I sat plowing through Céline's ingenuous prose, sipping tepid juice, defeat hunched my shoulders. I kept wondering how I'd ended up in such a ridiculous situation. Those so-called grand flourishes of my obsessive passion had painted me into a petty corner, prey to all those practical exigencies that seemed so unimportant when I was in the throes. Love was nothing but that tubercular degeneration that left *La traviata*'s heroine coughing up green spittle on her deathbed. I was a chump.

By the middle of the night before we were supposed to

leave, I fell into a watery, deluded state of mind. Since I'd mastered the cloying tone of my text, work progressed mechanically; the fingers on my keyboard took on the identity of someone else. My mind numbed into a state more profound than any opioid high and began to offer a pleasant sense of detachment. Contexts were melting away. What city was I in? Did I care? With a sardonic giggle I realized that this exhaustion felt like falling in love, which isolates you in an inflamed anesthesia, exiling all worries and concerns.

Dawn found me in this state, with another twenty-five pages to go. I'd have to take the text with me and work on the train, then e-mail it from the hotel. Sweeping papers aside, I stood shakily. The best idea was to find somewhere selling breakfast, then come back and pack. But wait a minute!—Romulus hadn't yet returned as agreed. He was supposed to come back the night before, and just as I'd suspected, or hoped, he hadn't kept his promise.

A shudder of release, almost ecstatic, went through my body. Like a too quickly accomplished reverse zoom in a home video camera, everything telescoped away. Then the trip was off, and so were we! I was slipping out of a cocoon, new skin exposed to air for the first time. I looked out the window at the empty pavement, baked by the previous day's heat. In the dawn light, there was complete silence; no one and nothing were in the street. I grabbed the key and went into the hall. Steadying myself with the wall, I clambered down the stairs, aware that my coordination was severely compromised by fatigue. This wasn't the time to fall, not at the very moment of my freedom!

The streets of Bucharest were almost empty at dawn. There was no sign of the miserable dogs; it felt as if the beggar kids from the park, Razvan and his desperate gang of Pinocchio bad-boys—in fact, all of the suffering that had hedged me in—had disappeared. Unirii was still and limpid, a huge, vault-less fissure that had opened just for me. The only disruption in the film of dawn was a garish spot of red and yellow on the other side of the square, announcing a twenty-four-hour McDonald's. There was so little traffic I could walk diagonally toward the McDonald's rather than approach it by those exhausting right-angle crossings usually needed to get through the square.

Because I felt as if I were teetering, I started to watch my feet to make sure I wouldn't stumble. That's why I didn't notice the apparition that sneaked into the square from Bibescu Vodă Street. Rearing on its hind legs, mouth gaping in a furious neigh, as if mocking my assumption that pain was gone, was a tortured horse, whose owner was beating it for shitting in the street. Attached to the horse was a wagon full of scrap metal that threatened to overturn as pieces of the metal clattered to the pavement, some landing in the horseshit. While I gaped in disorientation at the scene, the driver took my look as tasteless curiosity and directed some of his obscene oaths at me. The horse grew even more frantic, shattering the stillness with its neighs.

The scene sliced through me like a razor through paper, mutilating my previous feeling of release and freedom. There was pain and disorder everywhere, it seemed, and passion was just a momentary way of denying it. I'd seen horses like this several times around the city. They belonged to peasants and Gypsies who traded in scrap metal, and were known to cause traffic jams. This one, though, had appeared from nowhere like a ferocious omen, clattering through new resolutions and throwing me into confusion.

I hurried out of the horse's path and into McDonald's, where I gulped down breakfast. By the time I approached Mihnea Vodă, the dogs were awake, and their barking interwove with my footsteps when I crossed the parking lot. I needed to sleep, then get up and finish the translation. Obviously, the Black Sea was off, the tickets wasted; but I was hoping that this also meant the end of my pathological attachment to Romulus.

He was sitting on the couch with a packed gym bag and a boom box when I arrived. "Why you not ready to go?" he asked, studying my glazed eyes with alarm. "I had to get middle-of-night bus. Other was too packed. Train is leaving in less than an hour."

Obediently I went to our bedroom and threw some clothes into a bag. I shoved the printed-out drafts from the translation on top of them. Then, after putting the computer in its case, I went into the bathroom and began to splash cold water on my face, over and over.

XXVI

"Your eyes," said Romulus, "they look like a crazy person's."

I was standing at the mirror in a coma, water running down my face onto my shirt collar. In my hand was an open jar of Gerovital face cream. I was bringing a dab of it to my eye.

"Are you crazy!" he said, grabbing my wrist and wrenching the jar from my hand. "This cream is not for eye!"

He was right. I'd fallen into such a stupor that I'd mistaken the jar of Gerovital for a Visine bottle. Romulus grabbed a towel and wiped my fingers as if they were a child's. "Let's go!" he said. "We are late." I slung my computer case over one shoulder and my bag over the other, then followed him down the stairs.

Preposterously, in my state I was still planning to use the three hours in the train to push onward with Céline. At the station, which was thronged with some of the poorest people in the city, Romulus set me in a corner like a retarded relative, cautioning me not to move while he went to retrieve our tickets. A parade of Roma families, hoboes, grimy teenagers and peasants with enormous bundles wrapped in twine went by, some of them eyeing my glassy stare with a predatory expression. Soon Romulus came running with the tickets and hurried me along to the train, which started up as soon as we leapt on. A dull realization came to me that I was seeing a new facet of him, as caretaker. Well, I chuckled blearily to myself, if this ever lasts, he'll come in handy when I'm an old codger.

About what happened next I can't be certain. I remember taking the notebook computer out of its case and placing it on my lap, then opening it. Then I must have blacked out for an hour or so, because my next memory is of the computer back in its case and sitting securely on Romulus's lap. The train was already about eighty miles east of Bucharest near the city of Feteşti, right before crossing the first arm of the Danube.

What had woken me was a blast of humid air coming into our air-conditioned first-class compartment as the door of the train opened to let out some passengers. We were already entering a different zone, leaving the arid continental climate of Bucharest and the Wallachian plain. We were closer to the Danube delta, which farther northeast becomes a land of rich watery plains full of dense reeds, bamboo and birds.

I looked at my companion across from me, the only other passenger in the compartment. Completely disoriented, I began to rehearse my identity in my mind like an amnesiac trying to regain his memory. I was in a train with someone I'd considered my lover. But events had occurred that had disillusioned me. What exactly were they? At the moment, I couldn't quite recall. Instead, my mind floated to memories of other people in trains. I saw Lupescu sitting alone in her first-class car, opening her bag to look for something she'd hidden inside. But what was it? I just couldn't remember. I looked at Romulus again, sitting impatiently on the edge of his seat, fingers drumming against the window ledge, watching the passing landscape with bored eyes. His body produced a dim flash of its previous allure. Somehow the little man with the large beak of a nose and the hollow cheeks had been surrounded by a ring of magnetic energy. Intense pleasure was hidden somewhere within his inconsequential body. But how had it all come about? Where had the power come from? I stared at him in confusion.

After a brief delay, the train started again and crossed the Danube, then moved through marshlands and fertile-looking fields. Peasants with faces and pants stained by the dark mud, standing next to exhausted donkeys attached to carts, watched the train go by with doubtful, narrowed eyes. I stared down at the river, sluggish and clay-colored in the blinding light. A memory of standing beside it in winter, staring at two men cutting a hole in the ice, came to me and vanished; and I thought of Johnny Răducanu's tumultuous childhood on the banks of the Danube, somewhere north of here, when he rubbed elbows with smugglers and gamblers. I remembered that my literary hero Panaït Istrati, the self-taught street boy who became a famous French raconteur, came from the same place.

About ten minutes later, over an endlessly long bridge, we again crossed the Danube, at Cernavodă. The city is the site of Ceaușescu's ill-fated nuclear power station, which never succeeded in making all of its reactors functional. We moved along a canal and passed through Medgidia, not far from the vineyards that produce a large portion of Romania's delicious wines. Romulus said we were just a half-hour from Constanţa on the Black Sea. Still studying my drawn face with alarm, he began to hang all our bags as well as the computer from his shoulders. Then he grabbed the boom box. Obviously, he doubted that I'd be able to carry anything.

After we stepped onto the platform at Constanţa among a swirling crowd of Gypsies, workers and tourists, Romulus discovered that a bus had just left for Olimp-Neptun, our destination down the coast. He decided that lunch might be the best idea before we figured out another way to get there. So he lugged our bags through the center of the port town, and I followed, still feeling like a ghost, glancing periodically at the strong shoulders and tensed forearms, glad they were there to help, and gaping at the Greco-Roman remains, modern city streets and Turkish mosques, which made me think of Istrati's Turkish tales. I was happy that I'd stuck his first novel, *Kyra Kyralina,* into the case with the computer. It was supposed to be his best, and I hadn't read it yet. Then my mind must have gone blank again, because I have no memory of the way to Piaţa Ovidiu, where a statue of Ovid brooded, apparently ignoring the energetic scene around him. In the heat and bustle, it seemed hard to give credence to his famous complaints about being exiled here in the cold by Emperor Augustus in A.D. 8. With the voice of an effete elitist, he'd bitterly railed against the harsh winters and lambasted the table manners of the natives, before dying in frustration nine years later.

We gulped sandwiches at a café, and I felt a little energy returning. My zombie state withdrew somewhat, and Romulus began to look more familiar. I insisted we stop for a few moments at the museum across the square; but I should have remembered that if anyone had Stendhal's syndrome—that overwhelming sense of nausea and dizziness that strikes the visitor to a museum—Romulus did. He detests museums, not only for their official atmosphere, which reminds him of all the totalitarian pressures he's had to endure, but also for the vast array of knowledge on display that he feels he lacks. So he stayed outside with our bags, smoking and ogling the local girls, while I dipped in, blearily planning to look at the statue of an earth goddess I'd read was there. In my fatigued state I missed her, and fell instead upon the Nemeses, goddesses of retribution and equilibrium—twins, like Romulus and Remus. I lost track of the time contemplating their double nature, and thinking that revenge, with all its bitterness and aggression, had once been a valid cosmic force for keeping the world in balance. What had monotheism done but drive the impulse back into the subconscious, distorting it into a puritanical sense of self-righteousness? But the Nemeses would see to that. They stared at me like a foreboding, threatening to surge up from my subconscious and set things straight.

When I came out, stricken by vertigo in the change of light, Romulus seemed to be dying of boredom. He returned my bags, then pulled me past the square toward the shipyards, which stretched out before us like a menacing chessboard, filled with a thicket of squat tankers, masts and docks. On the shore was the casino that had once served as a pavilion for Queen Marie and company to welcome a visit from the Russian imperial family, in hopes, later dashed, of marrying a young Prince Carol to Russian Grand Duchess Olga.

Romulus pointed to the scene and chuckled gloomily. "Forty-three days I lived on one of those ships. What is word for that I would become? Merchant sailor. Then, when I go to Western European country or maybe America, who knows, I going to jump from ship."

"What happened?"

"I give up before training is over. Too harsh."

He walked over to a taxi and fell into a discussion with the driver that seemed like a dispute. Both of them were waving their hands aggressively in each other's faces, and Romulus even slapped the hood of the car with the palm of his hand. Then he signaled me over. "He going to drive us to Neptun," he said under his breath. "Good price."

We sped away with me in the backseat, and the road soon bordered cliffs, with dense foliage concealing the sea below.

In the front seat, Romulus and the driver had fallen into a jocular camaraderie. They had the radio booming and were regaling each other with jokes and tales of the transient's life, while I sat ignored in the back, gripping the top of the front seat as we swerved around curves. Finally we came down the long gravel road to our hotel, the Panoramic, on the sea at Olimp-Neptun. The lobby had an institutional feel because the hotel had been built in 1960 to accommodate the hundreds of thousands of Romanian, Czech, Polish, Slovakian and East German workers who went there for their summer vacation, forbidden to visit other venues. The desk clerks seemed at a loss about how to deal with the new, capitalist system. They demanded to see reservation slips, passports, local addresses and even train tickets, and they scrutinized my exhausted eyes as if I were a spy. Romulus and I paid two different rates, his for tax-paying Romanians, and mine, at thirty dollars more a day, for foreigners.

Our room was at basement level, looking out on the pool. It was pleasant but not air-conditioned. The air in it was humid and still. As I fought dizziness and unpacked the computer, intending to hook it up to the phone outlet so that I could e-mail all but the last twenty-five pages of Céline and beg for an extra day's extension, Romulus slipped quickly into the brief blue bikini I'd bought him in a Budapest that seemed so long ago. "You're coming?" he asked, without bothering to notice what I was doing.

"Of course not. You know I have to finish this."

He wasn't deflated in the least; possibly he was relieved. He grabbed a towel and peeled off his socks. "I love the fucking beach," he crowed.

I couldn't really argue with him. This was his Côte d'Azur. He'd been locked in a small country all his life, except when he could sneak out illegally. When it came to sun and sea, this was it for him. Still, I felt a sick shiver of envy as he pranced out of the room, looking marvelously lithe and slender in his briefs, with soft pink skin as smooth as a girl's.

I e-mailed what I could of the translation with a note and collapsed onto the bed. About two hours later, I got up and looked around the room. So this was where I was. Slowly it came into focus. I sat down to finish off Céline. Little did I know that her last simpering chapter was in a sense my death knell. Later, after it all became clear, I found the sound of her music intolerable. It would make me stop my ears.

That evening Romulus came in only briefly, to change out of his bathing suit and see how I was doing. He'd gotten a slight, healthy burn, and his face was shining with pleasure in a way I'd never seen. His eyes sparkled merrily, and he had the excited, quick gestures of a boy. Only then did it dawn on me how many young girls there must be on the beach, and I thought again of the figure he cut in the bathing suit I'd bought him.

I was asleep before he came back that night, and I rose at six the next morning to work, finally finishing and e-mailing the rest of the translation by about three in the afternoon. Romulus had been gone since he woke up at eleven, so I slipped into bathing trunks and headed for the water alone. It was a pleasant beach, a cove bordered by huge rocks on which large concrete structures in the shape of anchors had been placed to hold back the advance of the sea.

Weird thoughts about the sea filled my mind, coming from unknown impulses. I felt as if I'd come to the end of the sea as a signifier, in all the modern/romantic ways I was dependent on: the cradling sea, the sea of bottomless potential, the sea of adventure. The only metaphor about the sea that hadn't been deflated was "back to the sea"—a backward evolution, the sea as a kind of death—not only of the body, but also of development, the sea as a kind of degeneration. Moreover, I was just like any other traveler or tourist who goes to the sea looking for an escapist experience. I was trying to recapture some sense of myth in a world rapidly becoming uniform. All I would meet, however, was a simulacrum of what I'd left behind.

For years I'd believed I could escape that equation by seeking out sexual excitement and exoticism, taking risks and convincing myself that established monotony was about to be overturned. But now, what was there about my story that seemed so deflated? Was it just this horrible fatigue? Or was it that my imagination had finally been vanquished too many times by the facts?

I zigzagged along the beach, curious about the people who came here. Milling everywhere was every sort of human being, from enormous Slavic-looking women with big bellies and breasts in loud-patterned one-piece bathing suits to trim teenaged boys and their girlfriends lying bare-breasted on towels. I walked along the edge of the water until I came to a wire fence that separated the hordes from an empty expanse of beach. On the fence was a sign that I later found out announced in Romanian: "Danger! Deep Water." It was the beginning of Neptun, the satellite colony that contained the mansions of the *nomenklatura,* including a palace that had belonged to Ceauşescu. The sign was a duplicitous warning to hoi polloi to keep away, so that the beach could be enjoyed by the privileged. Beyond the trees on the hillside I could see a gleaming Rolls-Royce, and next to it a man dressed like a guard, holding a machine gun.

Near the end of the afternoon I found Romulus sunbathing on the sand, watching three teenaged girls apply lotion to one another's backs. His skimpy trunks revealed an obvious hard-on. I looked down on it with a contemptuous sneer and he chuckled rakishly. "I'm finished," I said. "I finished the translation." He barely reacted, and once more his detachment irked me, almost to the point of making me shout, "I finished the translation so *we* can have money!" But I repressed the impulse, and he said, "You know, day after tomorrow is my birthday."

"Yes, Romulus, I know. We're going to celebrate our birthdays together."

He shielded his eyes from the sun and looked up at me tentatively. "Bruce, you know, you are educated man. But for me, birthday is day to say fuck you to whole world. I must get drunk, go to clubs, have good time. You will do this with me?"

"Um, sure, but I got to admit it doesn't sound that appealing."

Romulus sprang to a sitting position. "Aha! Just what I am thinking. So maybe, you and I will spend day together. And in the evening, Bogdan—"

"Bogdan?!"

"Yes, you mind so much if he coming here for my birthday?"

"Wait a minute, Romulus. Where's he going to stay?"

"With us, of course. I sleep on floor."

"Romulus, that reception desk was like the police blotter. They're not gonna let him just come and crash with us."

"Ugh, worry always is only thing you do. I know how to take care of people at desk."

"How's he getting here?"

"Hitchhike, of course."

If I'd had a shred of hope about a romantic moment on our birthdays, it had left in a flash. Anger rose uncontrollably in me as I contemplated what I considered the injustice of the last few weeks, my slaving away at tasteless work so that Romulus could enjoy his birthday by the sea with his brother. Every cell in my body slammed shut steel shutters of protection. An icy haughtiness took over me. "You and your brother can stay in another room, Romulus. I don't want to share that room with two other people. We'll speak to the desk clerk and I'll pay for a second."

I suppose I was half expecting him to say he didn't want to spend his birthday night without me, but instead he said, "Thank you, Bruce. You know, the way we celebrate. This is not your cup of milk."

"Tea, Romulus! Tea!"

"Okay, okay, tea," he said defensively.

Our dinner that evening was hasty, and conversation clipped. It may have been an act, but Romulus seemed totally unaware of, even mystified by, what was bugging me. The seaside glow remained on his newly tanned face, and he wolfed down his food with relish. We were sitting in one of the mediocre restaurants with a terrace overlooking the sea, surrounded by affluent Romanians, the first I'd seen close up. They reminded me of Argentines or other members of the South American ruling class, with the men's too-tasteful Armani T-shirts in beige and black and the women's bleached, stiffly coiffed hair.

Romulus was a little frightened by my bitchy withdrawal, but he let it sail past him and still exulted at the luxury of this resort experience. Afterward, as we walked toward the sea to catch the breeze, we saw four beautiful girls dressed in the same blue-and-white outfits handing out safe-sex information for Durex condoms. Spying Romulus, whose body looked limber and feline in his tight T-shirt and jeans, they galloped over to us and held out their brochures. They had no actual condoms, the Romanian economy being what it was. When they learned that I spoke English, they began confiding in me in good-natured giggles about Romulus. He was such a hunk, they said, he must have a frequent need for the kind of protection they were offering. Strangely, he kept himself from picking up on their flirtatious provocations. It was at that moment I began to suspect that he had something much more interesting on his mind.

I think there was a rock concert on the beach that night, and when we separated by accident, I didn't bother looking for him. Instead, I chose to wander among the young Romanians yelping, clapping and dancing in the sand, until around midnight, when latent exhaustion from the last few days suddenly filled me with vertigo. I stumbled back to the room and fell asleep immediately. When I awoke at eleven the next morning, Romulus was gone again. Hiding sulking eyes behind sunglasses, I went to the terrace for breakfast, and brought along Panaït Istrati's *Kyra Kyralina.* At sundown I was still immersed in it and had even brought it to the beach, then later to lunch and cocktails. I was so enchanted by the book, which was written in the pseudo-archaic style of a fable, that I kept reading—I couldn't put it down. Gradually the novel's playful tale began whispering quirky alternatives to the maudlin state I was in. It was as if the story were meant just for me.

Born in 1884 to a Romanian peasant woman and a Greek smuggler who frequented Brăila's ports, Panaït Istrati never received an education beyond the age of twelve. Like Romulus, he floated from country to country, often as a stowaway, picking up odd jobs and sleeping in parks. He came to literature by accident when he happened upon Tolstoy's *Resurrection,* during a foolhardy jaunt to Egypt, as he lay penniless and hungry on the banks of the Nile. A year and a half later, after learning to write in French and having sent a twenty-page letter to, and received no answer from, the French writer Romain Rolland, who was a champion of the underclass, Istrati slit his own throat in a park in Nice. But in the hospital, the letter he'd written to Rolland, which had been returned marked "No forwarding address," was found on him. Rolland was contacted and was astounded by the work of this penniless transient who'd taught himself French. Istrati was brought to him at once. By the mid-1920s, he'd become an international literary luminary.

As I turned paged after page of *Kyra Kyralina,* it became clear that Istrati saw life as legend; his narrative had a biblical flavor. Exiles from marriage, child-rearing, schools, hospitals and all the other institutions of middle-class life, his characters lived according to one principle only: universal brotherhood. It was a rich, bisexual force that had nothing to do with permanence, security or faithfulness and a lot to do with the body. Neither was it that obsessive, narcissistic passion that bound Carol and Lupescu together and that took hold of me. There's a tenderness about the attachments of Istrati's characters that makes the most perverse situations feel natural, even winsome, fleeting as a breeze.

Depleted and demoralized, while Romulus philandered, I fled into *Kyra Kyralina*'s atmosphere of perfumes, cushions and patricide, learning the ways in which lovers who seemed much purer than I did turned their suffering into legends and poems. Little by little the beach and the sea dissolved, and the scenes from the book filled their place.

The story opened in Romania, before it had forgotten its Turkish roots—when gentlemen wore caftans and pointed slippers and women undulated with gestures that came from the harem. I saw nine-year-old Dragomir, blond and creamy-skinned, playing lookout at his mother's window, while she and her daughter, Kyra, tease and entertain salacious hookah-smoking admirers with rosewater-scented hands. Their dances intermingle Greek and Turkish steps. They drink tea and Turkish coffee, sip sweet fruit syrups and eat little Turkish cakes called *cadaifs*.

Little Dragomir's job is to give the alert when his father and brothers are returning, so that his mother's handsome lovers can slip out the window and escape. But at times, his attention wanders, especially when his beautiful sister Kyra is dancing seductively for her sensual admirers and gazes from under eyelashes dipped in kinorosse oil and eyebrows darkened with charred basil. Nothing seems more beautiful to him than her graceful movements, fragrant hair and laughing mouth.

At times like these he joins the frivolity, entertaining the visitors with his own serpentine belly dance. His nine-year-old heart knows only days of lazy sensuality, never suspecting that the afternoons of sweetmeats and languorous flirtation will soon come to a violent end.

Distracted one day by the swirling skirts and mad embraces of his white-limbed mother and sister and the faces of handsome gentlemen, Dragomir forgets to keep watch. Discovered by his irate father and brothers, Dragomir is beaten senseless, and so are Kyra and their mother. His mother nearly loses an eye and is locked up in an airless cellar by her husband. Meanwhile, bloodied Kyra is confined in a dark closet. And Dragomir, who has used a hookah to smash the head of the brother who held Kyra by the hair, is dragged off to his father's woodworking studio for punishment as a slave.

He escapes and frees his sister and mother, only to find that his mother's beautiful face is now swollen and disfigured, a condition she can't accept. She must leave her children, and will never see them again unless her eye, which is hanging from its socket, can be saved and she can return to a world of tasteful hedonism and sexual pleasure.

Kyra calls for revenge against their father and brothers, and enlists their uncle's help. When the night comes for them to be killed, Dragomir is racked with scruples and prays that he won't have to witness it. His prayers are not answered. Before his very eyes, a brother's skull is cracked open like a melon, while his father escapes. Dragomir and Kyra are taken to a hotel for safety, and their avenger pursues their escaped father.

During the day, they learn to sneak out of the back entrance and play in the fields among the wheat and tufts of wool caught on thistles from passing sheep. The outdoors teaches them a new sensuality that is just as pleasant and varied as the attentions of young men, and the wind on their bodies feels more pleasurable than caresses. At night, the young dandies, who've discovered their whereabouts, come to serenade them beneath their window. Kyra puts on the voluptuous gowns of before and goes out to the balcony, but the men are never invited up.

It's the lure of the Danube and its rushing waters that entice Dragomir, and he walks into them up to his chest and gives himself over to their swirling pleasures. When he and Kyra meet a wealthy Turk, who promises to take them on a boat along the river, they're fascinated. The Turk uses unctuous, elegant platitudes to lull the innocent children. He offers them the opportunity to dance and gives them luxurious clothes to wear. When their minds are reeling with delight from the opium cigarettes they've been given, they think they've gone to heaven. The Turk kidnaps them and takes them to Constantinople, imprisoning Kyra in a harem and forcing Dragomir to become his plaything.

It is here, during a six-year period, that Dragomir is corrupted for life, indoctrinated into every perversion and sordid pleasure imaginable. And during this period, the inner thoughts of the love object are revealed. All the abject misery of pleasing another who is more powerful pours from the pages of Dragomir's narrative, all the stark contrasts between the past, when sensuality represented freedom, and now, when it represents survival. After repeatedly surrendering his body to another, Dragomir's mind becomes numbed. His muteness resembles the helpless, passive world of plants.

At fifteen, Dragomir escapes from the Turk's clutches, but only to discover another kind of tyranny. "May all the devils take you, you scented lump of corruption!" he rails at his tormentor from the shore, never guessing that he'll soon find himself in a similar situation. The boy is beautiful and jaded, stupid as a concubine as a result of his shut-in years, but his rings and gold-embroidered fez make him look like the respectable son of a wealthy prince. In his pockets is enough stolen gold to live an idle life. Unfortunately, his head is empty of sense and principle; he has no idea of the value of things.

Then into his life comes a sensitive soul, Moustapha-bey, a caring aesthete who seems to offer Dragomir the understanding he's always desired. This wealthy, elegant and cultured man speaks exquisite Turkish and lives in a huge villa with a yard that stretches down to the Bosporus. Though he can never fill the void in Dragomir created by the loss of Kyra and his mother, he treats the boy with humility and empathy. Dragomir shares his innermost thoughts with him and finds a ready listener. Claiming to want to help him find his sister, Moustapha-bey sends female spies whom he bribes with gold into the harems to search for her. He offers protection to Dragomir, cautioning him never to enter the city center, where the Turk may be looking for him. He exchanges Dragomir's showy clothes for more reasonable, conservative attire and gives him the security of a well-guarded home with an intimate, quiet atmosphere. He even gives Dragomir a beautiful horse, whom he encourages him to name Kyra, as well as other expensive gifts, all emblazoned with her name, as if he expected that objects used to represent her were all that Dragomir needed to overcome his longing for his missing sister.

As the months drag on, it becomes ever clearer to Dragomir that the search for his sister is fruitless. Moustapha-bey swears that he is doing everything in his power to find her. But Dragomir's faith in him has grown clouded. Despite the pleasurable atmosphere of the peaceful home, despite the joyous hunts on which Moustapha-bey takes Dragomir, during which he rides the horse named Kyra, Moustapha-bey exhibits an overweening fault: he is a sensualist. And with this failing comes another: possession. Thus it is that when Dragomir loses faith in the search for Kyra, even suspecting that his wealthy keeper is not really looking for her, he begs to be set free. And Moustapha-bey, perplexed, refuses, claiming to fear what will happen to such a stupid and beautiful boy if he is left to his own devices.

In Moustapha-bey's concern is revealed a subtle elitism, which Dragomir begins to resent. Astonished that the boy could become repulsed by his dignified kindness, Moustapha-bey surmises that he must want women. He explains the error in such a desire, for even the most enticing women end up becoming "sluts." The comment wounds Dragomir to the quick, because he takes it as a condemnation of his enslaved sister. When Moustapha-bey offers him any woman from his harem or, if he prefers, the fourteen-year-old virgins from the countryside, who would rather be their slaves than married to some lout, Dragomir protests that any girl in her right mind would prefer freedom with a lout to slavery. Moustapha-bey softly replies that Dragomir may be correct, but that he should be more concerned with what is pleasant than with what is right, especially since they are the lords of the country and in a position to take anything they want.

He's become a loathsome presence to Dragomir, a rich man of bankrupt morals, and as his emotional hold over the youth is loosened, his discipline becomes more draconian. Dragomir is locked in his room all day or guarded by a servant during outings. When he falls ill after a foiled escape attempt and nearly dies, he finds the distraught Moustapha-bey prostrate before his bed, begging for forgiveness. But when Dragomir again asks to be set free, Moustapha-bey still refuses, saying that he can have anything else his heart desires.

Dragomir recovers and finds himself a pampered captive, locked in a posh bedroom day and night. In fits and tantrums he destroys every gift he receives, and smashes the beautiful furnishings of Moustapha-bey's house whenever he is let out of his room even for a moment. The mild-mannered Moustapha-bey never complains, but neither does he loosen his possessive hold.

Finally Dragomir escapes, with a new understanding of the evil and selfishness that exist among the respectable and privileged. Never to see his sister or mother again, he falls in with a wizened beverage seller, a truly generous man who's given up a past life of sensuality for one of chastity. For the first time in his life, Dragomir reaps the benefits of real friendship and finds an understanding father figure, who has no need for power or possessions. They travel the countryside together, making a simple living, sleeping in forests and fields. One day his gentle mentor is stricken by a heart attack, leaving him alone but with the bittersweet memory of their friendship, which asked nothing of him but his trust. Disaffected but experienced, Dragomir returns from Turkey to Romania, where he leads a marginal life as a seller of lemonade.

When I looked up from the last pages of the book, it was past midnight and the restaurant was closing. Waitresses and busboys were wiping down tables, and had been staring at my fixed face poring over the book's pages without daring to approach.

I paid, got up and strolled back to the hotel. The warm sea air seemed impregnated with images of the characters from *Kyra Kyralina*; I was white and rigid with the thoughts it had sent circulating through my mind. This, then, was passion from the perspective of the beloved. At that moment, I couldn't take it all in. It would be only later, when I'd climbed from the rubble of the relationship I'd so actively pursued, that I'd be able to face the parallels.

XXVII

Since I'd finished the translation, I would have been free to spend all day with Romulus on July 31, the day before his birthday. But that morning, when I rose early and walked to the beach and stared out on an unusually calm sea, pride and hurt pushed me into an unyielding position. Even the sea's glassy surface felt barricaded against me. Just as must have happened to Ovid as he looked out over the waters and thought of the distance that separated him from the warmth and comfort of familiars, I was convulsed with bitterness. Tears came to my eyes and, irrationally, I wanted to spit at the sea.

I suppose having Romulus beg me to keep him company would have been enough at that moment. It was, of course, an absurd demand. Even if he felt he owed me gratitude for the sacrifices I'd undergone to make us money, he would have had to hide it according to the very nature of his pride. That day he did, in fact, extend several cordial invitations for me to go with him to the beach or lunch, and I chillingly declined, preferring instead to walk along the rocks and stare at the water with the vain hope that it would suddenly approach, part and enfold me in a welcoming intimacy. What's more, I was suspicious of Romulus, thinking that he'd met someone—a girl, most likely—to compound his betrayal of me. With a kind of masochistic anger I wanted to see it develop.

That afternoon, I ran into him on the beach, where he lay alone, and the sight of his desirable body, with its muscular, elongated soccer player's legs and flat defined stomach, as well as his highly chiseled features, set my teeth on edge. Like an infant from whose hands a favorite toy has been wrested, I felt a tantrum brewing inside me, which I justified by the self-righteous excuse of having been turned into a mockery.

Later that afternoon, when the sea had changed to a vivid blue and was puckered by a breeze like skin irritated with goose bumps, I saw something that overturned some of the established attitudes I'd been depending on. Romulus was at a café, sitting with a girl, who was young, very young, and blonde. She was so tiny a thing that she had to be about a third my weight. Seeing me go by, he introduced me, sparing me the appellation "uncle" and referring to me instead as his "friend." Shyly—almost in terror—the girl extended a trembling hand, her eyes cast to the ground. Her voice was as quiet as a mouse's—about to be devoured by a fox, I thought grimly. Her purity unsettled me. She was just a well-mannered teenager, probably from a humble but stable family. I'd been so used to battling Romulus's competitive shrews and sluts, the jaded whores who filled my fantasies, encouraged by Elena, that it had never occurred to me I'd be faced with so mild a rival. Then for all these months I'd been preparing to do battle with a child? A wan ray of pity for her rose in me, a surprising note of empathy.

That evening, Romulus and I went to the most expensive of the four or five restaurants along the shore. It was something I'd imperially insisted on. No matter that stuffy establishments made Romulus uncomfortable. I was through limiting my life to please him. He made an attempt to dress for it, putting on one of two pricey items in his wardrobe that he seldom wore. It was a deep violet Ralph Lauren shirt

I'd bought him in New York, which brought out the gleam of his shiny black hair. His shadowy, photogenic face and the way his strong shoulders met the seams made it look like the perfect shirt. All of these charms, I reminded myself, were just snares bound to lure me into disappointment. Without so much as a compliment, I sat stiffly at the table across from him. Over his naturally suspicious eyes, his lips curled a bit in irony at my glum expression.

"If you're meeting that girl tonight," I said, "no problem. Eat with her. Or eat here fast and take off."

"I do not know about her," he said guardedly. "She want to go to Mangalia tonight." This was a larger town to the south.

"It's no fun hanging out with somebody who just wants something from you," I said cuttingly.

Romulus responded to the childish gibe with a defensive, mocking look. "I tell her to meet over there at seven-thirty," he said, and pointed across the terrace.

I dove for his wrist and looked at the watch. "Seven-oh-five already. That doesn't give us much time at all, does it. How about a drink?"

"You will have what?"

"Jack Daniel's."

"Me, too." It was spoken like a challenge. Romulus usually never touched anything but beer and wine.

"Make mine a double," I told the waiter.

"And mine."

Intermittently gulping our drinks, we gobbled the over-priced but mediocre food we'd ordered. "What time is it?" were my next words, with a full mouth and fake concern.

"Seven-twenty. I mean, twenty-one."

"I do hope she's there," I said in my best white-gloved Joan Crawford tone.

Romulus made that French-Romanian blasé gesture again, expelling air through pursed lips. "It doesn't matter."

"But it does, Romulus, it does. She was cute. How old is she, by the way?"

"Seventeen, she say."

"Tsk, tsk, robbing the cradle."

He chortled at the quip, but too much, with the vain hope of reestablishing familiarity. I cut it off by asking, "Isn't it time to go?"

He checked his watch again, "Seven twenty-three." Then he stared at me in annoyance. "Why you so concerned?"

"You know I want you to have a good time," I said with Crawford's purring insincerity. "Come on, Romulus, go over there. It must be time."

He stood abruptly and tossed his napkin on the table. "Good luck!" I called out ostentatiously as he walked away, which stiffened his walk.

While he was gone, I ordered another double. Nothing, but nothing, would stop me from finally having a good time. Under a passing cloud, the sea had turned leaden.

Romulus came back a few moments later. He gave a macho shrug.

"Not there?"

"I not wanna go to Mangalia anyway," he mumbled with forced unconcern. "Save that for tomorrow."

"Ah, yes, tomorrow. For your birthday. A real bash."

This time he missed the sarcasm. "Always my birthday is best day of year! We get—"

"I know, you get drunk, you fuck. You told me already."

"On your birthday will be different, Bruce. We have fine dinner or maybe even theater...."

"And who's going to pay for all that?"

As planned, the comment stung him. Seeing an inroad, I

went on. "I think I'll go out with Răzvan and his buddies for my birthday, Romulus. Hope you don't mind. Drink some beers, maybe get laid. You think Răzvan would put his legs over his head for fifty?"

Romulus scratched his chin, seeming to consider the proposition seriously. "Maybe...he do. I'm sure he do many things to survive."

The answer infuriated me further. I'd wanted him to say, But Bruce, I want to be with you on your birthday, so I called for the check, and when the waiter brought it, said, "Hey, let's have one more. Sort of a pre-birthday celebration for you."

"Bruce, my head spinning already. I am not used to the strong drink."

"Come on, Romulus, don't be a wimp."

"What is this word? Don't tell me—ah, I know. It is sudden desire?"

"That's 'whim,' Romulus," I said with pretended exasperation. Curiously, this wounded him more than anything else. He took pride in having learned several languages without a book or teacher. "And you're not," I said slurringly, now feeling the liquor, "a sudden desire. Or do I mean you're not a desire suddenly?"

Romulus missed my point but glared at the intention anyway, then rapidly slipped into a conciliatory tone. "So, what we do tonight? You want to go to disco, the one on the beach?"

"Sorry, I have plans of my own," I said as I stood up.

"And what is they?"

"I thought I'd go to Mangalia," I said, thinking quickly. "But I know this isn't your night to go."

Romulus stuck to his guns and nodded.

"Okay, then," I agreed, while a crushed voice pleaded inside me to stop the game.

Romulus nodded curtly and we separated. He went toward the disco, and I headed toward our room; then, after turning around to see if he was looking, I walked to the restaurant bar and ordered another drink.

The anesthesia of the alcohol was supporting my self-deception. I told myself that tonight I was really free and had damn well better be glad about it. This was the moment of power, I lied, when I was going to seize my own pleasure. I wanted to be just like him.

I was trudging along the highway in the direction of Mangalia, which is about a mile and a half south. The road led me past Neptun with its carefully guarded mansions. My eyes met those of a guard standing in front of one of them, in the harsh rays of a spotlight. Drunkenly, I cackled toward him, as if to say, You and me know the world's a fucked-up place. His body stiffened, and he moved his hand toward his gun.

There were plenty of tourists around me heading in the same direction, some in cars and some on foot. There was, I dimly remembered reading or hearing, a music festival going on down there. A garish sense of false optimism curled my lips into an inane smile fed by the alcohol; somehow I'd gotten it into my head that I was going to get laid.

The main street had been made to look festive, decorated with strings of red lights. In my blurry sight they looked like new bloodstains in the humid summer air. Mangalia was packed, just as I'd suspected. The majority of the people were young, and they lacked that sense of melancholy I'd often noticed in the faces of older Romanians. Along the street, a meaty teenager in a tank top was cooking corn on the cob on a charcoal brazier. The alcohol pushed me toward him, and boldly I struck up an inconsequential conversation.

It was probably only my American English that succeeded in charming him; otherwise he would have been annoyed by a middle-aged drunk trying to get his attention while he was working.

"Hey, where's the fun around here?"

He grinned at my casual tone and gestured with his chin toward the beach. "The concert just finished. But there are still the people over there."

"Who was playing?"

"You know Andrei?" he asked, expecting me to shake my head. I knew the group of two sexy girls called Andrei very well. They were the Jennifer Lopezes of Romania, with beaded hair, who sung with loose pelvises and swinging, pert breasts. I'd watched Romulus watching their rock videos countless times.

"Sure!" I answered a little too enthusiastically, and hummed the chorus of their hit song. He broke into an embarrassed, astonished smile and nodded along with me. "Take it easy," I called as I moved off, and seizing delightedly on the American expression, he called back, "You take it easy!"

The encounter had aggravated my horniness and filled me with a false sense of confidence, but when I got to the beach, which had carnival booths, rides and a stage, my spirits began to lag. I wandered among the laughing couples like a bachelor ghost, adrift and out of any context they could possibly imagine. I started back toward Olimp on the main road. Fatigue suddenly drained me, and my footsteps became leaden. Seeing a taxi pushing its way through the hordes, I signaled it and jumped into the front seat.

The driver was relatively young, about thirty, and he caught me examining his strong-looking hands on the steering wheel. They were stained with black grease from some kind of manual labor, which had also probably given him his lean, strong physique. Right away I noticed that he had a curiously elegant posture, a graceful crouch that would have looked good in expensive clothes. What caught my attention most was the position of his legs. They were spread a little too wide for driving, and the thighs were nonchalantly upturned.

My eyes locked to the sprawl; I was too drunk to move them away. He followed my line of sight, then looked back at the road.

"I'm going to Olimp," I said. "The Panoramic."

He nodded knowingly and then said, "You from America."

"Hmm, hmm, but I'm living in Bucharest. Came down here for a little vacation." His face darkened with misunderstanding.

"Oh, I don't speak Romanian," I said. "I'm really sorry." Then just for the fun of it, I added, *"Vous parlez français?"*

"Oui. J'étais à Paris. Deux ans." Then, still in French, he added that his name was Tristan and that he worked days as a mechanic at the train station in Constanţa.

He had mild blue eyes and something lax and cruel about his mouth, but I ignored the lower part of his face and concentrated on his eyes. Still, there was a facet of his body's tension that suggested ambiguity. The lean, casual elegance was a cover for something perverse. I was intrigued, and he seemed to like that, so I chattered on in French. As we went down the long driveway to the Panoramic, I suggested, "Why don't you come have something to eat with me?" He nodded and his slouch grew more pronounced. His legs lolled even more, as if he should have been wearing silk pajamas.

He knew his way around and led me to the closest restaurant, glancing at my gait, then taking in my face. I wasn't sure why I suddenly felt so cheerful, glad to be walking with someone fairly young, not bad-looking, masculine, impressing him with inconsequential information about New York.

The gleaming dark red lips of the leggy waitress greeted him with familiarity. A few casual comments passed between them with snickers and knowing looks. The waitress took off to get us some wine. He leaned closer toward me until I could see each individual eyelash. They were sandy-colored, a mixture of blond and dark brown. His full lips were slightly cracked, and there was a day's unshaven growth on his face.

"They're whores, you know," he confided in French, with a sly glance toward the waitress. As he said it, I let one knee graze his as if by accident.

He opened a pewter cigarette case and extended it toward me. For the sake of the gesture, I took a smoke between thumb and forefinger. As he lit my cigarette his mild blue eyes engaged mine insouciantly, but the mouth looked slack and absent. It seemed the very opposite of those people who engage you with a smile while their eyes remain vacant. He leaned back on two legs of the chair and let his legs loll open again. As he did, I thought I felt a bitter sadness waft from him, something metallic.

"You're here with somebody," he assumed, always in French.

"Just a friend," I assured him, "a Romanian."

Now his eyes looked bemused, the lips betrayed a hint of detached irony. "You need chauffeur?"

"As a matter of fact," I decided to claim, "I might need one for half a day. Especially tomorrow. I want to see more of Constanţa and some of the towns along the coast."

"Hmm, hmm," he nodded suggestively, as if I'd made a veiled reference.

"How much would you charge, say, for five hours."

He laughed as if I'd made a joke. "It depends."

After the wine, the waitress brought the food. I'd ordered a salad for myself, to conceal the fact that I'd already eaten. I picked at it halfheartedly and ordered another drink. As I ate and drank, he studied my manners as if they contained an answer to a question he'd posed himself. In the tension of the situation, I'd regressed to that old excitement. The black water beyond the terrace now looked soft, velvety and welcoming, with a note of risk that was enthralling. There was a small breeze. By the time we finished eating, I'd mutated completely. In my mind I felt I was projecting energy and warmth. It gave me the confidence to make my final gamble.

"Want to come back to my room?" I said, looking him in the eye.

Tristan nodded. I quickly paid the check.

As we walked through the hotel lobby past the desk clerk, I kept my eyes fixed straight ahead. "What about your friend?" he asked.

"Out for the night," I answered.

The beds were unmade, and the room was in disarray. Romulus's wet bathing suit lay on the floor next to a pair of my shoes. On the desk were his boom box and several of his tapes. I'd packed the computer and put it under the bed; I'd been worried about thieves.

Tristan perched on the edge of a bed and surveyed the room. His pale blue eyes seemed to click as he took in its contents. Suddenly I was struck with a feeling of awkwardness. Nothing about his posture indicated that he would decide to lie back and relax. The legs no longer lolled, and his hunch looked protective. Resolved to carry out my intentions, I pushed aside a crumpled sheet and sat down close to him. As I did, he reached for one of the tapes, read the name of the rock group on it and fingered it desirously. It was then that I reached toward one of the locked thighs. His elbow rose gently to push my arm away. His grasp on the tape tightened. I stood and moved away, feeling very drunk all of a sudden. "You'd better go," I managed to mumble, but his movement of rising was impudently slow.

"I'm sorry," he said with mock humility. "I do not do this kind of thing." Then he stood by the door like a stop-action frame, still clutching the tape.

"Put that down," I said, pronouncing the words evenly, in a tone you might use to control fear when dealing with a dog. He opened the door a crack and I took a step forward, extending a hand to receive the tape. He held it close, one finger rubbing back and forth over the edge, his eyes staring proprietarily at the boom box.

"It's not mine," I said, chancing another step forward. Then I reached out my hand again and pulled the tape from his. With the other I pushed softly against his shoulder, moving him aside so that I could swing open the door. He left a moment later, but not before fixing me with a steady gaze that seemed to say I was his debtor.

After locking the door, I fell back on the bed, but burying my face in my hands for only a moment. The ludicrous sense of a raw deal had returned, and like an old soldier, I rose for another quest. Disappointment and outrage, mixed with that desperate hope that comes from a survival instinct in the midst of defeat, impelled me out the door. The evening wasn't over.

Double vengeance addled my brain as I thought of both Romulus and Tristan. As if the weather were influenced by my roiling thoughts, it had changed. The breeze was gone, replaced by an eerie, starlit calm, like the hush before a disaster. I stumbled on the sand toward a spot of color that marked the entrance to the outdoor disco. It must have been past two in the morning, and only a few customers were clustered at the bar, while a single figure barely moved on the dance floor. It was Romulus, dancing alone, his violet shirt spotted by drink. He was making tiny shuffling steps to the rhythm of the music. His face was pale from booze and fatigue and probably disappointment. Nonetheless his hips swayed while his arms swung adeptly. It was a narcissistic dance, turned inward in a fantasy of popularity and fun, and his half-closed eyes seemed forlornly absorbed as he mouthed the words to the music. At the sight of me, his expression changed and relief flooded his face.

"Bruce," he said, extending an unsteady arm, "so glad I am to see you."

If truth be told, a surge of feeling had arisen in me at the sight of him, but I held it back with superhuman strength and merely replied, "How come?" Without giving him time to recover from the curt reply, I walked past him. I sat down at the end of the bar near a group of good-looking Romanian boys. I put my back to Romulus and ordered a drink, then tugged the sleeve of the boy next to me. "Would you like a drink?" I slurred, and surprised by his good luck, the boy replied, "Sure!"

It wasn't long before the other three had gathered around me. They must have ranged in age from seventeen to twenty-one, and all of them were fascinated by the friendly American. The one nearest me, particularly, had pleasant eyes and a graceful face and neck, attached to a flat, petite trunk. In the darkness illuminated only by red and blue lights, the skin of his neck looked satin. After buying each of the others a drink, I focused my attention on him. I was in that place I'd visited hundreds of times when drink, depression and a lack of context synthesized a certain suavity. It was a familiar role-play that came out with ease, half friendly but detached, loquacious with a tinge of exoticism. This all-purpose technique flattered him, leaving open the potential for seduction, but it also offered some foolproof retreats that could leave me looking like nothing more than a nice guy. Under my grooming, the boy performed, opening up to me about his life and disappointments. Unaccustomed to my wheedling words, he thought some miracle had brought him a confidant. He told me he was a university student who worked as a busboy at the resort for the summer. His salary was so miserably low that he could barely eat on it. As we sat softly talking, I sensed a shadow behind me. Then Romulus touched my arm and smiled in a way that asked to join the conversation.

"What do you want?" I said condescendingly, in a tone that must have embarrassed the boy.

"To talk to you is all," Romulus blurted out with a face that betrayed humiliation.

"So talk."

"Listen, Bruce," he said in a stage whisper he hoped could not be overheard, "seven hundred thousand lei [about twenty dollars] you gave me today is gone, and I borrowed from people at that table." He pointed to a table near the dance floor with two thuggish bodybuilders, one of whom wore dark glasses.

"Is it my business," I answered coolly, "if you borrow money from strangers?"

"Listen, listen, Bruce, you don't understand. They are getting, you know, aggressive."

With a hokey snarl, I reached into my pocket and pulled out a million lei. Turning my back to him so that I could face my new friend again, I passed Romulus the money. He took it and muttered a thank-you, but I didn't bother to answer. Behind my back, I could hear his steps shuffling toward the dance floor.

The boy was too cultivated to ask me about the transaction. However, from then on, conversation was halting. He'd obviously seen me in a new light. Moments later, he signaled to his friends and they all got up to leave. Incredible as it was to do so, I ordered another drink. As the aftermath of a fruitless evening passed through me in waves, I began to regret my behavior with Romulus. When I glanced toward the dance floor, an altercation was taking place. One of the thuggish men, the one wearing dark glasses, who was not only much more muscled but also much taller than Romulus, was standing, holding a raised index finger that nearly touched Romulus's nose. He was shouting at Romulus, who stood stock still, not budging an inch. The confrontation continued for several moments, until the thug gave ground. He walked out of the disco with his friend, shouting at Romulus, making threatening gestures with his fist.

I slid from the bar stool and walked over to Romulus, forcing a smile on my face. "What happened?" I asked as he stared at me with seething outrage.

"Nothing," he answered in an icy, mocking tone. "I wouldn't give him money."

"Why not?" I said. "I just gave it to you."

"Something better I need to do with it," and he threw all of the bills on the ground. "I am not your slave!" he spat, then gaped at me in outrage. This was the first time in our friendship I'd ever seen him express such fury.

It was one of those experiences that sobers you up faster than a cold shower. I gathered up all the bills, then reached out with a conciliatory hand to touch his shoulder. His face winced with disgust, and he wrenched my hand away.

"Come on," I said, "let's go back." We began walking toward the hotel.

"No one can treat me like you did," he sputtered, "just a moment ago."

"Romulus," I said, struggling for a weak excuse. "I was talking to somebody."

"You treat me like some whore asking you for money."

Then I made the mistake of a lifetime, by saying, "If the name fits, wear it."

His face contorted as if he'd been stabbed, and his eyes went hollow. Not since those early days in Budapest had I referred to the fact that I gave him money. Doing so would have changed the concept of our friendship, which I myself was always exalting, into something shallow and lurid.

Frantically, I tried to move the argument to a more reasonable level. "Okay. I was angry with you. Don't you care that I was slaving while you were out cruising girls?"

He looked me square in the eyes and said, "I hate you."

"What did you say?"

"I hate you! Now you know."

Back in the room, I made another weak attempt at putting the tantrum to rest. But for the first time ever, Romulus was out for blood. He flailed at the bond that suddenly seemed so demeaning. Each time he looked at me, he doubled over, as if he'd been punched in the stomach. Then he would whirl madly around the room, smashing glasses and flinging objects. He turned to the television and spat on it as if he were spitting on me. He lifted a chair and swung it back over his head, then aimed toward the glass door to the patio. I wrested it out of his hands and pushed him down on a bed. He fell back, and his eyes gleamed diabolically as he rubbed his hands together. "Let me tell you what was going through my mind all these months," he offered chillingly.

"Your money smells. The sight of your face make me want to puke in toilet." With these words, he lurched toward the bathroom, and I heard him vomiting.

I calmed down by telling myself that he was drunk, that it was the alcohol talking. What I didn't realize was that I'd crossed a prohibited boundary. By demeaning him in public as I gave him money, I'd branded the last eight months as whoredom. The gaffe had revealed how low I'd sunk, like Armand in *La traviata*. He throws the money he's won gambling in Violetta's face, in front of everyone. But even more trenchant—if I could have thought of it at the time—was the lesson from *Kyra Kyralina*. There's no more loathsome gesture a lover can make than to turn the beloved into a commodity. It's a heinous act, with both personal and political dimensions. It doesn't matter if the relationship truly is defined by one partner's financially supporting the other. The stigma leveled at the whore never takes into account that we all need a way to earn money. To libel the gain that the beloved draws from a romantic arrangement is to withdraw the gift of love itself. What is more, it indicts all forms of work and stigmatizes all workers.

Back on the bed, Romulus writhed under the loss of the one thing he'd held on to, his dignity. He searched his mind for every obscene word that could reduce me to his level. Hysterically, he drew a portrait of me as a monster deformed by possession. He coated with disgust anything that could have been construed as kindness before. He finished by leaping up and throwing all his things into a bag.

"Where are you going?" I asked in a panic. "It's three o'clock in the morning."

"To the road," he said. "I will sleep in the woods and hitchhike back to Sibiu at dawn."

"No, Romulus, please," I begged. "I apologize for everything."

324

But though my voice sounded reduced to tears, he continued with his packing. My brain swam with guilt and confusion, galloped through the memories of the evening. "At least let me give you some money for the train if you're hell-bent on leaving."

"Your money makes me sick," was all he would say. Each time this came up, he'd run to the bathroom to vomit another round.

Any anger I'd felt was now replaced completely by guilt. So desperate was I to escape the feeling that I started promising that it was I who would leave in the morning. He collapsed on the rumpled sheets in the bed next to mine. I turned out the light, and a pall of quiet settled over the room. I lay listening to his breathing, and after about twenty minutes, neither of us was asleep. My mind was in high gear, roiling in a maelstrom of conflicting emotions. Guilt had receded somewhat, and a bitter resentment was taking its place. His attacks still hovered in my mind, like ears ringing after an explosion. I knew that my behavior that night had been tasteless and futile. I knew also, or at least I thought, that I'd been struggling for eight months for his love. Regardless of the factors that had led to this, I knew I couldn't tolerate it. With a desperate hope that the storm was over and that things could be patched by some miracle, I heard myself ask, "Are you all right now?" and offer to climb into bed with him. His voice was calmer and sounded more rational, but his answer was, "No." I found myself trying to do it anyway, and he landed a blow on my face.

There I lay in the next bed, surrounded by broken glass, my face smarting from the smack, with an encroaching sense of injustice. An hour later we were both still awake and my distress continued to feel intolerable. Yet I hoped for a quick resolution that would release me into sleep.

"Romulus."

"What."

"If you can take back those things you said, we can forget it and go on."

"I can't."

The hurt congealed into a stony resentment. He, on the other hand, had fallen asleep with the labored breathing of a drunk. The thought came to me that I hated myself if I was willing to clear out for him. When morning came, and his birthday, he'd get a "salary" once more, a severance package, and be booted out. If his brother was on the way here, he could turn around and go home, too. After this trip was over, I'd go back to Bucharest alone and then return to the States.

Then, as I watched him sleep, a new fear overtook me. This was the first time I'd given him an excuse to hate me. The punch had flown at my face with such competence that I knew he was comfortable and capable when it came to violence. I remembered an experience I had had six or seven years before, during my Times Square period, when I'd indulged in a sort of fetish for some members of the Latin Kings gang who were hustling at a particular bar. One of them, a seasoned ex-con in his late twenties, had developed an attachment to me. We were spending virtually every weekend holed up in my apartment. His tales of gunfights and jail violence began to serve as a kind of foreplay. After conversations of this ilk, we generally watched heterosexual porn. Then I'd enjoy the thrill of his touch as we had sex in front of the screen. After several months of this, a genuine bond had flourished. But one afternoon my doorbell rang and I received a surprise visit. He'd probably been smoking crack—his pupils were pinpoints, his nostrils flared, and his jaw looked locked. I could hear him grinding his teeth. When

I told him I was working, he pushed into the apartment anyway. Rage rushed out of him unprovoked, and it seemed to have nothing, or everything, to do with me. As we talked, even a small gesture on my part, like standing up or moving a finger, produced a blood-curdling paranoia in him, a violent reaction.

I was careful not to show fear and to appear understanding. At one point, I somehow managed to walk casually into the kitchen and hide the knives. Then I convinced him that he was hungry and that we should go to the diner up the block to get something to eat. As he walked ahead of me and opened the door to the building, I saw a chance for escape. I let him pass through and then slammed the door shut, staying inside. I'll never forget the childlike look of dejection he gave me through the window of the door, before continuing down the steps. He must have gotten into some bad trouble later that day, because I never saw him again on the streets around Times Square.

The point is that I'd enjoyed similar rowdy tales from Romulus. It was the stories of car thievery, border gunfire and knife fights that had worked to attract me in the first place. Obviously, I was partly in love with his rage. Could it have been a simulacrum of emotions I didn't know I had? I'd always been half aware of this, but I'd never tried to sort it out. It was just too exciting, producing a sense of compassion in me, but also something more vicarious, something darker. All I knew was that the scars on his nose and neck from a knife fight had appealed to me, as did the stories of the brawls he'd gotten into when he was younger. Certainly he was no murderer, but tonight had shown that a large part of his rage had been in hiding. Now I wondered whether he'd ever be capable of taking all of it out on me. This was a line that I didn't want to see crossed.

Those were the thoughts that rushed through my mind as I wrestled with the choices, trying to decide whether I had the nerve to risk another scene in the morning by telling him to leave. As dawn crept into the room, I lay sleepless in confusion. Romulus's potential had been partly colored with the violence of my old Times Square buddy. Obviously, I wasn't thinking clearly, but this first sign of his hostility had opened a door of fear.

The phone rang, startling me but not even waking Romulus. I rose to answer it—maybe something was amiss with Céline Dion. Although the caller spoke French, it took me a moment to realize it was the taxi driver. I hadn't told him my last name, but he'd evidently made note of the room number. "I'm afraid the chauffeured trip is off," I told him in French.

"That's not what I was calling about," he said in a hushed, sinister voice. "It is very important that I see you immediately. I'm coming now."

"No, no, someone's here. What do you want?"

"I must speak to you," was all he would say.

"About what? I can't."

"You must. So I will come later, when you are alone." He hung up.

As I've mentioned before, homosexual importuning was illegal at that time in Romania. And Tristan had eyed the objects in the room with a strangely greedy look. I counted out approximately eighty dollars onto the desk for Romulus. Then I threw my clothes into my bag and grabbed my computer. To avoid the clerk in the lobby, I sneaked out by way of the pool into the dawn light.

XXVIII

The taxi driver who picked me up near the top of the driveway leading from the Panoramic wasn't Tristan, though I'd had an irrational fear it might be. I was in a sinister panic—afraid of a confrontation with Romulus when he woke up, but much more terrified of Tristan, who I assumed was coming to blackmail me. Somehow the two fears intermingled, one augmenting the other. I'd hightailed it up the gravel driveway at dawn with my bags swinging, my heart exploding with anxiety each time I saw a parked vehicle I thought might be Tristan's cab. Almost immediately, I found a taxi speeding by the entrance to the driveway and flagged it down with both hands.

This time I sat in the backseat rather than the front and told the driver to take me to the train station in Constanța. As we drove along, he kept examining my face in the mirror. It was pinched from fatigue, and my eyes were burning with my rushing thoughts. To avoid him, I glued my gaze to the blur of sunlit forest speeding by and thought of the rushing waters of the Danube, which we'd crossed twice on our way here, or the rich wine country near Medgidia, and Maramureş's vast stores of timber. All of these treasures and more had gotten Romania into trouble, time after time. One hostile power after another had tried to control the country's access to the Danube, its minerals, oil and wheat.

For the first time in my stay here, I felt part of this turbulent history. Gone was the romantic exoticism that had allowed me to play out fantasies of passion surrounded by foreign ways. Gone was the delicious electric charge that surrounded Romulus's body. In its place was a creepy urgency, probably closer to the true feelings of those historical and literary figures whom I'd drafted as part of my adventure. I was having the experience of anyone who stays too long, when the mundane ugliness of anyplace at all suddenly becomes too apparent.

This must have been why my tortured mind wandered. I found myself thinking of a depressing night of drizzle in Bucharest in September 1940, just a day after the cries of an armed and violent Iron Guard, Romania's Fascist militia, had echoed toward the royal square. Hidden in the palace on Victoriei were two white-faced virtual prisoners, Carol and Lupescu. The Iron Guardists were calling for the "she-wolf's" head. "Down with the Jew!" they roared. And they wanted the head of the king, too, for touching the flesh of a Jew.

In the middle of the night of September 7, the king and his mistress sneaked out of the back of the palace like hunted animals and dove into a waiting car. Along with about ten others, they were taken to three special railway cars prepared for their flight. It was, as they say, the end of an era. Carol's ten-year rule, which began when he returned to Romania in June 1930 to reclaim the kingship he'd renounced a few years before, was definitively over.

It looked like my romance with Romania, as well, was dead. When we pulled into the station at Constanţa, I scanned the street nervously for signs of the possibly treacherous Tristan. He'd told me he worked here, and that may very well have been where he'd called me from. Glancing in both directions, I got out and paid the driver. I climbed the steps to the platform, but when I reached it, a train was rushing by.

"Train! Where is it going?" I ask a plump, perplexed-looking woman, probably a maid in one of the hotels.

"Bucharest! Bucharest!" she calls out over the clanging of the wheels. Frantically, I run down from the platform and survey the street again. The taxi I've just ridden in is pulling away, so I run toward it and pound on the window. The driver rolls it down and gazes at me incredulously.

"Please. Bucharest. How much?"

His eyes take on that knowing gleam I've seen so often in this country. What is it—a cynical familiarity with the suffering of others? At the same time I can feel him using this insight to double the price.

"Two million lei." About sixty dollars.

Opening the back door, I jump in. "Sit in front, if you wish," he says. I shake my head. Once we start up, I reach over with half the money. He seems relieved, and I take in the back of his neck, not so much out of any particular interest but from a new sense of caution. It's creased and sunburned, over tired shoulders. He looks about fifty.

Our car speeds rapidly out of Constanţa and then gains the highway. He's one of those Romanian drivers I never got used to on the road. We lurch into and bump out of potholes, pass slower cars on a dime or careen around tight curves, nearly on two wheels. Obviously, time is money; and although he's probably getting more than three weeks' salary in less than a day, he's planning to press his good luck and make the most of it.

Slowly Romulus's anger and Tristan's possible blackmail recede. I settle into a listless mood that is part shock and part sullenness. I have a lot of reordering ahead of me. I had sublet my apartment in New York at least until October, but now I can't see myself sticking it out in Bucharest. Also, I don't want to be in the apartment like a sitting duck if Romulus decides to come back. Soon I'll need to find some work as well.

The uncertainties are so overwhelming that my mind drains. If only I could put my head back on the seat and sleep for an hour, things might get a little clearer; but I can't. Instead my thoughts focus dully on my recent existence and all the stories, characters and fantasies with which I've wallpapered it. I turn them over in my mind the way Tristan had insistently turned the tape over in his hands. I keep trying to solve the mystery of their lost allure. All of them have shrunk to distressingly human proportions.

It's said that Carol was blind to Lupescu's failings. He was so gaga for her that he was bowled over by her most banal remarks. If she told an off-color joke in the presence of someone who'd come from a higher level of society, Carol slapped his knees and howled so that the august visitor was doubly grossed out. Each time Lupescu fabricated a tale about a nonexistent noble relative, Carol listened with rapt attention. It was as if the image of her he'd imprinted on himself was permanent. He didn't need more input.

What is the great draw of the little man who has told me I disgust him? Pinning him under my scrutiny, like a frog to a lab board, I begin to subject his qualities to a merciless inquiry. I can't deny that the scars from knifings or border crossings struck me as badges of courage. And the uncommunicative eyes were dark ponds in which swam mysterious sufferings. They were enough, it appears, to silence judgments about banal underclass tastes, the fancy cars he wanted, a life full of soccer games.

If truth be told, the royal couple themselves led a ludicrously common lifestyle. During their years in exile and even when Carol ruled Romania, bridge games, boiled beef and mystery novels seemed to have been their daily fare. Lupescu was no intellectual, and even the gowns I've raved about turned out to be copies. The bric-a-brac they crammed onto their end tables was inexpensive faux Second Empire. She and Carol were scrooges, more interested in accumulating funds than in a glittering life. To top if off, the glamorous-looking Lupescu put on quite a few pounds by the midlife of her love affair. As Carol's face filled out, it joined his neck for lack of chin. It's the face I now imagine bent over a boring book on British military maneuvers or nodding out at the cinema in front of a mindless thirties melodrama to which Lupescu has dragged him. The opera of their love affair itself now seems like a trite women's picture.

These were the thoughts that assailed me as we sped through the countryside, punctuated now and then by the faces of impoverished rural laborers. It might have been the difference in region, but they lacked the magical focus of the faces of the peasants I'd seen in Maramureş. My eyes fastened to the deadened eyes of a group of fruit-pickers by the road. All I could see was their poverty, written on their bodies like a life sentence.

The driver asks permission to stop at a roadside stand to buy some water. He comes back with a piece of pastry and holds it toward me smiling, a look of sympathy for my drawn face. Although it's almost ten and I haven't eaten or slept, I decline it politely. We start back up, and I notice he's examining me again in the rearview mirror. Aware that something is very wrong, he delicately tries to start a conversation. To discourage him, I tell him that something terrible has happened that I don't feel like revealing. The remark embarrasses him as I'd hoped, and he moves his eyes away from the mirror.

A new notion has begun to absorb me. One of subtle but tantalizing proportions. It's occurred to me that passion itself is little more than a disorder. Stricken by obsessive thoughts of my life during the last few years, I begin to see all my treasured impulses as merely pathological. In the process, Romulus's importance shrinks to that of an incidental extra in the drama. The struggles I thought were directed at him were narcissistic flailings in a mirror. If he played any part at all in this complicated projection, it was only because he happened to have the correct proportions of an actor.

As the light of the projection dims, the shoddy theater that I've been sitting in and its all-too-human audience become apparent. The mystery of why the character of the beloved has so few lines is answered by the fact that the movie was never about him. This was, instead, a chaotic melodrama of non-Aristotelian proportions. No need to spell out the dreary plot—a petty tantrum against an overcontrolling mother, a fear of my encroaching age and her death, a feeling of low self-worth leading to a flirtation with my own demise—the synopsis isn't even worth mentioning.

The thought brings me to consider a historical figure I've assiduously avoided thinking very deeply about. The contours of his headstrong ravings in a way too much resemble mine; today his emotional excuses seem just too transparent. He was a principal character in the Lupescu affair and another foolish emotional obsessive.

His name was Corneliu Codreanu, and he was the fiery leader of the Iron Guard. Only now does his fatal mistake take on relevance for me. His entire life is a metaphor for the selfdeceiving tactics of passion.

Beginning life as an intellectual, an idealist, Codreanu was attracted at university to the patriotic right-wing Christian principles of a Professor A. C. Cuza. These principles, which grew into a dangerous nationalistic movement, were a reaction to Romania's constant partitioning by other countries, as well as its recent throes in becoming an independent nation. They were based on the gut feeling that there really was a true Romanian identity, sanctioned by history and by God—something beyond the greedy land-grabbing and cynical quests for power Romanians had had to endure.

In 1927, Codreanu founded an even more extremist religious-nationalistic organization: the Legion of the Archangel Michael. Closely associated with the more conservative elements of the Church, it promulgated the notion of the racial destiny of Romania. As its leader, Codreanu was a romantic figure, dressing like an operatic hero in the peasant's white garb, emblazoned with the red cross of the Archangel and riding a white horse. His holy task, as he saw it, was the purification of his country. The targets of his lofty, pious campaign were outsiders who he felt were contaminating Romanian culture—namely, Communists and Jews.

In late 1929, the more militaristic Iron Guard was born from Codreanu's Legion. By the mid-thirties, its cells honeycombed the country, swarming with disenfranchised peasants and lower-class Romanians hoping to find a sense of identity and self-worth for the first time in their lives. Some members of the Iron Guard had even won seats in the National Assembly and were becoming powerful enough to force King Carol into dangerous concessions. Codreanu had traded the intellect of his early years for unyielding energy and heartfelt intuitions. No one could tell him he was wrong; nothing could penetrate the bulwark of the pigheaded emotions that drove him. Only the pangs of a passion for belonging and for the complete unification of his people—an experience akin to love—could inspire his idealistic objectives. With patriotism as his catchword and

335

violence as his talisman, he came close to wresting control of an entire country.

The few photos of this modern prophet reveal him as one of Romania's most handsome historical figures. He had strong, regular features and dark, gleaming, swept-back hair. Under his slightly bobbed, aristocratic nose was a determined, vigorous mouth, and above prominent cheekbones were wild, piercing eyes. With his loosely buttoned collar and reared, heroic stance, he was the ultimate Byronic figure, radiating adventure and romance.

It didn't seem to matter that Codreanu himself was not really a "pure" Romanian. His birth name was Zelinski, and his father was of Polish origin. Like Lupescu, he fantasized his roots to match his emotional yearnings. Whatever drove him to excess was hidden from him by an immersion in mysticism and an unshakable belief in himself as a patriot. Lupescu and he were spiritual brother and sister, both convinced that any means justified their romantic quest. Until his death, he remained blinded by his enthrallment, never to get a glimpse of its shoddy underpinnings.

Codreanu was proof that passion, which bursts from the id with the blazing certainty of its integrity, is no solid element, but rather a gas that seeps uncontrollably into the farthest corners, taking on a life of its own. Strangely, Codreanu would find his archenemies, including Carol and Lupescu, often in league with, or at least contaminated by, his goals. Some say it was Carol's closest friend and aide-de-camp, a dandyish young man named Dimitrescu, who plotted with Codreanu to murder Lupescu. The chore was represented to the Iron Guard as a "sacred duty," and adherents eagerly took up the cause. But Dimitrescu merely saw Lupescu as a fly in the ointment in his dealings with Carol. He was just using the emotional, malleable Guardists toward his personal ends. Later, he cautioned Codreanu against it, fearing that the king would have a nervous breakdown if it happened.

In the end, Carol's government swerved unexpectedly away from the Guardist cause. The king began an aggressive campaign against Codreanu. In 1938 he had him and some of his partisans rounded up just as their Nazi kinsmen in Germany were casting aggressive looks eastward. Codreanu and his henchmen were sentenced to ten years, and on the road to a prison camp they were strangled. It was made to look as if they had tried to escape and then been shot, and they were buried together in a sealed pit.

Now the ghost of Codreanu became a scourge to Lupescu. It wouldn't be long before she found her home on Aleea Vulpache surrounded by a bloodthirsty anti-Semitic mob. Soon after, in September 1940, she and King Carol cowered at the palace, waiting for the car that would take them to the train station. And that is how two great passions came to a climax: with the corpse of Codreanu at thirty-nine buried in a common grave, and with a trembling Lupescu sequestered with her lover on a train rushing toward the border.

How ironic that an all-consuming passion born from idealism and convinced of its own integrity would meet such a crude end. Codreanu's followers were so blinded by emotion that they forfeited the objectivity and insight needed to control the consequences of their journey. They were, so to speak, head over heels.

As we pull into the outskirts of Bucharest, the driver glances questioningly at me in the rearview mirror. "Unirii," I say. It's one of about a dozen words I've spoken during the entire three-hour trip. I hand him the other half of the fare with a tip equal to about ten dollars and he beams with pleasure, then notices my drawn face again and conceals his happiness, as if out of respect for someone in mourning.

Our apartment on Mihnea Vodă is baking in the heat. Realizing that there's no longer anything to conceal in the bedroom, I sweep aside the curtains, pull up the shade and wrench the windows open. An uncustomary blast of air pulses into the room. I fall onto the bed, which still smells of Romulus and his cigarettes, but something hard collides with the small of my back. It's the large book about Brancusi's life and work, which I'd been thumbing through more than a week ago and which Romulus in his sloth, apparently, had never bothered to take off the bed.

As sleep finally creeps into my exhausted mind, I think of my precious Brancusi, considering whether he was one, of all people, who'd escaped the revolving door of desire and disappointment. The possibility shines forth as a shred of redemption, and my mind begins to reevaluate his interest in Oriental mysticism. But was it a willful ascent to a cosmic level, or just a distraction for a heartbroken lover?

Information is scant about his affairs and entanglements, although it's hinted that a disastrous love exiled him from carnality forever. I hope that he then moved to a higher plane, a love that took in the cosmos. Or were his abstract forms and monkish lifestyle merely signs of terminal isolation? Noguchi says that in his later years Brancusi became completely disillusioned with the French. He began to feel that aside from a few American collectors no one in the world understood his work. In his dusty studio on rue d'Arcole, his mind became more and more cryptic and more and more isolated. It's true that he accomplished a miracle: the abstraction of movement, a wedding of the life force and the intellect. But could it be that these accomplishments were the absolute and only prerogatives of a fantastically lonely man?

Unable to wrestle with the question, I take the book and place it carefully on the floor. Misery withdraws soothingly into blackness, rudely punctuated by the jangling of the phone. Laboriously I rise, and stumble toward the study. I pick up the receiver and say hello, but at first hear nothing but an indrawn breath. Then Tristan's voice comes insidiously over the line.

"You owe me something. I know where you are."

"Wh-where are you?"

"In Constanţa, but I can drive to you easily." The phone clicks to signal that he's hung up.

XXIX

Heels digging into the sand of the inclined beach, I look out at the whitecapped waves with a feeling of disorientation. What is there that makes these waters seem so different from those of the Black Sea? The foam laps rhythmically to the shore, then pulls back in a graceful gesture, as if insisting on reclaiming its privileged role as a signifier. And everything is blue. It can't be that different a color from the water at Olimp, but somehow I don't remember this all-pervasiveness. Glorious blue joining the blue of a clear sky rather than sulking with a blue-gray passivity.

I'm watching my dear friend Victoire helping an unknown little boy at the edge of the water, urging him in gently up to his ankles, then showing him how a flutter of fingers dipped into the water makes such pretty patterns. As she bends, her full breasts spill partly from her stretchy bathing suit and her abdomen extends slightly, forming soft curves that suggest the maternal and the comforting.

We've been here a week in Fécamp, Normandy, after meeting in Paris. By six a.m. the day after receiving the ominous call from Tristan, I'd fled to the airport, bought a ticket and was waiting to board a plane. I was hoping it would be the final gesture of my eight-month debacle. From the airport, I called Romulus to tell him that I was leaving and that he was free to claim the VCR and any other objects left in the apartment. He swore that he didn't remember a single word of his tantrum on the night before I escaped, but at the same time he put up no resistance to my decision. Out of concern for a possible encounter between him and the treacherous Tristan, I told him that story as well. Romulus, who'd awoken that afternoon with one of the worst hangovers of his life, said that a man had come to the hotel room asking for me.

"He may come back to harass you, too," I warned.

Romulus audaciously pooh-poohed the possibility, merely saying, "Just let him!"

I wondered whether he had revealed my location in Bucharest and given the phone number as a sort of revenge, and I mentioned it. But he swore he hadn't. What was more likely, he said, was that Tristan had a connection with the desk clerk that probably involved pimping, the same kind of operation Romulus had been involved in with the bellboy at the Bucharest Marriott. In fact, he confirmed Tristan's assertion that the waitresses at some of the seaside restaurants were part of a vast flock of prostitutes; he said that he'd been aware of it almost immediately. Part of his entertainment on the beach, though he hadn't mentioned it, had been observing the tiny cabals of petty crime going on around him, from hustling to pickpocketing of tourists. Hadn't I noticed? In the end, I believed him, figuring that Tristan had gotten the information about me from that interrogator of a desk clerk who'd demanded my address and phone number in Bucharest among other information.

Paris was a lush, impossible image to my traumatized eyes, and when Victoire met me at her mother's Marais apartment, which had been vacated for August, I crumbled and put myself at her mercy. Immediately, she called an artist friend who had a house in Fécamp and arranged this week of recovery. We soon left in her car, but not before I'd stocked up on several boxes and bottles of Neo-codion, a mild form of codeine available in tablets and liquid form in any French pharmacy.

Now here I sit, popping the pills or gulping liquid codeine from the bottle, mostly nonverbal, with a pale face. Victoire and her artist friend ply me with enormous platters of fresh shellfish entwined with seaweed. Or they lead me to the beach for a little sunning. On August 6, they sweetly surprise me with a birthday celebration, another feast of seafood with champagne. Victoire has wrapped a gently provocative gift for me. It's a piece of pumice soap, which she says is intended to scrub away the cares of the past.

Three days into our visit, I came to enough to realize that I was seriously broke. The $3,000 advance for Céline had already been spent, as had the money I'd received in advance for subletting my New York apartment. The other $7,000 from Céline would be swallowed up by the $18,000 in credit card bills I'd accumulated during eight months of loving Romulus. Luckily, the French Publishers' Agency in New York turned me on by e-mail to another translation that same week, a biography of the childbirth specialist Ferdinand Lamaze.

It was providing a routine. Every morning, I worked on it for about three hours, popping the codeine a couple of times an hour, to prevent reflection and keep my reaction to the death of my relationship with Romulus at bay. However, at the end of the week in Fécamp, it was apparent that I had nowhere to go. Victoire came to the rescue again, by deciding to install me at her mother's apartment in the Marais, where I could continue working on the translation until fall.

*

The day before we leave for Paris, I wake to a hot, prickly sensation. At first I think it's just a sunburn from the day before, though I'd been at the beach little more than an hour. But when I climb out of bed and look down, I'm aghast. My entire body is covered with red eruptions, some of which have already started to form pustules. The rash runs along my chest and abdomen and upper arms, down my legs and even across the tops of my feet. I dash to the mirror and discover that it stops at the base of my neck, leaving my face unharmed. A thought enters my panicked mind: I'm having a *Death in Venice* experience. Because I've been living for my senses, I've sunk into *pourriture,* like Aschenbach. Love, a terrible and degenerate illness, has ended in a full-bodied rash. The next, similar possibility is that it's the secondary stages of syphilis. I put on a long-sleeved shirt and long pants. Since Victoire is the soul of discretion, she never inquires why I'm dressed so uncomfortably or why I say I prefer not to go to the beach.

As soon as I get to Paris, I run to a doctor. In that scholarly way that French medicals have of approaching a problem, she interviews me for more than an hour about my experiences of the last few months. No, she's certain it isn't syphilis, but she does a test anyway, which comes back negative. The HIV test is negative, too. Finally I admit my codeine abuse, but to her it doesn't look like a drug reaction, either. Cortisone has no effect, and after several visits she surmises I'm having a delayed reaction to the insecticide in the electric mosquito repellent. She can't be sure, however, unless she sees the ingredients. Still, with that squeamishness with which the Schengen countries look upon their eastern neighbors, soon to be brought into the fold of the European Union, she decides to blame it on them. All she can think to prescribe is a mild antiseptic to keep the open pustules from becoming infected.

I kept it hidden. It didn't really matter anyway since I felt exiled from anything to do with the body, after my disastrous experiment in sensuality and passion. At the Marais apartment, which was a tastefully decorated converted maid's quarters, I fell into a monkish existence, plus the mind-numbing codeine. Victoire had gone back to the provincial university where she directed an art program. Most of the many friends I had in Paris were away for August, and my morale was such that I didn't feel like seeing anybody, anyway.

So I got lost in the dreary toil of translating, going down to the streets of the Marais, which happens to be the gay area, once a day for food, looking with remote, evasive eyes at the couples and cruisers I passed, feeling like another species. Then back I would come to my little garret, where I'd pop pill after pill, which, curiously, accentuated my focus on my work, until I felt as if I were in a black tunnel with only the squiggles of black on the white computer screen. Eventually, halfway through the night, the codeine would caress me in its swirling, persuasive embrace and create an anesthesia of warm, isolating intimacy. I'd fall onto the bed and drift into sleep.

Every few days I had to speak to my mother, to whom I'd lied about recent events. Half from pride and half from concern that she'd worry, I'd told her that Romulus and I had found Romania intolerable in the heat and that I'd managed to get him a tourist's visa to France. Now, supposedly, we were leading a quiet domestic life in Paris while I worked on the new translation. She said she was relieved that I'd come farther west. As someone who had, just by chance, escaped the horrors of life in Eastern Europe, she was at a loss as to how anybody could be intrigued by it.

One day I stand swooning before the mirror with an open

jar of Gerovital cream, convinced in my opiate intoxication that it holds all the properties of restoration that Ana Aslan claimed, plus more. I need only apply it to the mysterious rash and my skin will change back to normal with the speed of time-lapse photography. This doesn't happen, of course, but by the next morning, I swear that there's a noticeable improvement. Application of the Gerovital becomes a daily ritual. In my mind, I've altered the concept of rejuvenation that was its claim into one of spiritual purification. The cream, I believe, is drawing my corruption from me and restoring me to a state before I was poisoned by passion. I can't claim without a doubt that it helped. Still, over a period of about two weeks the rash begins to heal, then disappears. It persists only in the area where my upper thighs rub together when I walk.

Miraculously, the translation never stopped progressing with great precision in my highly medicated state. It was as if I'd reduced all consciousness to that particular part of my brain. All the anguish, self-recrimination and loneliness caused by recent events were exiled from the world. There was only me and my work, followed by that delicious but brief hypnogogic period when I fell into bed each night and the codeine coaxed me into unconsciousness. However, near the end of the third week, a strange thing occurs. During the twilight period, instead of sensual blankness, images begin to creep into the sinking into sleep. They're pictures of Romulus, shorn of the kinky urgency that drove me halfway around the world to be close to him, illuminated instead with a new kind of idealism. He appears like Dragomir in *Kyra Kyralina,* sweetly corrupted by a culture of enslavement, but simple and pastoral, adrift in a dangerous world of sensuality. Recriminations and disappointments slowly fall away from his name like an ear of corn being husked, leaving a tender and appealing innocuousness. Strange impulses of pity and tenderness float up to him from my heart. A joyful poignancy curtains the narrow horizons of his unlucky life. Bemused, I play with the images right into sleep, the way a child adjusts and readjusts a favorite toy that has been placed in his bed.

In the morning, the innocent image of Romulus is still intact. As I spiral deeper into the work of the translation, he reappears as a mascot, which I'm grateful to have. I don't know how the idea of wanting to see him again came to me, but each day it grew more urgent, until finally I called his cell phone.

I wasn't prepared for the fragile, uncertain voice that answered—the voice of a young, slightly disconcerted girl. It brought a picture of the insecure, nervous little blonde at Olimp into my mind, except that this voice seemed purer, sadder and more patient. At the sound of my voice, she was taken aback and lost a beat. Then gently she told me that Romulus was out. If I called again in an hour, I'd reach him. Perhaps because of my altered state of mind, the voice felt alchemical, even enchanting. It produced a hush around me, and I pricked up my ears.

After the call, I stood with the phone in my hand as an extraordinary awareness flooded over me. It wasn't at all that I was empathizing with the girl or even identifying with her. For the first time, I was *seeing* her, but in such a limpid light that it was almost like a vision. My position was unique, I realized with excitement, for experiencing what she was experiencing. I felt a young, frightened heart stirring with what she thought was love. I felt the heart skip when Romulus's hand, with which I was so familiar, touched her. I felt the strange confusion of her lips when his mouth pressed against them. And then, an enormous sea of sadness engulfed me, warm, rushing and strangely savory. All of her frustrations, the feelings of abandonment in store for her, and yes, all her ecstasies as well swirled around me. And at that moment, I felt intensely grateful, not for anything Romulus might have given me, but for her.

He and I spoke later that afternoon, and by then I was in a reasonable mood. He was polite on the phone, even a little cordial. What I was suggesting was that we meet in Budapest for a week before the summer was over and I went back to the States. As at the very beginning of our relationship, I cloaked the offer in business terms, not in a demeaning way, but with the preposterous hope that the cover of a financial arrangement would give him a sense of freedom and me a sense of detachment. He agreed fairly eagerly, even claiming that I didn't have to give him money; but although I was in dire financial straits, I insisted. Then, as if it were a casual question, I asked who the girl who had answered the phone was. "Just a girl," he said, and I let it go at that.

During the next ten days my mind again entered the tunnel of perfect concentration on the translation. And each night before sleep, the codeine brought the gentle blossoming of pristine images, like blips on a horizon. Only this time, I saw the girl again, always alone, waiting for Romulus, perhaps. She appeared like an idol in a clearing, in the preternatural light of a new discovery, around which I tiptoed with held breath.

Slowly, I diminished the codeine, a little perplexed that I wasn't going into withdrawal. And each day I performed the superstitious ritual of the Gerovital. Even though the rash was all but gone, I began to think of it as a preventive. However, it still hadn't vanquished the more stubborn eruption on my upper thighs.

As more energy returned during evenings, I took up some

of my old interests again, finding more books about Istrati in French bookstores than were available in English. I commiserated with his sad fate on the road to brotherly love. It seems he was in store for a terrific disappointment when he witnessed the long-term results of the Russian Revolution, which should have been a full-scale realization of his principles. Instead, upon going to Russia, he saw a new kind of tyranny and exploitation. Being an outspoken man and thinking he had little to lose, he wrote a book expressing his disillusionment with the Communist ideal. It alienated the entire French left, which had previously acclaimed him, and even cost him the friendship of his mentor Romain Rolland. Then he returned to his own country, and in the new atmosphere of Fascism under the reign of Carol II, his pastoral, sensual Oriental fantasies all but dried up. Communists in that country considered him a traitor at the same time that Fascists attacked him for what they termed his decadence. He died discredited in Bucharest in 1935, at the age of fifty.

On the last Friday in August 2000, almost nine months after first meeting Romulus in Budapest, I got on a plane. My reasons for the reunion were largely unknown to me, cryptic and buried in nighttime visions. But my heart was beating with anticipation.

XXX

Budapest is a dark world suddenly burst into color. My two previous visits were in winter, characterized by early nights that came even sooner because of the late hours Romulus and I kept. Budapest was just as I'd imagined, defined by my American Cold War childhood, which obscured the day-to-day life of Eastern Europeans with the sinister shadow of the Iron Curtain. From the first night I met Romulus on the Corso, Budapest was a blurred, intuitive space, buried in the depths of the id.

Now it's a city of salmon, pale gray, taupe, yellow and mustard, exploding before me in astonishing clarity. All of it is richly gilded by the light of late summer, which itself holds a note of ending. It's hot as well, and my upper thighs smart with irritation as I walk into the blinding light outside Ferihegy Airport. Romulus, who promised to meet me, is nowhere to be found. Now I'm walking along the Corso toward the spot where we first met, steps away from the Inter-Continental. My computer and heavy bags—containing everything I brought from New York and have been living on for the past four months—are at the four-star Mercure Korona, in the Pest side of the city, within easy walking distance of the spiky nest of the Parliament and the Danube waterfront.

I tried the Gellért first, but prices there have tripled because of several conventions in the city. Hordes have arrived to celebrate the thousand-year anniversary of Budapest's founding. As if to mark the inane level to which civilization has sunk, an enormous balloon, a dorky inflated bottle of Unicom, one of the national beverages, bounces on its edge on the opposite shore of the river not far from the Gellért.

Summer has vastly increased the stock of hustlers on the Corso, most of whom look Romanian. They lounge in the tiny parks, legs outstretched and arms slung over the backs of benches. For the first time since my rash, old desires stir at the sight of flat stomachs, dulled, predatory eyes in a young face or a hand scabbed in a brawl; but then a censor reminds me that these don't represent new adventures. They're just old stimuli, whose roots have been severed from the unconscious.

Suddenly I see Romulus in conversation with a battered teenager, but I'm disconcerted by the feeling that it's not really him. Holding his gym bag, he walks toward me with a sheepish smile, looking pale, unhealthy and older. His hair, which has been thinning since I've met him, now looks dyed, opaque and dead black in the bright summer light. It isn't dyed, I realize. The effect is just part of a strange new projection on my part, the opposite side of the coin of the former. Gradually, as we walk toward the hotel, the alien feeling recedes, and he begins to seem more familiar.

I'm in a cranky mood, scolding him for not appearing at the airport. It turns out he was there and on time. My plane arrived fifteen minutes early without my realizing it, and I must have left just before he came. We dip into a workers' bar farther down the Corso. It's full of weatherbeaten men barking wisecracks at one another with the raw vocal cords of the alcoholic or falling into exhausted depressions before huge beer mugs on wet tables. It's not far from the Szabadság

Bridge, where I went for my first walk when I arrived in Budapest for my journalism assignment.

By this time, the heat has aggravated what's left of the rash between my thighs. I keep wincing and readjusting my position on the bar stool. Romulus notices, but makes no remark. He's telling the story of his arrival here early this morning; and as he does, images flare up in my mind.

Stepping off the red-eye bus all the way from Bucharest, and before that, Sibiu, into the already stifling heat of morning. Going to a locker in the station to park his bag with its paltry contents. Wandering aimlessly on foot past Budapest's huge and brazen examples of state architecture, as memories pour in. Everything reminds him of the affair he had, which he represents as reaching furthest from convenience or exploitation and closest to love. No, not the affair with me. Not Elena, either, who he says was the one who called incessantly during my second trip to Budapest, the one he took to the movies and fucked in the toilets. This was the girl before, for whom he asked me to wire money from New York after our first encounter, the one he saw change from an innocent high school girl into a prostitute at the house for Asian clients. The one who got stabbed.

She and Elena overlapped. And she visited him in Sibiu several times after he and I met, before Elena came to live there. I was paying for it, I see now, making a quick calculation of dates. In fact, during our entire relationship, he's always had a girl. Or should I say we have? Now, with nothing to lose, he lets all his heterosexual affect out, as if I were a friend, a confidant. He believes, he admits, that for the first time in his life he was truly in love with that girl who ended up in the Chinese brothel. It was ruined, he thinks, by jealousy and possessiveness. Neither was willing to trust the other.

What's more, the relationship ended just as ours began. The dark, secretive eyes, swimming with mysterious suffering, that had attracted me so much, were really little more than mirrors of this secret of love and hurt, something I never considered. *I was in love, it turns out, with his loss of love.* Budapest, he makes clear, is excruciating now, just an empty stage set for an irreclaimable drama. He knows he's a permanent exile from love, and these buildings have become an unbearable representation of his loss.

Against my will, my mind accompanies this tale in narcissistic counterpoint. So, as I worked in New York to earn money for us, to get him a visa, to plan a life in Costa Rica, similar energies were radiating from him toward a girl whose life had been ruined by prostitution. And when I twisted and turned with codeine intoxication in the low-ceilinged bedroom in Syracuse, he, too, was twisting and turning in that Austrian jail cell, thinking and thinking of her. And when I called his cell phone from my mother's house, thinking I was reaching him in Bucharest, where I assumed he'd gone to apply for a tourist visa for the United States, he may have not been there at all. He may have still been in Sibiu, in bed with a soon-to-be lost love. She could have been lying right next to him as we spoke, listening to my voice coming over the phone.

As he speaks, my mind embellishes every episode from the past with paranoid flourishes. It sets up a scene with him and Bogdan in some club, laughing together at my naiveté as I come home from my job at the financial printing house in New York, eyes glazed from staring at the computer screen and mind in thrall to passion. It watches him in a lazy last embrace with a tearful young lover as I sit in a plane bound for Bucharest, trying to control the delicious shivers of anticipation. But does it matter anymore?

Abruptly the conversation changes to Olimp-Neptun. He

still claims complete amnesia about our vicious argument. I describe my flight from the blackmailer in a taxi. It would have made a magnificent montage if only I'd known what was happening to him at nearly the same time. On the first day of our arrival in Olimp-Neptun, shortly after he left for the beach in the revealing blue bathing suit, he met a girl, just as I'd suspected. It wasn't the little blonde with whom he'd been sitting at a café table, whom he never met again, but another, whom I never saw. But he'd spent most of his time with her during the days he was there. She was a prostitute of seventeen, on her very first travel assignment, and every night her pimps from Bucharest would come to her room to put her to work, moments after Romulus had left her for the evening.

In fact, I'd had a glance of them, late that last night at the disco on the beach. One of them was wearing dark glasses even though it was night. They observed Romulus dancing alone for a while. After he came to me for money, they pounced, one of them sticking a raised index finger in his face, warning him to stay away from their property if he valued his life.

"You mean those weren't just two guys you'd borrowed money from?"

"No, money is so I can get away from them, go someplace else to drink."

It was twenty-four hours after my flight to Bucharest, almost to the minute, that he began a similar flight to Sibiu with the fledgling prostitute. And just as I'd crept out of our hotel room toward the edge of the pool and traced my way around it to the beach, then up the long driveway to the highway, he and the girl had done the same. They made an early-morning escape in defiance of her brutal pimps. He was saving her. Even though the plan was to return to

Sibiu, where she would continue life as a prostitute, but now managed by Romulus.

The girl and her bewildered voice on the phone reappear. The eerie tenderness surges up, becoming more and more poignant. Romulus sees it in my eyes.

"What?" he says, startled.

There's no way to express the strange transformation that's occurring: my eyes becoming mysterious pools hiding dark excitements and inarticulate losses, just as his once were; and Romulus studying them in tantalized confusion.

The hotel room is larger than we're used to sharing, but it feels claustrophobic. It's as if the rhythm of our cohabitation has become lost. Romulus is expecting to perform the duties he imagines I'm paying for. But first he stakes out the twin bed nearer the television and sets up his measly corner in that way that the kept try to establish something of their own—despite the impossibility of fortifying its boundaries.

As he moves the ashtray closer to his side of the table and bunches up the pillow, my mind locks to a lost little girl waiting in Sibiu. Maybe sitting at the dinner table at his mother's house. Or alone, in front of the television, in the bed she shares with him—suffering small bursts of resentment that well up in her mind over his sudden departure. Fretting over who this uncle or friend or trick is—whatever he told her. Calming herself with a stalwart acknowledgment of the reality of survival. I wish I could be there to touch her shoulder gently and say, See, there's really nothing to worry about, from me anyway.

Like an unwilling actor drafted into a play whose script is too well known to improvise, I undress. So does Romulus. And as the T-shirt rises from the lean waist past the dorsal flare, there's a shock. His skin is covered with the same rash.

"Your back!"

"Is nothing."

I lower my pants and show him my upper thighs.

"Ah, you too." He shrugs.

"What is it?"

He expels the air through pursed lips. "I don't know. Nothing."

I describe how the rash looked at its worst, tell about my visits to the doctor and her theory that it was caused by the mosquito repellent. He listens to the tale with cynicism, and his reaction perfectly complements the Western European doctor's. "Always they thinking trouble comes from us," he snorts. "Is not the cause. This I am sure."

"But what are you doing about it?"

He frowns, as if to indicate that there are problems thousands of times more serious. I, however, have been wondering whether the disease is contagious throughout its entire course. I spent a fortune dry-cleaning Victoire's mother's bedspread before I left Paris. I'd even planned to keep the area of the rash away from Romulus when we had sex.

"Put all your clothes in that plastic bag over there."

"Are you crazy?"

"Do it!" A fearful hysteria has seized me, but even more vividly, a sense of poetic justice, the notion that both of us are contaminated by the deadliest disease of all. It doesn't matter who the carrier was; as Codreanu was proof, it's a germ that spreads uncontrollably.

Thus do we spend the next twenty-four hours in the hysteria of a symbol, gestated by my guilt and shame for the excesses of the past nine months. Half believing I might be right and half capitulating, he lets me send out all his clothes to be dry-cleaned. Naked and chain smoking, he obeys, and watches television while I read.

Above and beyond the absurdity of this symbolic behavior on my part is the real possibility that the unknown rash might be contagious. But even more important is the fact that sex had become a primary tool of my self-delusion. The impossibility of it, I think, will now reveal what there is of a real friendship between us.

I must have, on the other hand, underestimated the multiple vectors of contamination. For as we waited out the quarantine I'd imposed on physical contact, conversation deepened. The room lost its claustrophobia. A pleasant sense of companionship, which had grown up between us and seemed to have nothing to do with passion's fantasies, took hold. Romulus's brusque but graceful macho rhythms, the patience I so admired and that placid, animal manner of his, as comforting as the mute, sensual presence of a cat, began to flourish. Soft, unembellished stories of his sad childhood, tales of his dangerous travels and the thoughts and feelings he'd concealed from me while he'd had to masquerade as my lover, came out, bringing us closer. He revealed, albeit a little awkwardly, his shy respect for my intelligence and even some gratitude for the part of my behavior that he couldn't interpret as anything but generosity. He spoke, as well, of the miracle of trust that I'd provoked in him for the first time in his life. It was something he claimed he'd never experienced before. "You are only true friend ever in my life," he said again. I took the compliments graciously. But the thought did come to me that Romulus was having a bourgeois experience for the first time. In the world in which we all live, the only dependable alternatives to the chaotic rhythms, elastic time and changing allegiances of underclass life are really nothing more than that.

The disease, though, had been given a port of entry. As Romulus became more candid and as what was good about our friendship took hold, I began to overinflate what was happening. A new fantasy of future purity took over. I was seized with the notion that I hadn't really lost Romulus. All I needed was a little forbearance, the disease urged me demonically, in the way that demons convince an alcoholic that it's possible to have just one or two drinks. I ended up telling him that we would see each other from time to time, perhaps on a regular but intermittent schedule. Every few months I'd come to Europe for, say, a week. Because I was aware of his ongoing financial problems, some money would be part of the package.

"Yes, yes, good idea is this. Except."

"Except what, Romulus."

"Maybe I begin to feel the claustrophobia."

I couldn't deny that I knew what he meant. He was referring not just to his need for women but to that same feeling I'd experienced in the presence of my mother. The discomfort of a bond that felt incestuous. The tyrannical sense of another's physicality and need. But it wounded me.

"You'd rather me treat you like the other tricks you've had!" I sulked. "Pay you for a good dirty time and not give a fuck."

"Yes. Then I go and come when I want."

"As long as you get me off first, right?"

"Hmm, hmm."

"Do you know what you're telling me? That you don't want me to care about you."

"Yes." The answer, of course, went through me like a knife.

When the dry-cleaned clothes were returned the next morning, I asked him to leave. Gravely he agreed. "Is better this way. And you know, in Sibiu things are complicated."

"How so?"

"The girl think she is pregnant."

357

I was standing by the window with its sweeping view of the street. On the sidewalk was a Hasidic family on their way to the nearby synagogue. The father's wide-brimmed hat looked like a black hole in the strong sunlight, as did the mouse-brown wig of his wife. But their child, a toddler who kept lingering behind them as the wife gestured at her to advance, was wearing bright pink socks that drew the eye like a target.

"Maybe you find another Romulus on Corso," I heard him say. The notion of interchangeability irked me, and I didn't answer as he walked out the door.

By that afternoon, I was back working on the Lamaze translation. I had six days left in Budapest. The rental I'd arranged in New York was supposed to last through the month of September, but near the middle of the week, I called my tenants and concocted a terrible emergency about illness in the family. To my surprise, they were relieved. They were running out of money and had the chance of staying for free in a smaller apartment belonging to a friend. A refund of one month's rent would make that even more attractive.

With a dull feeling of finality, I slipped into a routine for the remaining days. I'd rise about ten o'clock and work on the translation with the television bellowing in the background. Punctuate the day with hourly doses of codeine. Each evening, about an hour and a half before sundown, I'd stroll to the river, cruise the hustlers like an automaton running on an outmoded program. As I'd suspected, most were Romanian. One, blond and practically preppy in attire, lured me to an expensive café. His annoying routine was marked by self-satisfied claims of upward mobility and contempt for his roots. He didn't associate with or speak to the other Romanian hustlers, he assured me conceitedly. He only pitied their ghetto mentality and their lack of honesty. It was he who told me about one of their tactics, conning a sentimental client by saying their father worked for the railroad and had just lost both legs. As was typical of his ilk, he tried to up the price when we were already climbing the stairs to my room. He saw no discrepancy between such a maneuver and his claims of bourgeois respectability. I left him standing on the stairs, after handing him the original fee, and went back to my room alone. In fact, despite my lab-rat repetitions of learned behavior, I never touched another body during that entire week.

On the second-to-last evening, I was mesmerized by a poignant and ominous image. Standing at the edge of the river in the ghastly pink glow of a particularly spectacular sunset was a man of about thirty-five. His scraggly reddish hair was matted over a pasty forehead. The cheeks of his once handsome face were hollow. As his head turned, he made a point of looking at me with blue eyes that bulged eerily from their orbits. His thinned lips over damaged teeth creased into a vulnerable, boyish smile.

Boldly the overaged male prostitute approached. As his face got closer, I took it all in. Obviously, he'd once been incredibly handsome. He had a Hungarian face, with a wide forehead, high cheekbones and tapered, delicate jaw. But the years had flattened and mauled it. The eyes protruded permanently, as if in fright. The cheeks had sunk into the shadows, among which undoubtedly lingered memories of poverty and drug abuse. The strong, aquiline nose had been smashed at least once, as evidenced by a bump halfway up its graceful bridge. The shoulders were burly from prison exercise or violence, and the neck parched by sun. Despite all this, the features kept their mask of boyish susceptibility, which was supported by a weak, affable voice.

"I was watching your kind and intelligent face," he said. "And I know you are the one for me."

EPILOGUE

Many things have changed since the events covered by the last pages of this memoir, which took place at the end of August 2000. Some have seemed to follow their natural course, but others turned out impossible to predict. Romulus went back to Sibiu, and I to New York, where slowly, I dug myself out with journalism and translation assignments from the financial mess into which I'd sunk. I tried to put the previous nine months out of mind, and succeeded to a surprising degree, except during moments when I would see a news item or watch a television show whose theme touched on male or brotherly friendship. Then suddenly, I'd burst briefly into tears.

Occasionally, I blamed myself for the end of my relationship with Romulus, supposing that it would have endured if I'd been more flexible and more understanding. My friends, as well as my mother, tried to be supportive by defaming him, claiming that I'd been duped by a cold and exploitative person and that it was a blessing that I'd finally come to my senses. Meanwhile, I continued to experiment with turning the experience into a book, a project that lasted four years.

About eight months from the last time Romulus and I saw each other, the phone rang. He was calling—not even collect—and wanting to know, he said, how I was doing. The conversation led to a reestablishment of our friendship and later to the routine relationship that I'd suggested to him on that last day in Budapest. In April 2001, I went to Romania for a two-week stay. We revisited Maramureş together, a visit that eventually became the subject of an article for *nest* magazine. Very quickly we fell into a more restrained friendship and discovered that we truly enjoyed each other's company. This developed into a routine of visits to see him once or twice a year. Soon, out of a nonchalant acknowledgment of my needs, Romulus again began to allow sex. Because I was able to keep the experience defined as a mundane concession to pleasure rather than the sign of a great romantic passion, our relationship continues happily along those lines to this day. He's not the same Romulus who appears in these pages, but a more mature man, bulkier and with thinning hair. His success with the ladies continues, and he's rarely without a long-term, though casual, involvement.

About a year after struggling to survive in Sibiu, he started working as a bouncer at the club that I'd visited, where his brother Bogdan had become the manager. This offered moonlighting opportunities for introducing willing young women to businessmen who visited the club. It's a fairly lucrative setup, which I suppose can be defined as pimping. But it's not in his nature to boss, manage or punish, and his relationship with the women from whom he profits often takes on the dimensions of a friendship or love affair. I'll admit that I encouraged it, because he's never had any way of supporting himself before. Today he makes an average of about $250 a month, which puts him on the economic level of a middle-class Romanian.

In 2002, the Schengen countries lifted their travel ban on Romanians. Romulus seized the opportunity by starting with a vacation in the Canary Islands. Then, with very little money left, he foolishly decided to continue to Paris. His

hoped-for final destination was London, where an underground network of illegal Romanian immigrants, including
his friend Ursu, were getting work in the construction
industry. He planned to get there by the Channel Tunnel
train, already the scene of the deaths of several immigrants
who sneaked into spaces near the train engines. Perhaps fortunately, Romulus's plan was foiled shortly after he arrived
in Paris. At the Gare du Nord, a hostile Turk, who felt that
too many illegal Romanians were spoiling his turf, slashed
Romulus's face with a knife, sending him to a Paris hospital
and leaving him with a dramatic scar from the end of his
earlobe to the corner of his mouth. I was awoken in the
middle of the night in New York by an emergency call from
the hospital and ended up having to pay not only Romulus's
but also his brother's and brother's girlfriend's fares back to
Romania. The scar is still visible but has faded somewhat,
and for me it adds a jaunty touch to his already dangerous
good looks. He detests it and hopes it will fade altogether.

Romania has changed immensely since my first visit there
in early 2000. In Bucharest, the illegal kiosks with their
bootleg liquor were almost all torn down by the center-right
mayor, Traian Băsescu, who was impatient for gentrification.
He also eliminated about three-quarters of the wild dogs, and
probably not according to Brigitte Bardot's specifications.
Băsescu became president of Romania in late 2004, and his
orientation is decidedly Western, with a view of getting the
country into the European Union.

Whereas cash machines were rare, they now proliferate,
and stores are filled with a wealth of new merchandise. The
folkloric appearance of horses pulling carts of scrap metal
in downtown Bucharest is a thing of the past, outlawed by
a new ordinance. However, the economy continues to lag,
and the distressingly low average income prevails. Romania

is still among the last of the Eastern European nations to be invited into the Union and will have to wait at least until 2007.

Eager for a tool to use in the conflict with France and Germany before the war in Iraq, George W. Bush speeded the entrance of Eastern European nations into NATO, and Romania now holds a place in that organization. Yet it remains, in my opinion, a conundrum in the equation of Western globalization, with one foot still in the East and the past—which could turn out to be the very thing that saves the new global uniformity from potential colorless-ness. Meanwhile the country's businesses continue to be privatized; and the dreaded Article 200, which prohibited homosexual contact in public and could have put me in danger for importuning Tristan, has finally been rescinded.

In January 2002, my mother died of heart failure at the age of ninety-eight. She died, essentially, in my arms and during an argument as I was walking her to her bed. For better or for worse, our relationship continued on its terms right until the end. The night before she died, and even the day of her death, we were still trading recriminations and tendernesses. One of her last statements to me was, "You eat too much." For the first time ever, the criticism must have stuck, because in the year since her death I've slimmed down considerably.

In Bucharest, my friend Alex Leo Şerban continues his journalism career and travels to film festivals, always re-turning faithfully to his native land and gracing it with his talents of criticism. Despite heart-bypass surgery, Johnny Răducanu, seventy-four at the time of this writing, leads a vibrant life as a jazz pianist, touring occasionally and enter-taining his fellow Romanians frequently at clubs, universities and concert halls. One highlight of my visits to Romania is dinner with Johnny and Romulus in Bucharest. Carmen Firan, the cultural attaché who so graciously received me at the Romanian Cultural Center in New York, writes poetry as before, but has branched out into fiction and playwriting as well. She's happily married to a Romanian gynecologist, Adrian Sangeorzan, who is also a poet, and they live in Queens.

Queen Marie, beloved by her people, and admired by other royalty, died in Romania in 1938 at the age of sixty-two, after being pushed to the sidelines by her son Carol. It was just two years before his flight from Romania, and nine before the eventual end of the monarchy. She succumbed to a bizarre cirrhosis, whose cause could not be determined. According to the May 29, 1937, issue of *Life,* the "Iron Guard's work was the guess of Rumanian observers March 12 when it became known that Dowager Queen Marie... was paralyzed by poison or 'gastric disturbance.' Marie, born an Englishwoman, is strongly anti-German." In addition, although there was no proof, certain people who took into account the tensions between her and her son, and the various cabals at court, surmised she had been poisoned. Marie's dream of greater influence over Romania through her son was never realized, and the quarrels that broke out between her and Carol, which affected the entire family, rendered her later years tragic.

The government of her son was pressured irresistibly toward Hitler, and it fell under the sway of the Axis powers soon after her death. When Carol and Elena Lupescu fled Romania in 1940, their train was attacked by members of the Iron Guard in Timişoara, near the border with Yugoslavia. According to Alice-Leone Moats, Lupescu hid in a bathtub on the train and Carol threw himself on her to protect her from a hail of bullets. The two made it across the border, then moved to a series of havens, including southern France and finally Spain, a neutral country; they lived off a stupendous amount of currencies, jewelry and national treasures that they'd stuffed into suitcases and trunks, but they were wanted by the Iron Guard to stand trial, and reviled by the United States government as Nazi sympathizers. Once known as the hope of a new Romania, Carol was now branded by Romanian newspapers as a "degenerate alcoholic and epileptic" who'd fallen into the hands of a satanic Jewess. Lupescu's residence on Aleea Vulpache was opened to the public and presented as a hellish fun house of decadence, despite the lack of evidence. In 1941, Carol and Lupescu reached Portugal; he crossed the border by hiding in the trunk of a car. They settled there, in Estoril, and set up their own faux court, although they were snubbed by a majority of the local and expatriate aristocracy.

Carol died in Portugal in 1953 and was buried there; Elena lived until 1977, in Portugal and France. Eventually, under the incorrect first name Magda, she became the subject of the following bit of doggerel:

> *Have you heard about Magda Lupescu*
> *Who came to Romania's rescue*
> *It's a wonderful thing*
> *To be under a king—*
> *Is democracy better, I ask you?*

In 2003, in a conciliatory gesture, Carol's body was returned to Romania. With it were the remains of Lupescu, who was buried separately, thirty feet away in a commoner's grave.

ACKNOWLEDGEMENTS

This book covers an intense nine-month period of willful exile. The story of Romulus and me is, in a sense, a tale of personal alienation, not only because of the time I spent away from my country but also for my attempt, unsuccessful as it was, to distance myself from an identity I no longer desired. Anyone who is aware of the intense isolation of the literary process will understand that writing this book extended my period of alienation, even more so because its story takes place primarily in a faraway country, which cut me off from the environment in which I was writing. The effect was exacerbated by my decision to finish most of the book in Florida, where I know few people. I think of Ovid exiled to Romania's Black Sea coast: my calls and e-mails to friends were full of complaints. There were, however, people who made some effort to lighten the load, and I would like to thank them.

First of all, of course, is Romulus, whose family name shall remain unmentioned, and who became distressed after I read him the chapter about my visit to Sibiu, saying he'd never understood I was so unhappy there, but who now takes great pride in this book, occasionally fantasizing that it could make him rich. Second, Ursule Molinaro, who died without seeing much of the current text but whose enthusiasm for the subject and for my writing in general encouraged me, even after her death. Third, Jack Murnighan, who sent me to Budapest to write the article for nerve.com that led to my first encounter with Romulus.

I have deep gratitude for my American editor, Ken Siman, whose decision to buy this book and shepherd it through the editorial process eased some of the disenchantment I felt about my own country and increased my hopes for a better intellectual future here. I also thank Anna Jardine, the most understanding and informed copy editor I've ever encountered.

I'm very grateful to my publisher, Payot & Rivages in Paris, which published this book first, in French, in 2004; to my generous French publicist, Agnès Guéry-Plazy, whose exhaustive efforts helped me win the Prix de Flore that same year; and to my French editors, François Guérif and Catherine Argand.

I thank Carmen Firan for her interest in this book and the information about Romania she supplied, and Leonard Schwartz for introducing me to her. And Doris Sangeorzan, who rapidly and expertly prepared a synopsis of Johnny Răducanu's Romanian-language autobiography. Thanks also to Toby Dammit, who wrote an electronic symphony around an excerpt of my text, which he performed with me in Paris and which sharpened my focus on the book.

I'm grateful to friends who volunteered to read the entire manuscript before publication: David Wax, Emily Blumberg, Mack Friedman, Eliot Michaelson, Catherine Texier, Walt Curtis, Michael Murphy, Tsipi Keller, John Evans, Susan Jill Levine and James Derek Dwyer; as well as those who read or listened to sections while it was being written: George Agudow, Peter Upton, Thierry Marignac, Japhet Weeks, Robert Houghton, Diane Clemente, Scott Neary and Carol Olicker.

I was also heartened by those editors who published early versions of parts of the manuscript, or spin-offs from it, including Jack Murnighan, Matthew Stadler, Joseph Holtzman, Ariana Speyer, Andrew Gallix, Jordan Heller, Bob Nickas, Nathan Deuel and Kelly McEvers.

Although this eccentric undertaking was often not without doubts that came from me and were projected toward those around me, I hope that those who helped will conclude that it's been justified.

Versions of passages from this book appeared in the following publications between 1999 and 2004:

> *Best Gay Erotica 2005,* edited by Richard Labonté and William J. Mann (San Francisco: Cleis, 2005)
>
> *Gobeshite Quarterly*
>
> *Index*
>
> *The Literary Review*
>
> nerve.com
>
> *nest*
>
> *Scrisul românesc*
>
> *Shout*
>
> *The Village Voice*
>
> www.respiro.org
>
> www.sixbillion.org
>
> www.3ammagazine.com

READINGS

Twelve books provided most of the information about Romania and its people, or inspiration during this project. In order of personal importance, they are:

The Bandits by Panaït Istrati, translated from the French by William A. Drake (New York: Alfred A. Knopf, 1929)

Kyra Kyralina by Panaït Istrati, translated from the French by James Whitall (New York: Alfred A. Knopf, 1926)

The Playboy King: Carol II of Romania by Paul D. Quinlan (Westport, CT: Greenwood Press, 1995)

Lupescu: The Story of a Royal Love Affair by Alice-Leone Moats (New York: Henry Holt, 1955)

The Last Romantic: A Biography of Queen Marie of Roumania by Hannah Pakula (New York: Simon & Schuster, 1984)

Brancusi/The Kiss by Sidney Geist (New York: Harper & Row, 1978)

Athene Palace by R. G. Waldeck (New York: Robert M. McBride, 1942)

The Saint of Montparnasse by Peter Neagoe (Philadelphia and New York: Chilton, 1965)

King Carol, Hitler and Lupescu by A. L. Easterman (London: Victor Gollancz, 1942)

Romanian Rhapsody: An Overlooked Corner of Europe by Dominique Fernandez (New York: Algora, 2000)

Constantin Brancusi, 1876–1957 by Friedrich Teja Bach, Margit Rowell and Ann Temkin (Philadelphia: Philadelphia Museum of Art, and Cambridge, MA: The MIT Press, 1995)

Ten Steps Closer to Romania, conceived by Antoaneta Tănăsescu and edited by Cipriana Petre; translated by Adrian Bratfanof; English version revised by Stefan Lupp (Bucharest: Romanian Cultural Foundation, 1999)

Other books that I consulted:

Brancusi by Ionel Jianou (New York: Tudor, 1963)

Brancusi and Rumanian Folk Traditions by Edith Balas (Boulder: East European Monographs, 1987)

Romania: The Rough Guide by Tim Burford and Dan Richardson (London: Rough Guides, 1998)

Singurătatea...meseria mea by Johnny Răducanu
(Bucharest: Regent House, 2001)

Bury Me Standing: The Gypsies and Their Journey by Isabel
Fonseca (New York: Vintage, 1995)

Balkan Ghosts by Robert D. Kaplan (New York: Vintage,
1994)

The Prodigals by Petru Dumitriu, translated from the
French by Norman Denny (New York: Pantheon, 1962)

The Story of Romanian Gastronomy by Matei Cazacu,
translated by Laura Beldiman (Bucharest: Romanian
Cultural Foundation, 1999)

The Black Envelope by Norman Manea, translated by
Patrick Camiller (New York: Farrar, Straus & Giroux,
1995)

Red Horizons: Chronicles of a Communist Spy Chief by Ion
Mihai Pacepa (Washington, DC: Regnery Gateway,
1987)

Journal: 1935–1944, The Fascist Years by Mihail Sebastian,
translated by Patrick Camiller (Chicago: Ivan R. Dee,
2000)